Spirituality in the Workplace

As we become more and more of a global trading world, the challenges of leading and managing within this turbulent environment and its associated, complex, interconnected markets and disconnected relationships are indisputable, so just how far can any change requirements be practically engaged with, whilst also keeping the employee at the organisation's central core? Today's business world cries out for people who can lead with a cross-cultural global perspective, who can lead from the heart as well as the mind and address and manage problems on not just an integrated local level, but also with a healthy, holistic perspective. The subject of spirituality has long been discussed within academic research, but there still seems to be a misunderstanding and stagnation of both its real meaning and application amongst business academics, the population and organisations alike.

This book aims to provide a realistic message to help those who are looking for some answers; for those who are looking for a way to advance their own skill-set and progress both their careers and the organisation's current standing; to move from being confused and insecure about strategies and tactics, to positively contributing to not only their own, but also to the employees' well-being and the business's overall purpose and intention. By basing the content upon real and relevant, interesting, modern-day perspectives, applications, requirements, opportunities and benefits, all combined into a manual for thought and a practical framework for action, this book will significantly and realistically move the subject of spirituality forward.

This book will be of interest to researchers, academics and students with a special interest in the, positive, influence of spirituality within the workplace and everyday healthy living.

Stephen J. Broadhurst has an Executive Doctorate in Business Administration (EDBA) and is an Independent Consultant, Change Agent and Expert in International Business Administration, UK.

Routledge Studies in Management, Organizations and Society

This series presents innovative work grounded in new realities, addressing issues crucial to an understanding of the contemporary world. This is the world of organized societies, where boundaries between formal and informal, public and private, local and global organizations have been displaced or have vanished, along with other nineteenth century dichotomies and oppositions. Management, apart from becoming a specialized profession for a growing number of people, is an everyday activity for most members of modern societies.

Similarly, at the level of enquiry, culture and technology, and literature and economics, can no longer be conceived as isolated intellectual fields; conventional canons and established mainstreams are contested. *Management, Organizations and Society* addresses these contemporary dynamics of transformation in a manner that transcends disciplinary boundaries, with books that will appeal to researchers, students and practitioners alike.

Towards the Compassionate University
From Golden Thread to Global Impact
Edited by Kathryn Waddington

Reimagining Faith and Management
The Impact of Faith in the Workplace
Edited by Edwina Pio, Robert Kilpatrick and Timothy Pratt

Analyzing Organization Cultures
Edited by Bruce Fortado

Public Sector Reform and Performance Management in Emerging Economies
Outcomes-Based Approaches in Practice
Edited by Zahirul Hoque

For more information about this series, please visit: https://www.routledge.com/Routledge-Studies-in-Management-Organizations-and-Society/book-series/SE0536

Spirituality in the Workplace

A Tool for Relations, Sustainability
and Growth in Turbulent and
Interconnected Markets

Stephen J. Broadhurst

Routledge
Taylor & Francis Group

NEW YORK AND LONDON

First published 2021
by Routledge
605 Third Avenue, New York, NY 10158

and by Routledge
2 Park Square, Milton Park, Abingdon, Oxon, OX14 4RN

Routledge is an imprint of the Taylor & Francis Group, an informa business

Library of Congress Cataloging-in-Publication Data
Names: Broadhurst, Stephen J., 1965– author.
Title: Spirituality in the workplace : a tool for relations, sustainability and growth in turbulent and interconnected markets / Dr. Stephen J. Broadhurst.
Description: 1 Edition. | New York : Routledge, 2021. | Series: Routledge studies in management, organizations and society | Includes bibliographical references and index.
Identifiers: LCCN 2020050307 (print) | LCCN 2020050308 (ebook) | ISBN 9780367861100 (hardback) | ISBN 9781003017691 (ebook)
Subjects: LCSH: Religion in the workplace. | Management— Religious aspects. | Spirituality. | Multiculturalism.
Classification: LCC BL65.W67 B75 2021 (print) | LCC BL65. W67 (ebook) | DDC 650.1—dc23
LC record available at https://lccn.loc.gov/2020050307
LC ebook record available at https://lccn.loc.gov/2020050308

ISBN: 978-0-367-86110-0 (hbk)
ISBN: 978-0-367-76584-2 (pbk)
ISBN: 978-1-003-01769-1 (ebk)

Typeset in Sabon
by Apex CoVantage, LLC

To first and foremost my mum Hazel, my best friend, confidante and greatest advocate, who I loved dearly and totally miss every single day x.

To my father John, who, although I was never particularly close to, it would be amiss of me not to acknowledge him and knowing what I know now, to whom I wish I had been a bit more understanding, tolerant and patient with. RIP Dad.

To Doggie Woof-Woof, for all his hard paw work and finally, to a Broadhurst who is very much with us, my son Charlie—full of life, energy and good-natured fun and long may it continue; who I am extremely proud of and love, more and more, dearly, every single day. "Hello *Shunshine—Dabza here*, you're a good lad xx."

Bless them all.

Contents

Figures and Tables

Tables

Acknowledgements

To my brilliant mum who without her, literally and absolutely, none of this would have been even remotely possible.

To my good friend Stephen 'The' King where certainly, without him, none of this would have been possible.

To Professor Nicholas Harkiolakis, PhD, where there are not enough positive words in the dictionary to refer to in describing him. All I can say is—"Thanks Dr Nick, for making this, certainly, possible."

To all of the fine individuals, who kindly and freely gave me both their time and candid testimonials. Brilliant!

To Professor Joseph Santora, Dean; Professor Alon Rozen, Dr; Saman Sarbazvatan and François Blanchet and all at École des Ponts, Paris; together with a special mention to Maurizio Travaglini and all of his/the team at Architects of Group Genius—all decent, inspiring, true and fair people.

To my longstanding and true best friend Rob Gray, always there to chew things/life over with. Long may it continue, me old, Sucre Lèvres, mucker.

Finally, lest not forget those individuals we come across who have a negative affect on our lives, for it is those that can have the most positive effect on the I—but only if *you* want *them/it* to, that is!?

A very sincere and deep thank you, to each and every one of you.

1   Setting the Scene

How many people dislike, even hate their job in the world? Thousands, millions—billions!? No matter how many, when it is *you* who is going through *it*, you feel like you're the only one anyway! Not everyone hates their job for the same reason. Maybe there's a toxic work culture, or a distinct lack of respect throughout the organisation. Perhaps even a basic "Thank you" from leadership and management, even when *we* go above and beyond their expectations and our pay grade, is significantly missing. Sometimes we can also find ourselves working far below our capabilities and abilities and we end up doing any old job, just to pay our way through everyday life. Sadly, some individuals think the world—the business—just *owes them* a living, in return for very little effort on their part. For other individuals, carrying out the same work, day in and day out, working for and with the same people can be dreadfully boring, monotonous, tedious and laborious. Here the phrase 'soul destroying' is frequently and often used. Where life and work, and even being at home, is a forever repetitive, constant drudge and drain. In any of these events, this can and must ultimately lead to disillusionment and prolonged stagnation for the individual, the employee and the business, which is not a fit or healthy position for anybody or the organisation to be in. At this point, the question is deafening from across the page, "Why don't these individuals . . . (if they are that unhappy and discontent), just simply leave and go and find another role?" The indirect flippant answer . . . the grass isn't always, perceived or otherwise, greener on the other side of the fence and even if it is, it still needs mowing and weeding! The direct answers: Laziness! Where the individual simply doesn't do anything to help either themselves and/or their situation to improve. Put even more simply, they cannot be bothered to look for or find something else—whether it be another job, or a new relationship which is more suitable to them and that they will like and enjoy doing and participating in.

To be fair, we also need to consider the fear of *uncertainty* amongst all of this. The fear of the future—the fear of the unknown. Fear is the one emotion which is the most predominant and powerful of human traits and to accept and overcome fear isn't easy. However, "Surely fear of the unknown and uncertainty are better alternatives than the current real fear and the demoralising experience of the quagmire in which they/we are currently stuck and are so unhappy in?"

At this juncture another question beckons, "Why don't organisations simply 'let go' these less-than-productive, perhaps disruptive and miserable employees?" This too isn't that simple with employment laws as they are so, instead, organisations have been trying to do this via the 'back door' since the start of the Industrial Revolution, that is, make the individuals' working life (which, by default, will also affect their home lives), as unreasonable and intolerable as possible, which they then leave either through (sometimes) unfair dismissal, or of their own accord. This 'act' of forcing them out, is usually 'the job' of the/their manager.

Controversially, it could also be considered, within both their work and home lives, some people secretly like, even 'love' being stuck in both misery and denial—moaning and groaning to whoever cares to listen to their "Poor me's." These individuals are always waiting for the right and easy option, or perfect moment to come along to 'just land on their lap', with little or no effort expected and regarded as being required by themselves and so certainly not given in order to *change their own lot* in their own life. For these people life revolves very much around the 'if only' game! "If only things were different. . . . If only I had this *and* that . . . or this happened, or if that person would only do this for me—I would be happy!" Further to this and significantly, 'everybody wants to either try to change or see another person changed, where the best place to start with, is one's self' (Buchman, 1961). What is forgivable amongst all of this is where the individual knows that they themselves have a problem (the problem is when they don't know that *they* are the ones who have a problem, this is denial), but don't know what they don't know in terms of doesn't know what to do, or where to go to seek help for themselves when faced with life's situations and circumstances.

Some individuals lead such painful, monotonous, poor and limited lives that the urge and need for instant escap*ism* through either drugs, alcohol, smoking, gambling, eating, sex and even work to significantly alter their consciousness and so *transcend* them into a (albeit temporary), artificial utopian/spiritual state is what they choose to turn to, for their particular 'help'. The linking of addiction to this spiritual longing and soul searching is certainly not new. From the Dionysian rituals[1] of the Ancient Greeks and the 'intoxicated'[2]—'soul' searching traditions of the native American Indians, the need for some form of, quick, 'high' experience still remains as strong and relevant today.

Be honest, when you either see or hear the word 'spirituality', what do you immediately think of? Commonly, when the words 'spiritual' or 'spirituality' are either read or said, the first thought in a majority of people's heads ranges from, "It's all just mumbo-jumbo," whilst conjuring up additional and prevalent images of people meditating, as well as crystals and 'high' hippies sitting cross-legged saying "Ohm" whilst listening to whale music/pan pipes, to (even making jokes about) Gandhi wearing a loin cloth! Some people (if you are not old enough to remember them, please feel free to Google them) relate spirituality to either Doris Stokes, Mystic Meg or Gypsy Rose Lee, that is anything to do with contacting the dead, fortune telling and/or 'seeing' the future. This, believe it or not, is considered to be, according to Leviticus 19:31 and Leviticus 20:27, a mortal sin!

Spirituality as a positive action has, perhaps, been one of the most confusing, misused and misconstrued of concepts, where it has acquired somewhat diverse and conflicting meanings, (Ratnakar & Nair, 2012), amongst—well!—everybody really. Even so, over the years, it hasn't stopped the subject of spirituality being extensively discussed, rehashed and repackaged within popular articles, self-help books and academic research as being the 'next best thing' which will change your life, usually with promises of making you rich[3] beyond your wildest dreams. Although these books have sold millions and millions of copies and achieved a multitude of *likes* on social media, not many individuals have been presented and so held up as being successful examples (apart from the authors of such) in achieving this untold wealth. Is there any wonder there still, even today, seems to be many misunderstandings around the meaning of spirituality—in terms of its practical application and the reality of what can *actually* be achieved, together with the substantial benefits which will be *realistically* gained, amongst the general populace and businesses alike!?

The fact that there is no one widely accepted definition of spirituality has also become the most controversial and confusing area in the entire discipline (Koenig, Koenig, King, & Carson, 2012). A central functioning definition may make the subject of spirituality easier to research, understand, drive business value and so strive towards, and as such this does, in many respects, require a pragmatic solution. The lack of a recognised definition also raises doubts regarding the ability to measure it, which has led to the conundrum "Could it be considered impossible to even be able to measure spirituality?" (Ratnakar & Nair, 2012; Koenig et al., 2012; Koenig, 2008; Neal & Biberman, 2003; Moberg, 2002). Taking the (more so business) view of what cannot be measured has no value, in there has to be a measurement in order to gain a factual understanding and realisation of the benefit, consequently, some, (mainly academic and [self] proclaimed guru's), individuals have found a way around this problem by defining their own construct to spirituality and then gone on to concoct different ways of measuring it, usually to suit whatever message or recommendations which they want to put across.

The truth is, within any instances and examples, spirituality is a step too far in many an individual's notions, never mind business academics and organisations alike. As such, these stagnated views of spirituality have become so fixed the whole subject now needs fresh and creative thinking, together with a new definition and construct, which has a more integrative and interdisciplinary outlook, to jolt and so move the whole subject forward and importantly keep the momentum going, in the right direction.

As we become more of a global trading world there is, clearly, a requirement for a more inclusive terminology which will bridge and encompass different and isolated streams of thinking and research, to form the important and relevant, interconnected market links and their associated relational behaviours, to all come together to truly form a route between the 'I' (the individual) to the 'you' (who you actually are), to the 'we' to the 'us' and finally back to the I again. Then to all *start* again in a continuous improvement loop. Spirituality does this by providing a vehicle, which uniquely links individual*ism*—the principle and priority of being independent and self-reliant—to collectiv*ism*—the practice and principle of giving a group the priority over each individual within that group.

Although simple, Figure 1.1 is intended to illustrate/reflect how the 'I' to the 'you' to the 'we' to the 'us' and (back to) the I are all outliers (a person or thing situated away or detached from the main body or system, or differing from all other members of a particular group or set). The intention therefore, throughout the following chapters, is to determine, realise and connect and reconnect these—*our* links accordingly.

The purpose of formulating and presenting a more pragmatic understanding and approach as to why, what, where, when and how spirituality could be introduced and be beneficial, is to position it and provide it as a realistic and accessible tool for sustainability and growth for not just the business entity, but also for the person who, as both its employee and as an individual, can use *it* within their home/personal life as well. By basing the writings of this book upon real and relevant modern-day perspectives, together with balanced and genuine unsolicited testimonials and so direct relevance, practical and feasible applications of spirituality

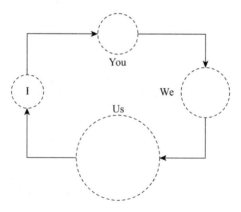

Figure 1.1 Determining the links.

in real life, the intention is to, at the very least, create a spark of interest in this fascinating subject. At best, the contained writings will significantly and realistically move the whole subject of spirituality forward, whilst also converting *it* into both a manual for further thought and a framework for practical action. What makes this book different is that it serves to invite the very idea that spirituality can be relevant and be practically applied to everyday life and so be of value to people, both as employees and individuals alike, up to and including any executive leaders, who all operate to survive in not just the hardnosed profit-driven world of corporate businesses but also (with a reluctance to say 'normal' after all—what is normal!?) day-to-day life.

No book about work would be complete without the mention of 'the Industrial Revolution' and this book is without exception; however, it has endeavoured to not just copy and paste the well-worn 'usual' into it, but to also intersperse it with, perhaps some lesser known, interesting and relevant trivia!

1.1 It Just Wouldn't Be the Same, Without the Mention of . . .

Prior to the Industrial Revolution, manufacturing was carried out in people's homes using either hand tools or basic machines. In general, most of these people worked in villages and small towns, where working and living within these small communities also provided the ability to directly pass on good values, behaviours and experiences from generation to generation, as a way of truth and so a decent way to live by. One advantage to this, by enabling and educating children in this way, meant that when they entered adulthood they would be ably equipped and knowledgeable and so to be able to conduct themselves well, within all areas of their lives.

In 1750, the Industrial Revolution marked a sizeable move to powered, special-purpose machinery, factories and mass production. While this period brought about an increased volume and variety of manufactured goods for the consumer and for some (mainly the owners) an improved standard and way of living, it also resulted in extremely grim employment and living conditions for the workers. Additionally, children were expected to and did go to work in factories alongside their parents and so they lost the 'life schooling' time which they had previously spent and benefited from with their families pre-Industrial Revolution.

The Industrial Revolution began in Great Britain and quickly spread throughout the world. Notably, Henry Ford introduced the first moving automobile assembly line in his Highland Park plant in Michigan, Detroit. This changed the manufacturing industry forever. After its introduction in 1908 and with the consequential success of the Ford Model T motor car, The Ford Motor Company became the leading manufacturer of automobiles in the world and its Michigan plant became the ultimate model for mass production. With this success, Ford's demand for more labour and together with the promise of high wages and shares in the company understandably attracted thousands of migrants and immigrants who were looking for work, to the Detroit facility. To manage and control such a large and diverse workforce John R. Lee, Ford's Head of Personnel in 1914, created the Ford Sociological Department. This new department quickly established a policy of rules and codes of behaviour for the company's employees that they had to meet, to qualify for their pay. However, the Sociological Department extended the company's rules and codes to also monitor (with a view to, arguably, helping) their employees when they were at home. Initially starting off as 50, but quickly rising to 200, these internal 'investigators' generally showed up unannounced, in effect carrying out night raids at employees' homes, in order to evaluate and make sure that they were virtuous. These 'checks' included ensuring both the house and its occupants were clean, marital relationships were being maintained; determining whether they had any illicit lodgers, how much alcohol the employees were consuming; checking that the children were regularly attending school; monitoring the households' spending habits, together with their bank records, to verify that each employee was making regular savings for the future. Although some regarded this as Ford's attempts at wanting his workers to be 'responsible—model Americans' (i.e. promoting patriotism and assimilation into the country), to what given standard was he measuring/forcing them to live up to and then in effect policing his employees against that standard is unknown! Whilst, given the massive amounts of immigrants and their inability to speak the English language (which was not claimed as him having contempt for other cultures—although it was never stated that it was *not* ever a part of it), Ford's intentions were also of an issue of safety, as a simple miscommunication on the factory floor could get someone killed. Some might suggest all of this was Ford's attempts at recreating the pre-Industrial Revolution where caring, morals and ethics, values and behaviours, which were previously enjoyed within the spirit of the community, were simply being (re)created within his culture. Others might say Ford went too far and rather it was all a deliberate method and intention of complete command and control, and asking such deep probing questions and intruding on his employees within the privacy of their own homes, in this way, were not appropriate of any company/organisation. Although at the time Ford's actions were applauded and tolerated (as his workers were dependent upon their wages), this management by virtue or even fear, depending upon how you view it, eventually gave rise to the Human Relations Movement,[4] but science, under the guise of efficiency and effectiveness, swung Ford's culture and whatever the reasons were behind it, fully back the other way.

1.2 Science, the Proclaimed Panacea?

During the Industrial Revolution, the human element of the organisation was viewed as a nuisance, a resource of uncertainty and variation to be reduced by science (Shenhav, 1995). People were regarded as unnecessary fodder where science, under the guise of industrial betterment and rationalist drive for efficiency, simply surgically removed any employers' moral and ethical considerations and guides for its employees. This systems rationalism resulted in cold thinking and approaches towards human relations, where the mass of (and still growing) implementation of automation and computers has led to a focus upon leading through cognition. Cognition is the process of thinking and the identification of knowledge by both understanding and perceiving—rather than using emotion, which is distinguished from reasoning or knowledge as being a strong feeling which is derived from one's own circumstances, mood or relationships with others (i.e. having an instinctive or intuitive feeling). Today, with employees burning out from working long hours and increasing amounts of work-related stress, little has changed in this 'scientific' cold thinking approach and application of leadership and management.

The present core of leadership education and application primarily focuses upon hard disciplines such as management (including faddish) styles, accounting, statistics and operational research, together with all of their priorities to find even 'better' ways to forecast, plan and control people through (results-driven [?]) numerical targets, performance numeration and performance appraisals that are nowhere near scientific but, ironically, are still considered *useful* in making *informed* decisions, whilst blatantly and largely ignoring human factors such as emotion and well-being, which are mainly viewed as irrelevant within today's interconnected markets and interconnected relationships. Where the never-ending drive towards maximising shareholder values within these companies always seems to be at the expense of the people who are carrying out the actual work, still the organisations are rarely deemed (only possibly 'seen' to be, via some creative accountancy and end-of-year reports) to be successful in achieving their own strategic objectives. This all points towards the need for new ways of leadership and management education, thinking and action, to ones which move beyond the current linear and mechanistic (certainly outdated—but still stubbornly current) methods, to ways to still invest in both automation and technology but *also* take into account and provide organic human growth and development. Perhaps it is time to dust off the Human Relations Movement!?

1.3 An Historical Account of Spirituality

The term and subsequent translations of spirituality first began to appear within the 5th century, but only became more common in the Middle

Ages. In Biblical terms, spirituality means being enlivened and directed by the metaphysical God, whilst also being motivated and compelled by the Holy Spirit, as opposed to a life which ignores and discards both of these influences. During the 11th century the meaning changed where, as opposed to the materialistic and sensory aspects of life, spirituality began to represent the mental aspect of it. In the 13th century, spirituality attained both a psychological and social meaning. Socially, it represented the role and domain of the clergy, that is the ecclesiastical against these temporary, worldly, possessions, the ecclesiastical against the secular authority and the clerical class against the secular class. Psychologically, it represented the realm of the soul, that is the purity of motives, affections, intentions, outlook and inherent characteristics and behaviours, together with the requirement of self-analysis of any associated bad feelings that were related to these characteristic traits.

During both the 17th and 18th century, higher and lower forms of spirituality were terms used to differentiate between the higher mental thought processes or cognitive behaviour and the lower biological evolution of the physical form. According to evolution, as humans physically and naturally evolve over time, they can also (through their *own free will*) evolve mentally through different ways of thinking and through the training and pragmatic action of their spirit. Spirit, within this context, is the non-physical part of an individual, which provides and drives their emotions and character.

After the Second World War, spirituality and religion separated, and spirituality leaned more heavily towards being more of an objective experience, in terms of one which is subject to natural laws. This was directly opposed to the view that a religious experience is a completely subjective phenomenon which is based upon religious scriptures, rules and dogma, rather than something which can be objectively trusted, experienced and so considered to be real. The gap between spirituality and religion became evermore apparent during the latter part of the 20th century, which saw the arrival of the New Age and the rise of the secular New Thought Movement (Hanegraaff, 1999; Sheldrake, 2013; Waaijman, 2007). Tracing its roots back to Aristotle and together with scientists such as Galileo, Newton, Einstein and Maxwell, who all researched and carried out powerful thought experiments in their respective (and since published) works, this secular spirituality accentuates humanistic ideas, behaviours and moral character. Where qualities such as love, compassion, patience, tolerance, forgiveness, contentment, responsibility, harmony and a concern for others are all part of life and human experiences which go beyond a purely materialist attitude of the world, but without necessarily accepting a belief in the supernatural and/or a divine being—in other words, they didn't believe in a God! At its core, this contemporary approach to spirituality focuses on the deepest values and meanings through which people can lead their lives by, thus enabling the individual to recover and/or discover the spirit of their very *being*, together with what is their true *self*.

The declining membership of religious organisations has led to the growth of secularism in the Western world which, in turn, has caused the current broader (totally mis)understood view of spirituality where the word *spiritual* has now replaced the word *religious* and is now more frequently used as such. This has only further added to all of the confusion, as those individuals who now speak of spirituality often describe themselves as being *spiritual but not religious*, without really knowing the difference. From a life experience perspective of spirituality, spirituality is now considered to be more real, true and so useful, rather than accepting any historical (authoritarian) religious doctrine, which is based upon pure faith in an unknown deity. Personal well-being, both physical and psychological, is an all-important attribute of this contemporary spirituality, although the majority of modern-day thinking neither embraces or even understands this particular approach to it.

This current thinking is mainly due to the study of spirituality being considered and approached from two sides. On one side, there is the interdisciplinary perspective which draws from elements of psychology, sociology, history and philosophy where each of these disciplines interact, even support and contribute to the actual practising of spirituality. The challenge in this instance is to further identify the strengths and truths within each of these areas and integrate them into a practical—workable—framework which is not only understandable, but is generic, specific and flexible enough to support both professional and personal life objectives. Which is, of course, the aim of this book. From the opposing side, the study of spirituality is regarded as an independent discipline amidst the academic sciences from which it must detach itself from, specifically from the discipline of history and philosophy of both religion and theology. To enable this is also another aim of this book.

Medicine, science, art, psychiatry, astronomy and spirituality all have their origins deeply rooted within religion and all have subsequently struggled hard to free themselves of any trace of its influence. None more so than spirituality, which is still firmly fixed and entrenched within many minds, so seeming to be perpetually associated to religion and/or mystical practices.

Detaching from the past, whether it be a discipline, a professional or personal history, a way of thinking and doing things, or as an individual or group, is not easy. But it can be done. It is however fair to say to somewhat enable this requires an open mind, imagination and creativity if the context of spirituality is to be seriously offered as a viable thought and practice to the business and academic community and the general populace alike. From this standing and deeply entrenched start the best way to approach this, at this point, is by gritting our teeth (as the following goes against years and years of thinking and publishing, which has been underpinned and repeatedly been reinforced by 'factual' spiritual statements and how spirituality should be viewed and practised) and set out by categorically stating and clarifying what spirituality certainly isn't all about . . .

1.4 What Spirituality *Isn't* All About . . .

Are you ready? We start with (and so henceforth never ever, mentioned again) spiritual clichés: Karma. Zen. Regeneration. Reborn. Light. Incense. Enrich. Nice. *Ohm!* 'Money is evil.' 'You've got to dance like there's nobody watching—love like you'll never be hurt—sing like there's nobody listening—live like it's heaven on earth.' Along with: 'That which does not kill us makes us stronger.' 'Don't walk behind me, I may not lead. Don't walk in front of me, I may not follow. Just walk beside me and be my friend.' 'The question isn't who is going to let me, it's who is going to stop me.' 'Choose a job you love and you will never have to work a day in your life again.' 'Nothing is impossible, the word itself says *I'm possible*.' Lastly, the certainly well-used and worn ones: Journey. Joy. Nourish and nurture, which are only mentioned once in short sections, just to dispel them—I promise! Finally, spirituality is not all 'touchy feely', tree hugging and being 'lovey dovey' to everybody; on the contrary, it is hardnosed and selfish. Perhaps, surprisingly, you certainly don't have to like everything and everybody, or even turn the other cheek upon being confronted. Far from it!

Over the decades, the word *spirituality* has been used so frequently there is now a risk of current works becoming so cheesy, saturated and fragmented that it will become trite and meaningless. Attempts are also still continuing to de-link spirituality from both religion and science, whilst also attempting to identify its own unique and various facets and dimensions. This makes trying to define the term *spirituality* especially difficult and still today, there is no one commonly agreed definition. Given the aforementioned ambiguity surrounding the definition(s) of spirituality and the continuous attempts to identify it through the exclusion of synonyms and the inclusion of both antonyms and homonyms, defining spirituality is often very confusing and highly misleading. For example, words such as forgiveness, leadership, empathy, meaning, courage, honesty, perseverance, survival, calling, membership, hope and faith are relevant to spirituality but not in the same context, concept and meaning by which they are currently presented and understood. Still (incorrectly) associated with religion and God, spirituality today also has absolutely no relationship (perhaps even more surprisingly than the previous points?), to: Happiness. Perfection. Servant leadership. Altruism/altruism. Love (for others). Selflessness. Perfection or mindfulness. In addition, spiritualism and/or cults—which are situated at the opposite and extreme end of the spectrum, at what is termed as the 'dark' side—are the highly controversial occult perspective and understanding of spirituality which comprises of witchcraft, Ouija boards, tarot cards, horoscopes and fortune telling. These practices have nothing to do with spirituality—this is spiritualism, not spirituality!

Amongst all of this, there are also numerous misconceptions and misunderstandings regarding various other spiritual words and their associated meanings which have become stubbornly entrenched, within both literature and the mind, such as struggle, anchor and humility and that spiritual individuals are not creative, are nonconfrontational and have no ambition for themselves, but only for others i.e. servant leadership and selflessness. All complete nonsense! Spirituality also isn't about poverty (although the experience of being poor is useful, as it is a great leveller for the individual, in determining gratitude and realising the difference between want and need); it isn't about denying yourself anything that you want. It's nice to have a bit of luxury now and again and there is certainly nothing wrong with that. The problem occurs when anything is taken to the excess. The main culprit to extreme excess being . . . the pursuit of happiness, and the pursuit of happiness isn't the same as ever actually reaching it.

1.5 The Pursuit of Happiness

Happiness which is considered, by many, to be a proxy—a measure to living life and in general, as well—and as such, is considered to be the driving force behind so much of our own world, in terms of how our own motives and actions set out to achieve it. Psychology has defined happiness as a subjective well-being; however, some theorists disagree with this and instead promote the idea of a *meaningful* life as important, or being more important than a happy and cheerful one. Within this context, happiness can also be described as (and is generally associated to) positivity which, in turn, supports good *behaviour*. However, the pursuit of happiness also supports bad behaviour when trying to achieve (the elusive) it. Negativity, such as misery and suffering, is generally associated with bad behaviour and although the individual experiences no real meaning and purpose to their life, their current state could be considered to be meaningful. The reason is because these people are, in the main, *desperate* (see Chapter 2, Section 2.14 Why Find the Spiritual '*It*' . . .) to get out of their situation and circumstances and will do *anything* to do so. Although this 'anything' also supports, for example, stealing to sell and/or selling their/your body for sex to receive money to feed a, addictive, habit of some kind, all of which are considered to be negative behaviours, we could also consider prostituting yourself for money and/or stealing in order to basically survive, maybe due to a safety issue such as escaping from an abusive environment or violent relationship for example, (see Christine S., p. 183), this could then be viewed as more of a positive behaviour!? This 'do anything' also leads us onto the, previously stated, 'meaningful' part of the equation. A life of debauchery, misery and suffering will either kill us, bring us to attempt/or actually commit suicide, send us to prison, or motivate us to change things when we have had enough of this/our particular lifestyle. This 'had enough' is when we have hit our rock bottom (see Chapter 2, Section 2.12 Suffering), so this behaviour (both positive and negative) and reaching our rock bottom, in relative time and space, are meaningful as they (could and usually do) lead us into seeking a more positive change for ourselves. It can also be considered that stealing, drug taking, fighting, cruelty, being greedy, sex and acquiring material possessions can provide the individual with, at least, a sense of their happiness and so meaning (but not purpose) to their life.

Some individuals 'love' their job but are paid very little for doing it and although they also have little in terms of possessions, they are happy with both their lot and life. Whereas, other individuals work hard for the *purpose* of acquiring the material goods and services which they think and hope will bring them happiness (and for an instant they, indeed, do so), but this superficial escap*ism* and temporary happiness does not bring any *real* meaning or purpose to their lives.

Working and together with living in a (relatively) nice house and with nice possessions, these individuals can also suffer and be miserable for different reasons, such as living with an addict and/or being burned out/ stressed out from work. Working all the hours in a pressurised job, trying to pay for everything to which they (and their partner, if they have one) have become accustomed to. Going on holidays to exotic places. Enjoying fine dining. Personal registrations on their expensive car/s. Nice clothes and jewellery. Keeping the kids in private school and (trying to keep up the repayments on their mortgage on) a beautiful house are all the trappings of success. It all sounds and looks idyllic, but these/they can also all be heavy millstones (i.e. heavy burdens[5]) around one's neck. Any number of these things and more besides can cause misery and suffering from the pressures of being (or at least appearing to be) successful. These individuals, however, although they may eventually do so, will not be as 'fast' to hit their rock bottom as quickly as the debauched individual does.

Spiritual support groups (over 50 of them at the last count) exist to help and support those with an excessive addiction, rather than an excessive lifestyle (for which there is none, again at the last count). Sad but true. Suffice to say, more individuals *commit suicide* living in opulent-driven misery and suffering (through the stress of maintaining their 'position in life' and, especially, if they literally lose it all—in terms of their possessions and so sometimes and consequently their mind[6]), than those in the addictive and/ or poverty world of misery and suffering. However, more individuals *kill* themselves in terms of both losing their own identity (i.e. your *self*) and through *unintentional* suicide, caused by the hardships of their lifestyle in terms of their addictive and/or poverty-driven misery and suffering, rather than the, aforementioned, individuals who commit suicide, whilst living in opulence-driven misery and suffering. In any of these previous scenarios, it appears that both the psychologists and the theorists are right, as none of these individuals are leading a 'real' meaningful and purposeful life, only, at best, maybe a subjective happy one, at worst an objective escapism one. Aside from Al-Anon (a spiritual support group only for the family and friends of alcoholics; see Chapter 3, Section 3.6 Spiritual Support Groups: Fellowships), at least the (typically regarded) dependant addict can seek help from a relevant 12-Step spiritual support group/programme, whereas the (not so typically regarded)—(considered non) dependant 'addict' has nowhere to go. All in all, regardless whether it is subjective or objective, perhaps we are being coaxed, even persuaded, into looking for meaningfulness and happiness in the wrong places.

1.5.1 *The Pursuit of Happiness, in the Wrong Places*

These 'wrong places' often involve an extreme and dangerous view of what an individual thinks achieving happiness and being spiritual actually both mean, that is, that they must be completely *selfless*. As such, this 'selfless requirement' has become securely anchored within the (severe mis)understanding of what both achieving happiness and spirituality is really all about. It is hereby stated, and it cannot be stressed and underlined enough: *Spirituality has nothing to do with either happiness, or selflessness! Absolutely nothing!* Such a claim goes against thousands of years of thought on this subject and here's why.

It has long been peddled and so believed that the following 'anchors' are regarded as being the underlying foundations of spirituality that some individuals have to adopt and live their lives by. Anchors such as perfectionism: The state of being complete and correct in every way. This essentially means being flawless, needing to always be exactly right and to always act both morally and ethically in everything that they do. Unconditional love: The need to love and be loved. This is centred on the constant drive to form social bonds and to develop mutually caring (whether reciprocated or not) relationships with other individuals. This is all dangerous stuff and more worryingly, readily accepted assumptions of what spirituality is made up of and what the individual' *must* undertake to consider themselves to be spiritual. 'Made up' being the operative words.

Spirituality has also long been associated with servant leadership. People centredness is, (considered to be a 'universal agreement'), at the heart of servant leadership, the aim of which is to (happily) *selflessly* serve others. Disturbingly, existing empirical research on servant leadership supports the hypothesis that the servant leader *must* adopt the previously mentioned universal agreement, as it is core to the whole spiritual archetype (Fry, 2003; Greenleaf, 1998, 1978, 1977). Following Greenleaf's writings on servant leadership, for well over two decades, there has been little to no progress regarding this concept and proposal (Fry et al., 2007; Greenleaf, 1998, 1978, 1977). "What is the truth?" "Can an individual be obliged to be truly selfless (Smith, 2014), in ensuring the well-being in all aspects of another person, even the world in which they live in?" This is at the heart of the problem and a major error in the understanding of the word 'selfless', where being selfless is a disease within ourselves, or a *dis-ease* which we feel within ourselves (see Chapter 2, Section 2.14 Why Find the Spiritual '*It*' . . .), in its own right. This disease and/or *dis-ease* is an actual illness and is called co-dependency, or CoDa for short.

Although more of this subject will be discussed (see Chapter 2, Section 2.9 Co-dependency, Servant Leadership and Altruism), co-dependency also encompasses altruism. Altruism (aimed mainly towards 'required' spiritual traits) refers to an individual being morally obliged and purely motivated in benefiting others, without receiving or expecting anything in return. In addition, where one person is distressed altruism causes distress in the 'spiritual' individual, who then feels personally responsible for removing the other person's distress and discomfort which, in turn, relieves their very own distress and discomfort. The cycle thus continues. What is really disturbing amongst not just servant leadership and altruism, but all of the aforementioned spiritually 'required' traits, is through constantly feeling that they need to help and do, so pleasing and 'warming' the hearts of other people, the 'spiritual' individual starts to lose their own identity and their own sense of self. Paradoxically, if the answer to servant leadership and altruism is (and not to put a too finer point on it, but both of these are tantamount to problematic addictions to perfectionism and giving themselves/all to others) the quest for spirituality, then the ongoing solution must be—ironically—the quest for spirituality!

Science is a 'connaissance approchée' (Bachelard, 1927) that is, it comes closer and closer to truth without ever reaching it. Which is just like spirituality. Achieving perfection is regarded as the universal need to always be right and to reach the ultimate truth. Although there are individuals who class themselves as 'spiritual' and as such have totally convinced themselves that they will find this truth in their lifetime, they tend to be very disappointed when they go to bed at night having not achieved this universal need and truth, constantly 'beating' themselves up and wondering what they have to do next and where they have to try (even) harder, in order to be perfect tomorrow. As we know, tomorrow never comes! Although spirituality does seek to come closer and closer to the *truth* (with 'seek' being the operative word), the important difference being this seeking of the truth is about finding *The Self*. The spiritual individual also knows and accepts, that actually and finally, getting to this *truth* is unachievable. They will never ever reach it. It cannot be done. Instead, spirituality is all about progress, never-ever perfection. Frankly these spiritual anchors of perfection, servant leadership and altruism all boil down to self-abuse! All spiritual super struggles for deluded idealists.

Although they both share the connaissance approchée (Bachelard, 1927) science is not an appropriate instrument to seek the truth within spirituality. Scientific theory must be subjected to systematic empirical testing, in order to judge and determine the accuracy of the predictions which have been generated by it. 'Science does not apply within spirituality, as there is no need to test cause and effect relationships in areas of human experience which rely upon faith, as scientific theoretical models that are accepted upon faith are determined to be fixed, invariant and true' (Fry & Smith, 1987). Therefore, science is not considered to be an appropriate instrument to seek truth in areas of human experience and as such, has left the study of spirituality in the subjective humanistic world.

SIMON P: "My background and profession are purely scientific, so that kind of [spiritual] stuff doesn't really fit to the/my remit, but I think, erm, when I actually spend time thinking more about me, I suppose there is some element of spirituality within me, which I don't realise."

Within spirituality, there is no place for absolute truth and neither are there higher standards for the fixation of belief, as individuals often let their limiting beliefs control their lives. Instead, there is an acceptance that the (spiritual) individual will never be 'finished', that is they will never reach full spiritual maturity; this is all about *'progress not perfection'* (Al-Anon Family Group UK & Eire, 1992, 1997; Wilson, 1988) and accepting that they (and others) will always be *work-in-progress*. The task, therefore, is to assess and fix what is out of kilter within themselves and to resist the temptation to 'play games', in what is a deadly serious human situation or dilemma. This is, perhaps, the difference between spirituality and religion!?

1.6 The Difference Between Spirituality and Religion!?

Scriptures, rules and dogma of religion can be restrictive in terms of what is and isn't to be worn and what can and cannot be eaten. On that note, "What happened to not eating meat—only fish on a Friday, as this was once considered to be a sin and now, today, it doesn't matter!?"[7] "What happened to all of the previous meat-eating sinners—are they still in hell, or have they had their (in death) sentences suitably reprieved?" Some religions don't allow the drinking of alcohol, tea or coffee, or donating or accepting blood transfusions. Sadly, many terrorism acts and wars are also conducted due to religious ideals and beliefs. Overall, within religion and through interpretation, there can still be an overwhelming environment—a self-righteousness and attitude—of 'we are right and other people and religions, are wrong'. This is not to say religions have no value and while there are commonalties between spirituality and the major world faiths, they also differ from each other in significant ways. Spirituality is an *essence* defined as the core nature, or the most important qualities of a person or thing, that is, the construct of an individual. Although there are no standard rules, scriptures or texts, spirituality believes in what is right and what is wrong. The spiritual individual does not have to pray and if they do, they do it alone—not for 'show' in front of others. Religion is a 'form' which consists of a transcendent series of texts, practices and beliefs which are shared by a particular community, who are also (on occasions) expected to and indeed do regularly pray together. Religion also involves a belief in a metaphysical God. The very foundation of religion is *faith*, where even some teachers of religion neither understand nor practise faith whereas spiritual individuals, even the atheists and agnostics, make room for faith together with the belief, not necessarily in God, in a higher power (Hill, 2011; Ruse, 2010).

1.7 Higher Power

A vast majority of spiritual people, even atheists and agnostics, replace a belief in a metaphysical God and instead have a belief in a/*their higher power*.

PAUL J: "What is bizarre, is I don't really know the difference between an atheist and an agnostic, but at one point in time I described and regarded myself as being one, or both of those. Did I believe in going to church? Absolutely not! Because I previously had Christianity as a religion and that didn't sit well with me and it didn't sit well with me for many years. Do I believe in something now? Yes—absolutely! With what is going on in my life, the people who are helping me are all from my spiritual support group and that says something in its own right—that's power in its own right, of a higher power!"

EDWARD P. H: "I have been a Buddhist for over 20 years and as a Buddhist I don't believe in 'a God' as such, no! Buddhists don't believe in a God and there are some very strong arguments, from a Buddhist point of view, that there cannot be a God. However, that is a Buddhist view—I personally don't actually really know, but I feel that there is something out there Steve that's much higher, but what that is I really don't know."

Having a higher power reaffirms that the individual may be powerless, especially over other people and a multitude of situations, but they are not helpless and they are not alone. Some individuals have been known, amongst others, to use nature, animals and plain gut instinct as their higher power, but for many other individuals their higher power is the people who make up *their* particular (support) group. These groups all share a common aim, to look for solutions to a problem . . . which is achieved through both individual and collective wisdom and the strength and support which they get from those who understand what the individual has gone or is going through. In other words, they have empathy with one another. Others choose and have, in addition to their groups, an individual sponsor, one who has mainly been 'around' spirituality for a longer period than they have and so know 'some ropes' in terms of knowledge, experience, application, the pitfalls and the benefits of having a spiritual programme and being spiritual, which they are prepared to share on a connected, one-to-one basis.

1.8 Introducing: *Paracoaching*

The role and *aims* of the spiritual sponsor are to *freely* share their experience and to support others, by giving encouragement and providing some hope, whilst also acting as a trusted guide and confidant. It is a privilege to be *asked* to be somebody's sponsor, as the individual (acting as a receptor) is seeking an additional, perhaps more, focused stimuli in terms of a connection; a resonance and empathy with another person with whom they can and will share their very innermost secrets and seek guidance from. The sponsor, although a connection, is a person who is *not your friend* and as such they aren't biased, instead they are non-judgemental. The sponsor is somebody who (can and will) impartially listen to concerns, questions or problems, as well as clarify and put a different perspective on 'sticking points' as to when any doubts occur, or help if and when there are any blockers which need removing. This facilitates and enables the receptive individual to both *learn and develop* and so progress and *continue* to move forward. However, the sponsor does not measure progress; although they do serve as a useful reference point, the emphasis is always upon the individual to take their own self-responsibility for *all* things, particularly in discovering and acting on their own weaknesses and to recognising and building upon their own strengths, in order to reach their full potential. Self-responsibility means taking appropriate and proportional action, when naturally required and obviously needed. Realising and taking self-responsibility, for example, your health and/or the well-being of your small children, should be a natural given. Extending this given instinct to knowing the part that you play within unhealthy personal and professional situations and relationships, taking self-responsibility also includes what positive actions *you yourself* have identified as a *requirement* and so can then *choose* to do, in order to take yourself from where you are *now* by learning from and changing your own life and situation, to not necessarily take you to where *you want* to be—but where you *need* to be. This emphasis on 'want and need' may seem pedantic (although this is discussed further throughout the following chapters, especially Chapter 2, Section 2.10 Want and Need: Now and When), but there is a distinct and significant difference between these two areas. Basically, a want is something that people desire to have, which they may or may not be able to obtain, and even if gained, it might not be a good or right thing to have. A *need* is something which is required to survive, so ultimately it can only be a good thing, as it will always be significantly better than what you had and/or who you were before you had it. Although spiritual support groups do just that—they support through interconnectedness, a sponsor is there to connect with the individual and to *freely* facilitate this want and what is actually needed process, by energising and assisting the individual to enhance their *personal skills*, when they are *called upon* to do so.

Usually employed and so *paid* to do so, a business coach clarifies the vision of the business and plans both long-term and short-term *goals* to take the organisation and its employees from where it/they are now to where it/they *want* to be. Good coaches evolve, are flexible and can readily adapt to new theories and skills. They require knowledge and understanding of business operations and processes as well as a variety of styles, skills and techniques which deliver improvements in organisational performance in order to reach its full potential. They also understand 'a one size does not fit all' businesses and, as such, know how to make their approach bespoke enough to fit the different needs for different organisations and interconnected groups but not, in the main, to make their overall offering fit to different individuals, so avoiding a connection with them. It is *they*—the business coach who identifies the requirements, motivations, desires, skills and thought processes and also assists in the *learning and development* in enhancing the *business skills* within the group which, in turn, will deliver the overall organisational objectives, but not necessarily the individuals' own, professional or personal, objectives. Through listening, guiding, encouraging, motivating and (overtly) supporting the interconnected group, the business coach is also (covertly) assessing and providing feedback on their strengths and weaknesses of the contained individuals within the group to the key stakeholder/s (note, not to the individuals themselves), together with any obstacles as to the rate of *required* progress of the required objective. Although these business coaches have the required support of the stakeholders and as such are able to make informed decisions which will move the initiative (to a degree) forward, they do not have any recognised and 'real' authority to do so. A business coach is *not your friend*, or is really 'interested' in an individual (hence having neither the desire or need to want to build relationships and have a connection with them) unless they are being awkward and are, either directly or passively, standing in the way of business progress. It is then down to the stakeholders to deal with the situation as connected individuals rather than the, suitably detached, business coach having to do it themselves. The business coach, more than likely, will not be a permanent employee of the business. They are a sounding board—a source of information, purely employed (often on a temporary contract) to facilitate and ensure improvement in business performance. Therefore, any sense of loyalty and commitment to the business is somewhat lost.

With both a sponsor and business coach having many impressive and progressive traits and professional and personal skills, it makes sense to consider a hybrid—an effective and efficient amalgamation of these two functions and their connected and interconnected relationship abilities to, perhaps, be hereby named and henceforth to be known as—a 'paracoach'.

Although the 'paracoach' conceptual role is being offered as a viable option and alternative to the present leadership and management styles, it still doesn't answer the overall purpose of this book as there still remains the difficult question, "How can the subject of spirituality be developed and extended so that it is both treated and regarded as being a serious business approach, initiative and application to its use within (turbulent) interconnected markets and interconnected relationships; whilst also being appealing to and so can be considered amongst all people, but still being bespoke enough to allow the individual to change their own particular situation and circumstances for the benefit of not only themselves, but also for others and the overall purpose of the business?" This question, together with the conundrum as to what this spirituality is and isn't all about, continues to be obligated to answer.

Notes

1 Overcome by emotions and passion, the individual is driven to a self-destructive frenzy of excess.
2 Intoxicated: Emotionally excited, elated, or exhilarated—as by great joy or extreme pleasure.
3 The author of the highly successful book *Think and Grow Rich* admitted that it was deliberately titled this way—to give the impression that it was about making vast amounts of money. Spoiler alert: It isn't and doesn't!
4 Where personal development, growth and employee goal-setting are considered as essential to effective businesses. It also emphasised that motivation is derived from team goals and greater production resulted from encouragement and positive reinforcement.
5 The literal hanging of a millstone around the neck of the person placed in deep water is mentioned as a punishment in the New Testament (Matthew 18:6), so causing the 'naughty' individual to be drowned.
6 It is considered that accumulated riches can gain such a powerful hold on an individual that they lose all sense of value and virtue.
7 The Catholic Church defines meat as the flesh of warm-blooded animals, so eating fish is permitted on Fridays. The practice of abstaining from meat on Fridays is centuries-old, but in 1985 the Catholic Church in England and Wales allowed Catholics to substitute another form of penance in its place.

2 What Is *It*, All and Not, About?

At the heart of spirituality, there lie many tensions and paradoxes. This has created an ongoing, often mistaken perception, mystery and ambiguity, which have been and still are interpreted in many different ways across different countries and cultures, businesses, interconnected groups and both connected and singular individuals alike. To this, let us first of all start with determining some baseline definitions and thoughts around the core areas of the subject matter.

2.1 What Is Business?

The primary purpose of a business is to fund the costs of operating that business, as well as to maximise profits for its owners or stakeholders, through offering quality and value through its products and/or services to customers who are willing to pay for that value, with cash or equivalents. Although (and since discredited) Milton Friedman (1912–2006) viewed the responsibility of any business is to increase its profits and any corporate attempt to promote 'desirable social ends' 'is highly subversive to the capitalist system' (Ebenstein, 2014; Friedman, 2007). Friedman considered the sacrificing of profits for social interest as being wrong and that employees are only contracted and so are paid to carry out a job to the best of their ability and this is where the employer's responsibility ends (Freidman, 2007). Since then (although to some extent the debate has continued), it has been accepted that the pursuit of profits is neither 'wicked or immoral'.

2.2 What Is an Interconnected Market?

Our world economy and society are now interconnected by markets and supply chains, communications, technology and travel. For consumers an interconnected world means more choices and more competitive prices on the goods and services which they want. For those companies who are trying to reach the consumer, this means more competition and increased pressure to anticipate consumer trends, but what comes with this interconnectedness is an unprecedented opportunity to tap into new markets.

2.3 What Is an Interconnected Relationship?

When two things are related, they are connected. When a number of things are related, they are interconnected.

2.4 What Is Work?

"What is work?" Although the question may seem trite, analysis of the relationship between work (an activity involving physical or mental effort carried out, usually for money, in order to achieve a purpose or result) and suffering (where, although suffering can be caused in a variety of different ways, 90% of human suffering is caused mentally through causes such as anger, fear, hatred, jealousy and insecurity), provides an equation where work is not separate from suffering and when life at work suffers then the individuals' home life suffers as well. Vice versa, when home life suffers work life suffers as well—although amazingly! It seems it is totally acceptable, even the norm, to allow work to have a negative impact on our personal lives but problems within our personal lives are strenuously advised to be ignored, discouraged and disregarded as being irrelevant in business. Of course, taking this viewpoint and 'strong' advice only exacerbates the overall suffering, for the 'bottled up' individual.

One of the trickiest things to remember is when you've got troubled times at home it is not that easy to simply 'leave them' troubles (as previous management courses/books/practices have told us to do so) at the factory gate or office door. Personal problems such as divorce, a troubled marriage/relationship or money worries often become so overwhelming they threaten to sabotage all aspects of the individuals' life and when you are advised that to talk about your personal problems at work is strictly taboo, as it is considered to be 'unprofessional', this is hard for anyone. Equally, discussing professional problems at home and/or in the pub/bar/cafe could be considered as being a lot easier to do, but to the 'receiver' it is hard hearing the same old thing over and over and over again. How to lose colleagues, family and friends by influencing them to 'roll' their eyes and avoid you!? To avoid this eye rolling and avoidance means that you have to continuously put on a 'front', but behind this front, with all what's going on in your life will, more than likely, be 'bottled up' and as such 'eat' you up and so be 'killing' you, from the inside—outwards.

Where anger turns into a hardened resentment and where sadness turns into hardened depression, in trying to avoid reaching these points may mean the individual seeks to 'escape' their 'situation' and negative thought processes through the use of illegal, mainly artificial, drugs such as cannabis, spice, cocaine, crystal meth, MDMA, heroine, etc., or via legal ones such as alcohol, smoking, gambling, food and even sex, and/ or by a legitimate medical help/intervention of some kind such as therapy, Cognitive Behavioural Therapy (CBT) and/or antidepressants. All, whether it be unconventional and/or conventional, of which can have very unpleasant, cause and effect, side effects.

Happiness releases endorphins. Endorphins are also used to reduce our perception of pain and act similarly to drugs, such as morphine and codeine, but whilst some (albeit temporary) happiness and relief can be obtained (as previously mentioned) from the use of artificial illegal and legal, methods (by way of ingesting them, i.e. snorting and/or injecting—especially between the toes when all of the individuals' veins have collapsed—or, (but not for smuggling purposes), sticking drugs up the backside[1] and/or vagina[2] and/or poured through the eyes,[3] to name but a few) and materials, but as quickly as numbness from pain and euphoria is experienced, these concoctions of 'happy enhancers' can also produce profound ill health, as well as rapid and violent mood swings. These mood swings then generally cause and are associated with highly volatile, unpredictable and dysfunctional situations which lead to, both connected and interconnected, relationship problems. Additionally, say an unpredictable event such as a world pandemic where people are restricted in having to stay in their homes or, more commonly, where they find themselves 'stuck' within a work environment—where they are often thrown into a situation, having no choice as to who they have to spend time working with and then have to go home and live with others who are (also) considerably awkward and difficult to be with, together with any of their associated challenges—can all very quickly expose unhealthy cycles through being forced to spend time around not only other *people but also with ourselves and our own thoughts*. Few will recognise both home and work as being melting pots which can either create positive exchanges—where individuals and many different people can exist and come together in one place, often mixing different ideas and so producing something new and useful—or negative ones instead, and more commonly, where these situations become a breeding ground for a bottled-up and so forced, stress-related melt-downs.

2.5 Stress

Stress can be defined as 'the degree to which you feel overwhelmed and unable to cope, as a result of pressures which are unmanageable' to us. At its most basic level, stress is a response to pressures from either a situation or a life event. Stress symptoms can affect your body, your thoughts, feelings and your behaviour. Psychologists claim that feeling acute stress, or short-term stress, is beneficial as it provides determination and focus, which helps the individual to finish tasks and achieve goals. Then, the actual achievement of those goals makes us feel good and so is also an important part of good mental health. For most, this infrequent stress is inevitable, even good, such as, for example, planning a wedding, moving house, preparing for exams, starting a new job, meeting somebody new or doing something new for the first time. With awareness and a little skill, the impact of negative stress is only temporary and not particularly serious. However, intense or constant amounts and regular frequencies of this low-grade acute stress, over a long period, can also cause ill health. The point being, every individual has their own 'tipping point', the critical edge where moderate, tolerable stress transitions into bad chronic stress. Signs of this chronic stress fall into three main categories, physical, mental/emotional and behavioural. Not many of us manage this particular bad stress very well and as such are unable to recognise the signs that we are approaching the critical point and so cannot, consciously and deliberately, step back from the edge of it.

2.6 Work and Suffering

Compulsive working is chronic as the individual (termed as being a workahilic), seeks to alleviate personal psychological stress and, due to the release of associated adrenaline and/or other stress hormones by approaching work in this way, is highly addictive. Known as process addiction, interestingly, those who suffer from unmanageable work procrastination, or work aversion, are also categorised as being workaholics.

The number one cause of employee absenteeism is due to minor illnesses: colds and flu, headaches and stomach bugs. The number two cause of absenteeism is due to mental health issues, the suffering of stress, depression and anxiety. One in every six workers, at any point in time, will be experiencing problems relating to work-related stress. Within the UK alone, over 15.4 million days are lost to work-related stress each year. These unplanned sickness absences cost UK businesses circa £8.4 billion a year. This equates to 70 million lost working days p/a and £15.1 billion a year in reduced productivity at work. A further £2.4 billion a year is spent on replacing staff who leave their jobs because of mental ill health. Disturbingly, all of these figures are increasing, exponentially, year on year. The main reasons which have been cited for sickness absences due to mental health and stress include workload demands, job insecurity and (unhealthy) interconnected work relationships (i.e. bullying) and lack of a work-life balance—burnout and (connected) family issues, which all lead to low morale and disengagement of life in general. Whilst also factoring in employees who are not committed and so 'give' (and so get away with) the least that they possibly can to their jobs and to the organisation, as well as those who also tend to find excuses not to go in to their place of employment (i.e. take fake sick days), the overall impact on the economy, productivity and the 'bottom line' within the global economy is enormous!

Everybody goes to work to earn (some) money, usually to make for themselves a better life and/or to buy and do nice things for either themselves and/or their families. Nothing wrong with that! Some people work extremely hard for very little pay and they are the happiest people in the world. Other people work extremely hard for a lot of money and they are so stressed out it's unbelievable! Within the last decade antidepressant prescribing rates in England alone have more than doubled to over 70 million prescriptions. More than 80% of doctors admit to over-prescribing antidepressants to patients with depression, anxiety and stress. These doctors state they are often forced to prescribe these drugs because appropriate psychological therapies or social care for mild to moderate mental health conditions are simply not available. Many medical people also don't believe that you should 'just take a tablet and that's simply going cure the issue'. They don't! At best medications provide a temporary fix by taking the 'edge off' the symptoms, but they do not provide a root-cause solution to the individuals' underlying issue/s. Cognitive Behavioural Therapy (CBT) also has its critics and limitations. CBT only addresses the individual's current issues instead of the underlying causes to these issues, or any of the wider problems that the individual is experiencing where either their careers or other people all too often have a significant impact on an individual's health and well-being.

2.7 Moods and Feelings

Moods and feelings generally come and go on their own, but not many people can wait for this to naturally happen. By accepting what we feel, when and where we feel things, is all part of experiencing what it is like to be human, without the need to judge either oneself or others. This is the difference between being human and being a human being. Emotions are complex, they are states of feelings which result in physical and psychological changes that influence both our good and bad behaviour. As humans, we experience and have a wide and rich range of emotions. A majority of these emotions are activated by what we say and do and hear. Sometimes our emotions seem to simply 'come upon us' without any clear explanation as to why, as nothing has really changed in our day to cause this change. In some instances, we take on other people's moods or, more succinctly and accurately, we *allow* ourselves to take them on—either what these others do or say influences, enhances or exaggerates how we are currently feeling and can even put us in a totally different mood, at the drop of a hat. If we are in a good mood, we want that feeling to last forever. When we are in a bad mood, we may try and change it to a good mood through having fun by, say, going for a walk or drive somewhere, eating and/or drinking, listening to music or having sex, all with the intention of altering our present emotional state into another more preferred one. As previously discussed, sometimes we also try and alter/force our mood changes through artificial means such as taking drugs or drinking alcohol, or gambling, etc.

Spirituality is, first and foremost, learning about yourself and coming to terms with who and what you *actually* are. To enable this, we need to take a good long and hard look at ourselves, in terms of how we use our emotions to conduct our resulting good or bad behaviour. From this perspective, it helps to recognise and determine our daily moods and feelings with a view to either naturally accepting, controlling and stabilising the variations, through decreasing the highs and increasing the lows, by recognising and removing the influences behind our emotional challenges and changes and so removing the risk of triggering them entirely and with uncontrolled irregularity (see Figure 2.1).

However, this doesn't mean that we all become emotional robots, far from it! Spirituality isn't about denying feelings which are either comfortable or uncomfortable, as all feelings will, and do, eventually pass. Spirituality is about recognising, managing and avoiding our internal feelings before they become hardened and so manifest themselves into unhealthy outward-facing characteristics. Through this self-reflection we can then start to understand our negative drivers and how they are affecting our lives, with a view to us controlling them as opposed to them controlling us.

Although feeling pain in life is inevitable, suffering from a feeling is optional. At this juncture, it is important to note, spirituality is not being offered as the panacea and ultimate cure-all, but it does have a direct impact on life by helping people recognise, minimise and avoid stress and unhealthy, confrontational, situations. Many (of this type of spiritual) individuals, the world over, state that as their general well-being (greatly) improves so they not only have less time off work through being sick, but also have better home relationships as well. It is also recognised that as an individual's spirituality improves so does their physical and mental well being increase to the same extent, in effect, cause and affect! These,

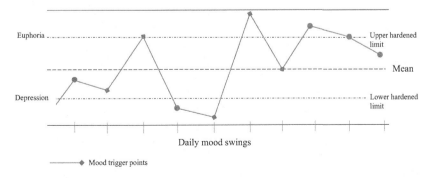

Figure 2.1 Emotional variation.

particular, individuals have come to realise that by taking one day at a time as it comes and not dwelling on the past, or projecting horror for the future (there is a saying, that if you have one foot in the past and one foot in the future all you end up doing is pissing in the now), they are not as stressed as anybody else, because they are alright and they know that they are alright and importantly, they know that everything is going to be alright.

2.8 The Beginning of the Spiritual '*Not*'

Spirituality is not frozen in time. There are no sacred texts, or a requirement to believe in a metaphysical God. *Truth* and *trust* are viewed as a matter of continuing evolution, even revelation! Spirituality is not promoted. Has no formality. Consists of no unnecessary trimmings.[4] Requires no reverence.[5] Has no authoritative figures. Doesn't 'work' through just paying lip service to it (i.e. 'Insincere agreement to something or someone, is to consent in one's words while dissenting in one's heart'). In a continuous and conscious search of *the truth*, spirituality cannot simply be absorbed by someone imitating a sponge. Practising spirituality isn't a matter of appearing in a congregation and putting a little 'quiet' money onto a collection plate. Spirituality provides the individual with significantly more freedom and helps to unlock old ways of thinking and behaviour, which will serve as a new and powerful stimulus for positive change.

Spirituality is not about being or seeking to be perfect as, in the main, we are only human and as such, this means that there is naturally a bit of bad in good people and a bit of good in bad people. Spirituality is about constantly minimising the bad, whilst accentuating the good and progressing to be the best that you can be. To enable this, spirituality means and entails (sometimes re)gaining your *own* morality and life. To do the next right thing, whilst letting others to just get on with their own lives.

We cannot control anything or anyone and spirituality has a very clear view on this, in that you cannot influence or try to change anybody and neither should you. As humans we have all been either cursed and blessed, at the same time, with *free will*. Free will running riot to do good or bad, legally or illegally—whatever we *all* want to do. "How does this help?" For example, if we take the view, as an individual, that we don't like what other people say, do or how they conduct themselves, even if we don't like or agree with them, if that's what they choose to say and do and they are *happy* saying and doing what they are doing then that's up to them—it has absolutely nothing to do with us. However, having free will and knowing that actually *you* can do something about your *own* situation with a change of attitude and way of thinking, gives *you* a much wider scope on and how you deal with difficult and unpleasant situations and other people.

Significantly, if the relationship with another party is *broken or toxic*, either physically and/or mentally, we then have three choices: to either stay, leave or ask the other person to leave us. In all of these choices it is important that we detach with love, that is, to let others simply get on with their lives and face their own consequences (even if this means that the other person dies) without having any ill will, worry, self-reproach or guilt about what may, or may not, happen to them, while we get on with our lives, in or out of the relationship. This is not about not caring. Detaching with love allows another individual to lead their own lives, whilst also providing them with the dignity and space to make their own life choices, to make mistakes and (hopefully) learn from them, whilst we get on with our own life choices. Having free will means having a choice—this means that we have empowerment. Empowerment is not the same as control. Empowerment means that we realise that we have choices, however difficult those choices may be. "But what is a broken or toxic relationship?" "Is it something that we have with others, or something that we have with ourselves, and what is it that prevents us from leaving one and/or having a healthy relationship with either another individual or ourselves?"

2.9 Co-dependency: Servant Leadership and Altruism

An addictive behaviour is a stimulus that is related to an action which is both rewarding and reinforcing. Co-dependency (CoDa) is where an individual's sense of wholeness (see Chapter 2, Section 2.14 Why Find the Spiritual '*It*' . . .), happiness and self-worth are interlinked, entangled and locked in and so their very survival is *literally dependent upon those of others* and if left untreated it becomes more and more serious and destructive, as the person loses all sense of who they actually are. Altruism refers to individuals being morally obliged and purely motivated in benefiting others. Way beyond obsessive, they say that when we die our lives flash before our eyes and if this indeed is the case, with co-dependency it is somebody else's life that flashes before your eyes. Come the day, perhaps this is a 'sobering' thought—in every sense of the word!?

Despite the appearance and rise of the term co-dependency, no standard or recognised definition exists, as there is no current agreement as to whether it is a mental sickness or a condition, a normal response from abnormal people, or an abnormal response from otherwise normal people. It still hasn't even been agreed whether the term co-dependency should be hyphenated or not. What is known is that co-dependents perceive themselves as being completely unselfish, dedicating themselves to the happiness and welfare of others and in doing so ceaselessly and selflessly putting aside their own interests in *trying* to satisfy other people's various wants and needs. Co-dependency is a dysfunctional one-sided relationship, where one person relies on another and/or others for meeting nearly all of their emotional and self-esteem needs. Consequently, these people constantly feel 'burnt-out'.

In addition to selflessly serving, caring, pleasing and benefiting others, these individuals are also 'enthusiastic' in trying to rescue, save, caretake and 'fix' them, that is, to repair another person, in terms of converting attitudes and behaviours into the way that they (the co-dependent) believe the other individual and 'things' should and must be—*their* perceived right way for *them*. This is unhealthy. For the co-dependent, this (constant) effort to fix others provides them with (not just meaning and purpose, with regard to their own lives) a particular 'fix' (i.e. a 'drug') where they seek to require, acquire and derive a necessary, wanted and needed amount of validation and happiness from their, fixated, efforts to fix this other individual(s). This wanting and needing continuously drives the co-dependent individual to compulsively seek ever more validation and happiness via an ever-increasing control of the other, to an extreme which the individual would do just about anything in order to have their 'fixes' to enable them to, literally, function. These fixes and functions are all symptoms of a severe dysfunction within themselves; in effect, it is a way of avoiding one's *own true self.*

Signs of co-dependency include having difficulty communicating honestly, including having a hard time saying "No!" in a relationship. Co-dependents also have trouble identifying their own feelings and making decisions in a relationship. They also value the approval of others, more than valuing themselves. They have poor, or non-existent boundaries. They also fixate upon their own mistakes. Lack trust in themselves. Have poor self-esteem and confuse pity with love. Thereafter the co-dependent relationship can become enmeshed, as it brings with it many perceived 'mutual benefits' where two individuals, in effect, become one identity and so reliant upon each other equally as much for their overall sense of value, worth, well-being, safety, purpose and security. More simply, this enmeshment is when the individuals' sense of wholeness comes from another person (see Figure 2.2). Collusion takes place in this particular

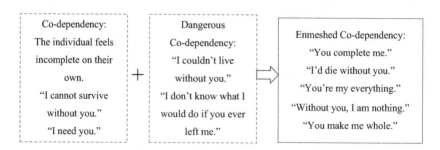

Figure 2.2 When two halves don't make a whole.

situation where, more often than not, there is an abuse of power by one of the participants within that relationship.

Applying this diagrammatic representation within an organisational context, our first thoughts might be to assume that there is a dominant co-dependent relationship between the organisation and the employee. Assuming that the organisation requires a metaphorical 'fix' (i.e. a 'drug') in terms of wanting and needing employees in order for it to function, it is the manager who supplies the enablement and so is the enabler of such (i.e. the action of giving someone the authority, or means to do something), where, in this instance, the manager then becomes a metaphorical 'dealer'. The manager/dealer through seeking and sourcing of individuals to act as employees, in turn, satisfies the *wanting* part of the organisation. It is then the employees who satisfy the *needing* part of this particular 'fix', in time and space. Employees are needed for the business to (*properly*) function (we will come onto the '*properly* function' part in the next section/paragraph Chapter 2, Section 2.9.1 The Next Paragraph: Who Is Co-dependent Upon Whom?) until the organisation requires 'more' employees or replacement employees. Thus, the manager moves away, once again, from their main role and goes back to being a 'dealer' again in order to satisfy the organisational wanting through seeking and hiring . . . the (new) employee, this then satisfies the need of the organisation . . . who then wants more . . . thus the cycle continues. This cycle goes on until the organisation becomes too 'sick'—sick through being 'heavy and bloated' i.e. costly caused by, such as, weak economic conditions and/or poor customer service and/or increased global competition, etc. This is the point when the business, in order to survive, needs to 'detox' so having to become 'lighter' by mainly 'letting their employees go'; in effect making some of their workforce redundant, by, more easily, firing them through circumstances and so nothing that was directly due to being their fault. This is ironic as the organisation has, far more, difficulty firing them when something is directly the employees' fault, due to Employment Law/legislation. In effect, they have to become leaner in their operations. However, during the economic good times and/or attracting lots of new business and/or having a good grip on the workings of an interconnected market, the craving returns and the dealer/manager and the employee/s are back in (the) business,[6] in every sense of the word. This is until the organisation becomes sick again . . .! However, this still begs the questions, "Who is co-dependent upon whom?" and if anything, "Does altruism play a part within all of this?"

2.9.1 *The Next Paragraph: Who Is Co-dependent Upon Whom?*

Just like we need food, water and sleep to ensure our well-being, in order to be fully active and so be able to function *properly and so to survive,* the organisation also requires healthy sustenance in terms of good methods (i.e. in the form of its processes and ways of working) to ensure its well-being. As without any basic necessities both we and the organisation would very quickly and surely fall very *sick* and even die—closing either our 'doors', or the business's doors for good! Therefore, it can be considered an organisation cannot fully function effectively or efficiently without its employees. As such, if it was/is being 'fed' artificial materials or, in this case, 'toxic' individuals, it would thus create an unhealthy environment/culture to operate within. This is indeed, in many, many instances, the case in point, but this will be discussed further in Chapter 4 (see Chapter 4 Culturing Cells).

A dominant loop is the one that principally controls the system's behaviour over a period of time, such as a manager. A manager also has *collusion* power, in a way that they can think and say to the employee "Your survival depends upon me. So, if you don't want me to cut your way of surviving, you're going to have to kow-tow[7] to me." This collusive power and control are, understandably, accepted as being within that of the manager's remit and requirement. In many ways this sort of ('dealing', 'fixing', hiring and firing) hierarchy of controlling power goes on in every business structure, doesn't it? To enable the leader and/or manager to function, they need to lead and/or manage somebody else/ others, because without employees they have no specific reason, purpose and/or meaning to fulfil within the organisation. Opposed to this, employees are more than capable in carrying out their work without either seeing their manager or being directly managed all of the time. In effect, the employee can, to a certain point, function ably without a manager, but a manager cannot function ably without employees. However, the employees' job, their very existence within the organisation and so their livelihood seems to revolve around the *need* to keep their manager 'happy', by providing this individual with their own 'power fix'. This power fix comes by the employee saying and doing the 'right' thing whenever they, the manager, is nearby and within sight and/or earshot of their subordinate. This saying and doing the 'right' thing in front of managers, unbelievably and commonly, goes above and beyond simply being able to do a good job; if the manager takes a dislike to you then, eventually, being 'managed' out of the organisational door is a distinct possibility. Either that or the manager goes out of their way to make their subordinates' life an absolute (collusion power) misery and thereon the employee is left with little, or no choice, but to leave. Suffice to say, people don't leave an organisation—they leave their boss. There is enough published data which says 79% of people leave their roles because of their manager. This statistical fact (at the time of writing) provides confidence as to where the true collusion and so destructive behavioural relationship occurs. Equally, if you are 'dreadful' at your job but the manager likes you, you then have a far better chance of surviving, that is, staying employed within the organisation. This is regarded, in spiritual terms, as putting personalities above principles, as opposed to (the spiritual individual) putting principles above personalities. We all know that putting personalities above principles goes on in most organisations but, especially upon reading it in black and white, this does come across as being both brutal and unreasonable. This finally comes to the heading question and the conundrum, "Who is truly co-dependent upon whom?"

Having an ego distorts one's thinking. Many managers and leaders have massive egos, which they need to 'feed' on a professional level and, presumably, on a personal level as well. Together with both a desire and justification in the manager wanting and needing to exist in their particular role (even perhaps seeking promotion from it) comes the requirement from the employees to satisfy this/their managers' particular desire, justification, ego and need to exist within the organisation as they are aware that, if they do not do so, they risk losing their job through, for example, insubordination. The manager benefits with having their ego fed from having their role of responsibility within the organisation and they also receive an additional benefit, the justification to exist in their/ that position of authority, which is provided by the employee (the subordinate) recognising the power (collusion or otherwise) that the manager has, in that they need to both do and say the 'right' things whenever the manager is around. The employee benefits from this transaction, as they feel obliged and so motivated in partaking in these exchanges, as they receive the benefit of staying in their job and being paid for doing so. All in all, we can safely say, there is no sign of any altruistic intentions from anybody within this scenario.

Having control and power over employees could be considered to be the manager's 'fixes' to their need to exist. The employee then becomes the enabler, that is, a person giving someone the authority or means to do something (where previously, it was the manager who was the enabler via sourcing and recruiting, etc.,) to satisfy their manager's requirement. As previously mentioned, if an employee is capable of carrying out their work but is not liked, they will not *directly* satisfy the manager's egotistical 'craving', so the chances are the employee will be discarded either to another section, or out of the organisation entirely. However, because the manager has the aforementioned power of 'your survival depends on me' as such, they can also feed their ego through having the ability to discard you, in whatever shape or form they choose, which, perversely, also validates their position within the organisation. There is a phrase for these managers: they have become 'drunk' on the power that they have. This power is the managers' (or leaders' for that matter) 'drug' of choice and without it, they would certainly lose their professional and, perhaps, also their personal identity. Which all comes back to, both professionally and/ or personally, their losing their sense of *worth and self* (see Chapter 1,

Section 1.5.1 The Pursuit of Happiness, in the Wrong Places and Chapter 2, Section 2.14 Why Find the Spiritual '*It*' . . .).

In effect, on one hand, the employee could be considered to be co-dependent as they need the job and will, at least on the face of it (see Chapter 4, Section 4.3 Sabotage and Section 4.3.1 Silent Sabotage), feed the manager's egotistical needs whilst, at the same time, also validating both their own and their manager's position in the organisation through being submissive and/or subservient (and more than likely, the manager will also be submissive and/or subservient to their boss for the same reason) to their manager. On the other hand, the manager could also be considered to be co-dependent as they need the employees for them to function and justify their position, as without employees there would be no need for managers, or leaders for that matter. Finally, the organisation wants and needs leaders, managers and direct workers to *enable* it to operate and so, it could be further considered, it has an enmeshed relationship with all of its employees. What is also interesting is that the employee, through their particular co-dependency, nearly always feels compelled to stay (whether this be through fear of losing their job and/or fear of the unknown and/or having no self-confidence and/or not hitting their rock bottom at work yet . . .) despite their desirable transferable skills—within a toxic managerial interconnected relationship. Phew! We got there, at least for this section. The question still hangs though, amongst all of this, particularly within an organisation, "Who is co-dependent upon whom?" (see Figure 2.3).

A co-dependent's being and even survival depends upon having unhealthy relationships and meeting the needs, wants and gaining the (ongoing) validation of others. Altruism refers to individuals being morally obliged and purely motivated in benefiting others, without receiving or expecting anything in return. An organisation's very being and even survival depends upon having healthy relationships, through having 'healthy' employees and meeting the needs of its (loose cog) customers (at

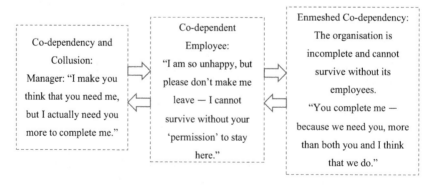

Figure 2.3 Who is co-dependent upon whom?

last we mention 'customers'; see Chapter 4, Section 4.1.2 'Us and Them' Now Becomes 'Us' vs 'Them'; Figure 4.2 Which way to turn: Nowhere to turn!?) and having their (ongoing) validation to survive. The organisation as an entity consists of enmeshed co-dependency, where many employees make up its whole. However even if one or two or more left its employment this wouldn't adversely affect the organisation, or even if it did, it, arrogantly and complacently, considers that 'nobody is indispensable' and that there are plenty of (external) 'others' on the job market, who would (happily!?) take their place and so continue to satisfy its—the organisations overall requirements. This may be true, but finding the right and proper employee who needs and wants a job or, indeed, wants and needs a job (see Chapter 5, Section 5.3 Work: Spiritual Drivers and Motivators) is a different matter. Any organisational resource requirement is satisfied and recruited by its managers (who benefit others, by providing them with a job), where these managers also have egos to satisfy which, in turn, are satisfied by the employees as they feel obliged to feed their managers' egos and are motivated to do so at the risk of losing their job . . . and so the previous 'co-dependency and addictive' transactions continue. However as we become more globalised and interconnected, this co-dependency, together with its associated collusion, enmeshment, egotistical fulfilment, various 'fixes', overall wanting and needing and (destructive) relationships, will become ever more apparent and there will and must come a time (which is *now*!) where these unhealthy, interconnected and connected, relationships must rapidly dissipate in order for the business to be both be truly fit and healthy. Where it is no longer good enough to just survive, the organisation and its employees must all grow and all prosper together.

The similarities and commonalities between servant leadership and co-dependency are abundantly clear. Servant leadership is built upon the belief that the most affective leaders (or individuals) strive to serve others, by responding to *their* wants and needs rather than accruing power or taking control. This is clearly not the case within some existing organisations.

Enmeshed organisations respond to their employees' wants—as it provides them with work and then fulfils *some* of their needs, by providing them with *some* money to fulfil (again some of) their own, both survival and pertinent, individual wants and needs. However, organisations do not have direct power and control over their workers; this 'having the power and control' is allocated and delegated to the function, role and responsibility of its managers. *Altruism* is the willingness to do things which bring advantages to others, even if it results in disadvantage for themselves. It's where individuals, who follow such attributes, subordinate their own interests and well-being for the sake of others. Organisations, together with their leaders and managers certainly in this respect, are definitely not altruistic. However, "Can altruism be related to the employee(s) who bring their attributes and skills (although, the fly in this ointment of this point is they are being paid to do so) but subordinate their own interests in a job which they (not all, but potentially all could) affectively hate and duly suffer as a consequence from, for the sole benefit of their organisation together with its shareholders or investors?" As previously discussed, this suffering is mainly caused through bullying and harassment (see Chapter 2, Section 2.6 Work and Suffering), by the collusive—direct power and control which the leader and/or manager has. These leaders and managers also provide the required resource to the organisation, where this all again comes back to the co-dependency debate. From a spiritual perspective, either at work or at home, it's an illusion to think that you have such power and control over another individual. Perhaps all of these individuals, in whatever shape or form, are avoiding their own true self?

Acquiring spirituality, together with its interdisciplinary outlook and application, does enable the individual to realise and overcome both the *dis-ease* (see Chapter 2, Section 2.14 Why Find the Spiritual '*It*' . . .) within themselves and the disease—the illness of co-dependency. Spirituality enables the I—the Individual—to form healthy relational links between and beginning with and from themselves to the you; their connected true selves to the we, but no longer the co-dependent to the us; the recognised interconnected individual*ism* to the group (but not emmeshed) collectiv*ism*; to all come back to the *I*, the free willed—the *Self* again.

Knowing the *Self* and how and when to accept the things that cannot be changed, but also knowing and having the courage to change the things that can be changed and having the wisdom to know the difference, is the fundamental spiritual key here. As testified by . . .

HEATHER P: "Realising this is really hard to do, especially when you're a control freak like me, just constantly trying to control everything and everyone to, mainly, stop bad things from happening."
SIMON P: "I now feel a lot calmer only being in control of me and my emotions."

Living with any (false) expectations, from either another person and/or living in a forever increasing dysfunctional environment or culture, desperately and obsessively wanting a desired positive outcome to our problems, is too much for most of us. Our thinking and behaviour become distorted, by trying to force our *own solutions* to the situations and/or onto other people. When these forced solutions fail to satisfy the problem/s, we then become irritable and unreasonable without knowing it. We make the mistake of blaming the situation or even the failed outcome, together with our feelings and behaviour, upon everything and everyone else that are around us. We apportion blame to everything and everyone for 'things' not being up to *our* expected standard—even lashing out when things are not appearing to go quickly enough, or the way *we* want them to or go, or in the direction that *we want* them to go in. Hence, there are many psychological and emotional benefits from separating love and care and concern for others from wants and needs in unhealthy situations and relationships.

2.10 Want and Need: Now and When

Living in this world of instant change, instant coffee, instant answers from the internet, instant money from the cash machine, instant service at the shop, bar or restaurant and of course instant gratification, it is understandable that we then come to be conditioned to expect, even demand, instant change to things, situations and, even, other people. To think, see, have and do it my way seems to be the modern-day mantra. Although interestingly, but not usually, we seem not to want to apply the same instant requirement of change when it comes to ourselves. Procrastination aside for the moment, patience, it appears, is no longer a required or wanted virtue in this want-it-all and want-it-now world!

Although spirituality offers a positive and optimistic view of life, even when the individual is experiencing disappointing situations and outcomes, certain media have pitched the notion that positive thoughts alone have an all-encompassing power over wanted results, as well as physical and mental healing and well-being. This is certainly open to doubt and criticism. "Can it really be true, that negative thinking is at the root of every trial and tribulation that we face in our lives?" If that is the case, "Is it really conceivable that all an individual has to do is positively *think* their way out of an unpleasant situation and/or horrendous suffering?"

The proposal that positive thinking is capable of mental regeneration or physical healing now abundantly appears within the self-help world as the panacea to everything that both the head and the heart desires. There is a plethora of commercial books sold and countless pilgrimages that have been undertaken which promote such promises as the ability to have access to untold riches (meant to suggest money) and enjoy mega health for the rest of our lives. Sadly, it is all nonsense! Steve Jobs (the Apple chief executive) significantly delayed having operations and chemotherapy for nine months after being diagnosed with a pancreatic tumour. Despite pleas from family and friends, he tried to cure himself through acupuncture sessions, drinking 'special' fruit juices, visiting spiritualists and using other treatments which he had found on the internet. He died after the cancer spread elsewhere in his body. Some cancer experts stated that Mr Jobs may have extended his life, or even survived, if he had been more prompt in accepting bona fide medical treatment. Before he died, the 56-year-old acknowledged he 'had made a mistake' by not seeking conventional treatment and medication sooner. Asking why "Such a smart man could do such a stupid thing?" Steve Jobs admitted that he thought 'if you ignore something you don't want to exist you start to have magical thinking'.

Generations and millions of westerners have travelled to places such as, amongst others, India, Peru, Cambodia and Indonesia in the hope that they will find some sort of magical spirituality to 'rub-off' on them and thus help them to get closer to enlightenment and/or be healed from sickness. This book neither offers nor promises this particular return on its investment. It does, however, take the view that peace of mind is everywhere, is readily available and is literally free to anyone who cares to find it, and as such, they can easily just stay closer to home.

2.11 The Beginning of the Spiritual *'Is'*

It's like trying to describe the taste of an orange to somebody who has never eaten an orange before. You can't do it—it's impossible—it's a bit orangey!! "What the hell does that mean!?" Trying to define the term *spirituality* is difficult, mainly due to the multitude of existing religions and variety of 'spiritual' practices which have emerged and, hence, have been conveniently labelled and accepted as to what spirituality is all about. This has meant that the very word itself conjures up a very general, vague and broad concept, which can be thought of and approached in a variety of different ways. As a consequence, there is no one widely accepted, all-encompassing and conclusive definition of spirituality. This has created a tremendous and still unsolved dilemma. On one hand, having no clearly agreed definition could cause the subject of spirituality (within both an academic and business context) to go into oblivion through the apparent lack of clarity and certainty whilst, on the other hand, not having a definition provides a flexibility, which allows for a greater interpretation and so increased creativity and progression of what is, in itself, a powerful construct and application. We may not know *yet* how to define spirituality (this 'yet' will be covered within Chapter 3, Section 3.2 A Fully Considered Spiritual Definition), but we know *it* when we see *it* and despite the fact of the academics inability to provide a precise definition has, so far, not prevented people from successfully practising *it*. Theologians have criticised the expanding definitions of spirituality as being driven by a therapeutic feel-good culture which focuses upon individual*ism* and desires. Because spirituality is generally considered to be 'something good' (i.e. it provides well-being and life satisfaction), "Isn't it achieving the desired outcome?" Concurring with this, the following are real and unprompted testimonials, which all provide new, but somewhat vague, definitions of *their belief* of what spirituality is—but interestingly, as each one means something to each of these individuals, they must all be both relevant and true, within their own right!

PAUL J: "I don't think you can call it my spirituality; I call it . . . who I am as a human being as a result of my spirituality."

JUDITH K: "It's beyond words; it isn't something that can really be explained to someone as it's got be a personal to the self—it has to be an experiential thing."

STEVEN I: "It's a personal code. It's a personal belief system which influences all of my decisions."

GEMMA H: "I don't understand all of it, but it's something that guides me through life."

JOSEPHINE B: "I find that hard to answer, because it means everything to me and it affects everything about me and what I do."

CHARLOTTE D: "It's individual to every person—it's different for everybody, so everyone has different definitions, but to me . . . it's believing in something."

RACHEL M: "I cannot put a label on it, as it's a very personal thing to me."

ROBERT A. G: "I find my spirituality leads me down a certain path, which means I am more open-minded about my needs, feelings and goals, rather than unnecessary wants and monetary desires. Whatever the outcome I also believe in being positive, so I am never frightened to walk into the unknown or a challenging situation, because I know if I don't I will never evolve as an individual."

Although in themselves these definitions are all new—fresh and creative, there is still a question of a single new overall definition and construct which has a more inclusive, integrative and interdisciplinary outlook. What is evident from all of the previous definitions is however spirituality was and is defined, it always references the 'self' in the first person (i.e. the 'me' or the 'my' and/or the 'I').[8] This self means looking after number one—even within a business context—becomes the priority. This also draws another very interesting parallel, even a distinct similarity to a business and the spiritual individual where survival(*ism*) is common ground, in that they both do all that it takes for *themselves* to survive.

2.12 Suffering

For those that live, or more precisely just exist, in a dysfunctional environment at home and/or at work and as such are experiencing horrendous suffering through physical, mental and emotional abuse and so can no longer cope with these unhealthy situations and/or individuals which are causing the *dis-ease* within us, this 'life' is a constant drudge, gloomy, unhappy and unmanageable. Constantly worried and on a (very) short fuse, we feel out of balance and synch within ourselves, others and generally the world around us. It feels like never-ending dark times and not belonging, being 'square pegs in round holes', where we feel lonely and frustrated in all areas of our lives and desperately unhappy! Where dreams are built false hope, if only's, what if's, but's and maybe's and then we wonder why they shatter, leaving us constantly disappointed when our dreams have failed to materialise, only to be constantly replaced with the thoughts of "What on earth do I do next?" These thoughts usually perpetuate into implausible decisions and (more) continuous, even the same, futile actions to try and alleviate our situations and circumstances. We resort to distorted thinking and feeling alone, unable to comprehend or talk about/articulate our mired situations and how bad they actually are, but "What's the point? Nobody will understand my 'unique' situation anyway?" This is (stinking) thinking and lifestyle which is not providing anywhere near a real life. When we constantly feel frightened and worried and can see no positive future, where these acute problems and merry-go-rounds dominate both our thoughts and our lives. For those with so many negative things going around and around in their head which they desperately need to offload, because they feel so ill and believe as all else has failed, they are prepared to go along with *anything* that helps them. This is rock bottom!

What is the meaning of a real life? It means experiencing success and failure and failure and success and then further failure and then further success . . . with lessons taught to us throughout via trial and error . . . constantly learning, unlearning and relearning "What *it* really is all about!" Where the measure of both failure and success is inside us—not 'out there' and compared to others. We are our own benchmark, not for others to judge us. This continuous (self)education and practice is a life-long affair, from which we grow.

2.13 The Beginnings of the Spiritual '*What*'

Political, business or social solutions do not deal with the root problems of dishonesty, greed and fear. Personal change from these problems must precede any economic recovery (Buchman, 1961). Spirituality promotes everyday life as its principal purpose (Sheldrake, 2013); however, it is also important to realise that just because you have spirituality and you are spiritual doesn't mean that bad/unpleasant things aren't still going to happen to you. It is how we manage these trials and tribulations, events and situations internally which allows us to effectively deal with them externally. Life is full of ups and downs, the ups are to be appreciated with gratitude and the downs as 'temporary failure', however long this temporary period lasts. From this, these temporary failures will teach you how to make stepping stones out of all of your past and future mistakes, where we begin to view them as positive *lessons* to be learned from. Where no matter how uncomfortable they may be at the time, we eventually realise that failure teaches us the value of everything, where success is very much gained from every single failure. This is the truth. Success and failure, good and bad times, nothing stays the same for ever. The only constant, therefore, is the relationship to oneself. This is the art of self-mastery. So, it then must follow, there can be 'no truth' without a change and transformation of ourselves (Foucault, 2005). However, before we can have access to this truth *it* requires 'work' on the self, by the self, for which we must take our own responsibility (Foucault, 2005).

At this moment, we may not *yet* know what this truth is, or even how to define *it* or measure *it*, but we do know the spiritual *it* exists and is practised by many the world over, by millions and millions of people.

"But what is it that initially compels certain individuals to find the *it* in spir*it*uality, in the first place?"

2.14 Why Find the Spiritual *'It'* . . .

Desperation! Feelings of pain, resulting from complete and utter failure. For some individuals either murder or suicide has literally been contemplated as the only 'seen solutions to escaping' what the individuals think are unique (to them) situations, problems and issues which cannot be overcome. With nobody to turn to, nowhere to go and no hope and faith for the future, these people believe when (temporary) defeat overtakes them in this way, the easiest and most logical thing to do is to quit. This is sadly and exactly what many, many, many people do. Especially at Christmas time and other emotional anniversaries.

Neo-evolutionism describes the idea that individuals constantly seek to preserve a familiar style of life, unless great change was forced upon them by situations and factors which were beyond their control. 'Suffering' can either force an 'end' to the individual or force a new beginning for them, and so suffering becomes the main motivator to each of these outcomes. Even when suffering and totally defeated, some individuals will not accept spiritual help. Others look to spirituality even if they have a healthy bank balance, a 'decent' partner and house and are generally regarded/seen as being successful, even super successful, a measure which most people aspire to. However, 'something' is still missing in their lives. This is usually explicit as to what they think achieving happiness actually is—take the fable of a group of multi-millionaires who are gathered in a room. When a billionaire walks in and says to them, "You are all doing okay but, come on . . . look what *I've* got!" "How do you think the multi-millionaires were feeling after that?" Were they happy with their lot, or did they now want to be billionaires? Whatever our lot is, we should—we must not desire or strive to be better than other people in the normal everyday (excluding competitive sports, etc.) world or wish to have, or more of, what they/others possess. But such is human nature! Instead, spirituality simply supports the striving to be better versions of ourselves. The point being, a majority of people have a *disease* (i.e. they are *ill at ease* with themselves; therefore, they are *dis-eased*). Happiness is elusive and fleeting and being at ease (not necessarily happy) with oneself is not easy. Where *something* meaningful from life is missing, it feels like a despairing hole in the soul that, no matter what, cannot be satisfied or filled despite all our best efforts to do so. Where the 'something' is missing, 'something' has to be found—but not through artificial stimulants. For many, spirituality is the last resort for finding their 'missing something', after which these individuals then know their greatest success comes just one step beyond the point at which defeat is about to overtake them, and then they know they have found their something.

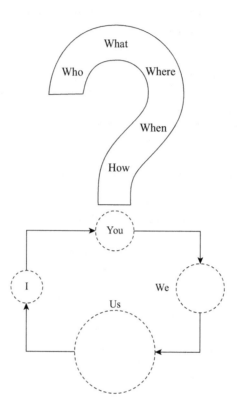

Figure 2.4 Who, What, Where, When and How creates you—*the Self.*

That *something* is the *real truth* of *who you* actually are and *what you actually need to question about yourself, to enable you to become and connect with your real Self* (Figure 2.4).

Spiritual maturity is the capacity to withstand ego-destroying experiences and not lose one's perspective in the self-esteem building experiences which follows and through which this form of spirituality is intended to come about. Having spiritual maturity, one also recognises both themselves and others as being 'simply human'. Spiritual maturity (as opposed to an individual's 'spiritual immaturity') is defined as someone asking themselves (with particular reference to the mind) 'what ails me?' This is different for each individual. It is through the ailed individual's exploring their own immaturity that they seek a change of their behaviour in order to reach a level of spiritual maturity which specifically includes knowing oneself. The *self* means one's own person. An individual's essential being, distinguishes them from others. In psychology the self refers to a person's experience as a single, unitary, autonomous being which is separate from others. This type of self is referred to as the *I*. The *I* equates to the total being of a person—their uniqueness, awareness and qualities which distinguish them from others. An individual is a single human, separate from others and as a human being distinct from a group. The word 'individual' is all about being a single entity, which cannot be divided; however this is somewhat debatable when it involves co-dependency (see Chapter 2, Section 2.9 Co-dependency: Servant Leadership and Altruism). Your *self* is your identity. When someone else gets to know you, you reveal your true—good and bad—self to them. If the subject of your thoughts is *you*, you're thinking about *yourself*. Your whole self is all of the components of what makes you.

2.15 The *Self*

Spirituality, in the first instance, is *learning* all about the *Self* (hereon in, the self) and the only thing that you can control is *yourself*. "How many of us really step back and think about this?" "How many people actually think it is, should and must be, the responsibility of others to make up for their own shortcomings?" Ironically, learning more about your *self* also helps you to learn more about others which, in turn, leads to healthy relationships with both ourselves and other individuals. In essence, looking after *yourself* and your own well-being is being *selfish* but, paradoxically, because you become your own top priority, these selfish actions can make you better at being nicer and kinder to other people because you feel well and so you have got something positive that you are able to give to others, which is being a decent and fair person.

From an organisational perspective, "If we are not well how can the organisation be expected to be well, in terms of being fit and healthy to compete?" To coin a phrase, an organisation and we are only as strong as their/our weakest link. Becoming selfish, tending and looking after ourselves, will enable us to be more healthy and be more willing to give to the organisation, (and to other people). Although this cannot be a 'one-sided all take and no give' on the organisation's (or by other individuals) part, this 'give and take' understanding has to be reciprocated; in effect, this is cause and affect! Where doing nothing and doing everything, good and bad, has a cause and an affect. Everything!

Interestingly, the overall construct of the *self* and *selfishness*, together with cause and effect/affect, are of both persistent and of principle importance within not just spirituality but also within any organisation. Spirituality is, first and foremost, learning about your *self* and coming to terms with who and what you are, through actually realising and taking responsibility for living your own life and even doing business on your terms, doing what you want to do and when you want to do it (preferably legally and legitimately of course) and not putting *others* before yourself. Understandably, whatever you choose to do will cause something else to happen and paradoxically whatever you choose not to do (i.e. including doing nothing) will also cause something else to happen, even (believe it or not!?) not happen (which will be further discussed within Chapter 2, Section 2.28 Contradictions and Chapter 3, Section 3.4 All Sorts Attract All Sorts). Within a busines context, simply doing nothing is not considered to be a viable option, but maybe it should be and maybe this 'doing nothing' is riper than what is cared to be seen and admitted to within an organisation, especially when it comes to making decisions! (See Chapter 2, Section 2.28 Contradictions.) However, organisations never put others (i.e. their competitors) above themselves and sometimes not even their customer is elevated to this higher position. Businesses look after number one, in every sense of the phrase. Although most people associate the word 'selfish' as a negative thing, it is actually a very positive experience and application. Spirituality within this context is described as *selfish*, in terms of what the individual *needs* (but not necessarily *wants*) to do in order to achieve more meaning and purpose out of their own life and to survive. The purpose of any business is also to be selfish, by providing meaning and purpose to achieving a profit and to survive (see Chapter 2, Section 2.1 What Is Business?).

Consisting of *you* and so the *self*, putting this into further perspective, spirituality is self-healing, self-reflection, self-awareness, self-worth, self-respect, self-esteem, self-recognition, self-sufficiency, self-responsibility, self-support and self-control which all contribute towards self-development. A kind of SWOT analysis. However, all of this self-development comes with a very high hurdle of not just getting over any *self-doubt*, but also learning to not just like but to also love the self.

2.16 Self-Love and Love of Self

The need for recognition . . . the need to be included . . . the need to be recognised, the need for at least *seeming* to be, whether it be true or false, successful—this is the part the ego plays or, in some instances, the super ego comes into effect! Differentiating between self-love and love of self, self-love is the source of hostility and arrogance that creates our ego, around which everybody must see and accept our point of view. The egotistical individual can see no other point of view other than their own. This is a state of mind which is closed to the real feelings and situations of others. There is no room for ego in spirituality. Love of self is only when we appreciate our own dignity and value as a human being that we are able to have compassion for others. Self-lovers are different from those who love themselves, as self-lovers tend to wear a mask of false humility which they 'hide' behind, and from which their own importance is exaggerated and so justifies unto themselves the wrongs that they do to others. True humility (which is significantly different to being humiliated) comes from the love of the self, the realisation that both ourselves and situations are seen and regarded to be what they really are. This is the blueprint for progress. To enable this blueprint for progress we have to realise, recover and find our true selves. The challenge, therefore, is for spirituality to function in a cognitive process, which leads a person from having a perceptual acquaintance of themselves to having an intellectual understanding of themselves; in other words, it is a quest to find who you are, your *self*.

2.17 Your *Self*

Prior to their spirituality, looking back, many individuals felt like they didn't exist . . . not even a doormat, they were underneath the doormat! From this situation, recovery doesn't happen overnight. Sometimes, it takes a fair while of unwinding from this highly reactive stage to get us back onto an even kilter. Even then, there are still parts of us, as a human being, that make us feel that we are not good enough. This is understandable, as after years of abuse and being manipulated we can have deep and ingrained feelings of being unworthy. Having low self-esteem and low self-worth and valuing ourselves can be quite a challenge, considering where we have 'come from' and what we have seen and experienced. These negative feelings can also provide a 'hair' trigger where the individual easily, immediately and (really) overreacts to someone who they feel is not valuing them because internally they are not valuing themselves. This is because they perceive within that others only value them to the degree that they are valuing themselves. This challenge in the valuing of the self is due to the, essentially destructive, *isms* which lie within all of us. When they are brought to the 'surface' by a particular situation and/or circumstance, we (and everybody else for that matter—because of the immediate, really high, volatile reaction we give outbound and they receive inbound) discover that our isms are raw, sore and tender to 'touch' (hence the expression 'to hit a nerve' with someone), which has been caused through years of emotional response conditioning. This (negative) emotional response conditioning has constantly challenged our self-esteem and confidence and as a result has significantly worn us down, so our isms, and obviously we, become sensitive to touch. As a consequence, the inevitable twists and turns and difficult things in life to work through become ever more erratic, because as individuals we are always at the mercy of being up and down, down and up and thrown all around, due to our highly volatile and delicate, worn-down, emotional state, mainly as a result of where we are always, seemingly, being exposed to (through and by other people) situations and events being constantly 'sent' in our direction that are designed to throw *us* out of our, emotional, kilter (see Figure 2.5).

"Recognise anything?" Deprived of the power of feeling any positive responsiveness, instead only being subject to constant disappointment,

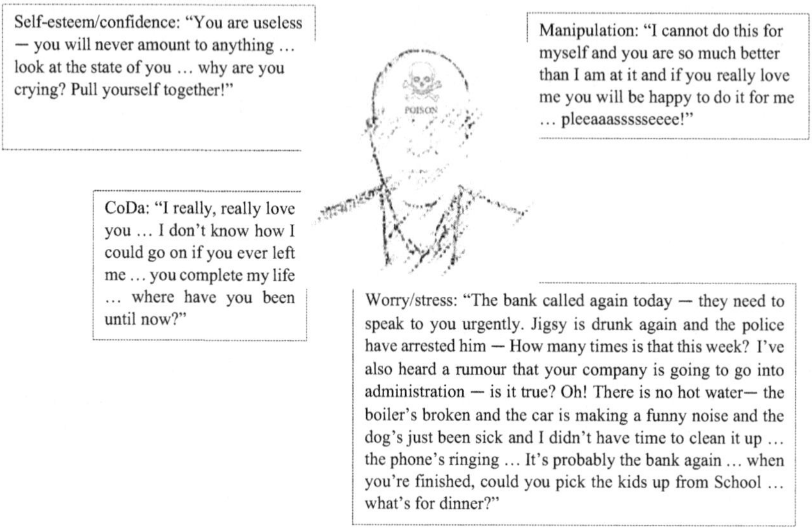

Self-esteem/confidence: "You are useless — you will never amount to anything … look at the state of you … why are you crying? Pull yourself together!"

Manipulation: "I cannot do this for myself and you are so much better than I am at it and if you really love me you will be happy to do it for me … pleeaaasssssseeee!"

POISON

CoDa: "I really, really love you … I don't know how I could go on if you ever left me … you complete my life … where have you been until now?"

Worry/stress: "The bank called again today — they need to speak to you urgently. Jigsy is drunk again and the police have arrested him — How many times is that this week? I've also heard a rumour that your company is going to go into administration — is it true? Oh! There is no hot water— the boiler's broken and the car is making a funny noise and the dog's just been sick and I didn't have time to clean it up … the phone's ringing … It's probably the bank again … when you're finished, could you pick the kids up from School … what's for dinner?"

Figure 2.5 The *turbulent* environment of emotional challenge.

scepticism, sarcasm, denial, jealousy, shame, fear, obsession, loneliness, confusion, manipulation, martyrdom, risk avoidance and shame, being the victim and having self-pity become the individual's main obsessions and so their dominant emotional drivers. Where one and all cause both physical and mental health decay, this leads the individual to their inevitable suffering.

Avoiding the truth . . . we (commonly and understandably) take the viewpoint that all of *our* troubles and anxieties are caused by *other* people. We believe that if only they would treat us better, differently, then *we* would be alright. We cry as a result of *their* behaviours and the way that they treat *us*. *They* cause *us* to worry and be angry because of their continuous crazy antics for which *they* blame *us* for *their* doing. Surely, they are the ones who need to sort themselves out—not us! Then, "Maybe we are to blame after all?" These blame doubts then begin to get a dangerous grip in our heads. If we love them just that little bit more, if we do or say something differently, dress differently or be better in bed, then (surely) they will change as a result of our new and continued efforts. We certainly try, but to no avail. Therefore (we think), our indignation and self-pity are justified and reasonable and our resentments, grudges and revenge tactics are suitably proportional, just and fair under the circumstances which they put us in as, after all, we aren't the guilty ones— they are! So, surely our light of reason and balance must shine through to them as, again after all, we have become rather adept at seeing and pointing out other people's issues and character defects; if all of *their* actions are the cause of *my* problems, "What can *I* do about that?" apart from continually showing and teaching them the error of their ways and most importantly keeping on 'rubbing *their* nose in it all'. Based upon subjectivity, our ego has suitably convinced us of all of this. This subjectivity is where ego and false pride plays the main part within us, as we have allowed another person to affect, ambush and dominate us into our 'stinking thinking'—suffering and misery. This blinds us to our own liabilities, which are holding us back. These liabilities, thus become our blockers to reason and improvement!

The difficulty being, when faced with any unpleasant situations or issues, many of us have learned to make irrational choices, which are based solely upon our feelings. Hence these particular feelings can be described as an emotional state or reaction which provides us with a feeling of either sadness or happiness, based upon an especially vague or an irrational idea or belief, which and in turn will prompt our resulting feelings. Psychology defines happiness as a subjective well-being. Although we see the pursuit of happiness as a fundamental human right and we work hard to acquire material goods and services to try and enable this pursuit, we also take the view that persuading others into both being someone and doing what we think they should—no must do and be—will (also) make us happy.

This has created a lot of the problems in the ways people behave, because they feel like they've only got this one life and so they believe that they have to buy and/or build a nice (material) lifestyle for themselves by having a 'respectable and well-defined' job' (on many levels we are defined by our vocation; one of the very first things we are asked when meeting somebody for the first time is, "What do you do for a living?"), together with meeting the 'right' partner and having a nice house (maybe), getting a dog, and then a 'chocolate box' life is inevitable—"Isn't it?" Happy days! All that then remains is where the individual *has* to make their 'right' partner perfect and then do all they can do to make their mark on the world, by impressing other people and being seen as (super) successful before they die, as they (as previously mentioned) believe at that point it's all over for them. Finito! There are no pockets in shrouds to put all your money and material goods in! Incidentally, just as a point of interest and aside from interpretations, nowhere within the Bible does it actually mention the word 'happiness', and 'happier' only appears once!

As such this comes back to "Are we are being coaxed into looking for happiness in the wrong places." In any event happiness is only temporary, but that doesn't stop us from forever seeking the constant high of it, artificially or otherwise. At the other end of this particular feeling spectrum comes a downcast one. If we have a general low mood, this makes us feel sad, this can then turn into feeling anxious and/or panicky, which can further lead into low self-esteem and confidence. This usually leads to the lack of sleep, which then makes us feel irritable and unreasonable, which then leads to anger, so we then look for happiness in the 'wrong places' and thus this cycle goes on and on and on—spiralling out of control and never ending, until we either *end* it through murder or suicide (see Chapter 1, Section 1.5 The Pursuit of Happiness) or end it when we have completely had enough of the situation, through a change of attitude, approach to life and appropriate, positive, action (see Chapter 2, Section 2.14 Why Find the Spiritual '*It*' . . .). It isn't until we learn to accept our feelings as either temporary, or ignore them until they pass, or accept feelings for what they are—just feelings—not facts that we can learn to adjust our thinking in order to overcome our negative bias, so our feelings no longer have the power to dominate our thoughts and our lives.

Spiritual programmes are designed to recognise and discover our *isms* (which usually accompany aggression) and through additional and appropriate group membership support and participation progress goes beyond these isms, in terms of recognising and learning how to constructively manage both the inner negative feelings and their associated outer destructive behaviours.

2.18 Nitty Gritty *Isms*

First the good news: spirituality helps you to have feelings and emotional intelligence.

Secondly the bad news: spirituality helps you to have feelings and emotional intelligence. What is meant by this is we start to develop a conscience. Those who attend spiritual support programmes *feel* the dark *isms* of, amongst others, guilt, anger, hatred, despair, resentment and numbness—being broken and unable to think straight and/or *feel* normal and/or be unable to react normally in everyday situations and circumstances. They have unpleasant feelings of indifference, possibly because of someone and/or something that has shocked and upset them in their past, or through having gone through horrible experiences, or they just simply feel awkward for no (immediate) reason. There are many words that people feel awkward with, for example: Cancer. Loneliness. Love. The word "No!" Please. Thank you. Failure. Redundancy. Spirituality. Termination—Death. An *ism* is defined as 'a negative bias' and interestingly, *isms* are not words that end in -*ism* and so are not stated within any dictionary. Instead, the ism meaning is derived from alcohol being a symptom of the underlying illness—alcoholism—and taking the *alcohol* out of *alcohol*ism, what is left is the *ism* part of the illness. Fear. Anger. Envy. Jealousy. Sorrow. Regret. Greed. Arrogance. Self-pity. Guilt. Resentment. Inferiority. Lies. False-pride. Superiority.

Ego. These common and collective problem 'isms' are all (stubbornly) central and rooted within individuals' minds, blocking and stopping us from moving forward. By making us feel flat, like there is no mojo or juice in our lives, we feel like we are, in essence, a one-dimensional being—being constantly and inconsistently 'blown around' just by our negative traits . . .

Where Figure 2.5 exampled the individual 'amidst a *turbulent* environment of emotional challenges' (usually coming from a third party), Figure 2.6 is a representation of how these external challenges influence our internal isms and so our rational thought processes. It is considered,

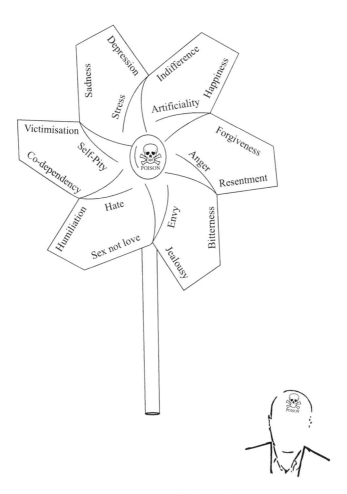

Figure 2.6 The one-dimensional windmill of emotional *isms*.

in spirituality, that it isn't the external circumstances which destroy us as an individual, but the way which we think about them and where, undoubtably, this 'stinking thinking' goes on to trigger our irrational external actions.

We can feel fragmented and unconnected through struggling on a daily basis with the never-ending negative emotional conditioning to what is being thrown at us and what we are exposing ourselves to. There can be no surprise, therefore, that our isms weigh heavily on our minds, seemingly and firmly embedded within our brain synapses and so our very psyche. We become trapped by and within our negative feelings and emotional cycles. To break out of these (unhealthy) cycles and ism merry-go-rounds, before any course of appropriate action can be determined, we need to know ourselves in terms of uncovering and recognising our strengths and building upon them, whilst also needing to know our own weaknesses which are preventing us from moving forward with courage. Having courage, on this occasion, requires not 'staring' at these isms, or beating ourselves up over them, but having the strength and bravery of being able to look at them in our 'rear-view mirror' with a view to rooting them out, before finally letting them go.

2.19 The 5S's

The 5S's are defined as a methodology which results in a workplace that is clean, uncluttered, safe and well organised. The aim is to help to reduce both waste and optimise productivity, with the intention of building a quality-driven (both physically and mentally) work environment.

The term *5S* comes from five words:

- Sort
- Set in Order
- Shine
- Standardise
- Sustain

Each 'S' represents one part of a five-step process, which is designed to improve the overall function of a business. Benefits to be derived from implementing a *5S* programme include:

- Improved safety
- Higher equipment availability
- Lower defect rates
- Reduced costs
- Increased production agility and flexibility
- Improved employee morale

- Better asset utilisation
- Enhanced enterprise image to customers, suppliers, employees and management

The 5 S's are a very practical hands-on tool, as they involve assessing everything that is past and present to be fit and ready for the future, in a relative time and space. The past, as a precursor, is assessed by taking stock of what we have, and we can then move onto the present by removing/throwing away what's unnecessary, before logically organising and keeping everything clean on a regular and frequential basis. This is the foundation to what then becomes relative for the future, which could be tomorrow, next week, next month, or next year, etc. Simultaneously sustaining and continuously improving the situation in the now ensures the overall efficient and effective function of the organisation tomorrow etc., thus keeping this cycle of sustainment and continuous improvement going—indefinitely.

2.20 The Spiritual 5S's

At this point, the previous 5S initiative might sound a tad off-piste and abstract in relation to spirituality, but we can strike some similarities. . . . After taking stock (i.e. of something accumulated over time; to make an overall assessment of a particular situation; to give serious thought about one's character and actions, typically before making a decision) of ourselves, we undertake a process of self-reflection. This self-reflection, what can also be known as emotional reflexivity, is a skill which is an important remedy to any (now and future) dilemmas that we will (not may) encounter. Where the future could be tomorrow, or next week or . . . next year, etc. Defining reflexivity as 'the process of critical self-reflection on one's biases and preferences', the more self-aware and forthright the individual is and becomes the better their understanding and perspective of the situation of which they are facing. If we are messed up and disorganised together with cluttered thoughts, in essence, "How can we decide, as an individual, what the next best thing is for us to do if we only have 'rubbish' in our heads, or we have little or nothing to base the decision upon?" Therefore, logically, the *goal* for ourselves is to be 'uncluttered' and 'clean', in order to be free from our historical *dis-ease* (see Chapter 2, Section 2.14 Why Find the Spiritual '*It*' . . .). Consequently, as we will be healthier and feel safer in ourselves, we will have better overall well-being and be well organised so that we are then able to make good (assertive) decisions through having clearer thoughts and actions, both in the now and for the future. In effect we will gain and have a higher availability in our mental capacity for (more and more) positive thinking, through having lower (ism) defect rates and so achieve both an increase in personal and professional performance, through being able to use our own assets in a more constructive way. "How enterprising is that?"

The *aim*, therefore, is to significantly reduce our 'waste' in terms of our inherent isms in order to optimise our own productivity and performance, or—putting this in more down-to-earth terms—we want to increase our mojo, if you like and prefer this terminology! With the, serious, intention of building quality-driven (both physically and mentally) health and well-being for ourselves, to help in enabling and realising this, the following 'Spiritual 5S's' come from five words, where each of the following 'S's' represents one part of a five-step process, which has been designed to both understand and so improve the overall function of us, as human beings:

- Self-analysis: The analysis of oneself, in particular one's motives and character
- Self-actualisation: Considered as the drive or need, which is present in everyone
- Self-realisation: Motivating and influencing one's own potential
- Self-development: The process by which a person's character and abilities are gradually developed
- Self-awareness: The ability to focus on yourself and how your actions, thoughts or emotions do or don't align with your internal standards

Also, if you're highly self-aware you can regularly and objectively evaluate your *self* (see Chapter 2, Section 2.14 Why Find the Spiritual '*It*' . . .), manage your emotions, align your behaviour with your values (whilst also understanding correctly how others perceive you) against a particular 'spiritual 5S lens' and how (these individual five lenses) all influence each other and merge together to form the whole *Self*.

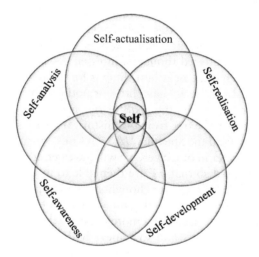

Figure 2.7 The spiritual 5S's.

Although it is considered that an individual's spirituality *begins* and so is principally motivated through suffering, their spirituality actually *starts* with the *doing* (i.e. *the action*).

Through our self-reflection, we can now start to understand both our negative (blockers) and our positive drivers and how they are affecting our lives. The *goal* therefore (and as previously discussed) is to recognise and reduce and/or remove our isms. The second lens, self-actualisation, refers to us recognising the need for our personal (and professional) growth and development throughout our life (Maslow, 1962). This is the highest level of Maslow's hierarchy of needs (Maslow & Lewis, 1987; Maslow, 1964) which, according to Maslow, represents the growth of an individual towards the fulfilment of their highest needs (i.e. their *needs*, not their *wants*), which is required to enable them to reach a more meaningful life. American psychologist Carl Rogers (1902–1987), one of the founders of the humanistic approach to psychology, created a theory which implicated a 'growth potential', which aims to integrate, congruently, the 'real self' and the 'ideal self', which results in the emergence of a fully functioning and relatively balanced person. Within this the individual desires to use their abilities, to be everything that they can possibly be. The third lens is self-realisation, being open-minded, understanding and influencing around and about one's own possibilities and potential. Through the fourth lens, self-development, the individual is actually realising and taking responsibility for their own potential and possibilities. Throughout all of these Spiritual S's the (*suffering*) individual is very much influencing the 'to be', by initiating *their own* activities here in the 'as is', for an improved well-being and quality of life.

Throughout the spiritual process the individual learns, gains or regains good (news) feelings such as how to laugh, have compassion and have love of self, as well as tolerance, forgiveness, gratitude, humility (not humiliation), real (not artificial) pleasure, appreciation, to take exciting risks, have hope, faith and courage to live their lives by and achieve well-being. The fifth lens, self-awareness, is having the ability to focus on your *self* and how your actions, thoughts and emotions (i.e. emotional intelligence) are having an effect on not only yourself, but upon other people as well. If we cannot determine any benefits but only negatives from a situation, circumstance and/or relationship, we then can revert back to the appropriate lens to work out why, together with what to do and not to do next! This means doing some more self-reflection, with a view to identifying and rectifying the root causes of our (particular) slip—note 'slip' not termed as a mistake!

2.21 Self-Reflection: Root-Cause-Analysis

Taking stock, termed within spirituality as 'taking a personal inventory of ourselves', then acts as Root-Cause-Analysis (RCA), which then allows us to understand and so (finally) 'dig out' the (deep) roots of our various isms and blockers.

When undertaking our 'searching, fearless and moral' personal inventory (Anonymous, 1978) as the name suggests, it has to be searching, fearless (note the word 'fearless' and not 'fear' [which stands for False Evidence Appearing Real]) and morally thorough, in order to pinpoint, dig-out, and rid ourselves of isms, hair triggers and blockers.

To do this, we need to go back in time as far as we can remember—up to and including the present day and leaving nothing out, we start to write all of this down. The general rule, of thumb around this is, if it comes into your mind it goes in and on the list! Nothing is omitted through either shame, embarrassment and/or fear, as any paperwork can be destroyed, or a file on a laptop can be permanently removed from its memory afterwards. This is where the *courage* part starts to also come in as this exercise as this can be uncomfortable, even excruciating! As it is, many people put off, ignore or stall at this particular, important, requirement through either shame and/or fear of being confronted by the 'truth'.

"So, what is this fear behind this reluctance to be confronted by the truth?" After all, we have all done things which we are not particularly proud of, but "Why have we felt the need to bury these memories and events deep down within ourselves, never to be revealed?" In spiritual terms, we say that we are only as sick as the secrets which we keep. This basically means a secret that is kept in the dark grows and becomes more harmful, because you must continually lie to yourself in order to keep those secrets, which means that you are being dishonest by pretending and attempting to be someone you are not. Exposing your secrets allows you to 'see' your *self* accurately and as they are released, they (start to) lose their power. After years of building walls around ourselves, removing those blockers can be uncomfortable and frightening. We start to realise that we have emotions (the 'bad' news) where fear, stress, arrogance and conflict seem to have been forever the dominant traits within us: the fear of not knowing; of uncertainty; fear of other people but not just from 'danger', but also from their constant undermining and ridiculing of us, from which we have learned to protect ourselves—almost by becoming immune against it and numb from it all! Even fear of fear itself. Fear can also be experienced through lack of self-esteem. This, in turn, can trigger unexplained thoughts and feelings of worthlessness. Although this feeling of worthlessness may seem to be bizarre in that nobody is actually worthless, it is understandable, therefore, that we put walls and blockers up, and (perhaps over-) compensate for them with an inflated ego, in order to protect ourselves. Within all of these instances and occasions it has been and is far easier to blame somebody and something else, rather than do the 'demolition' work required in starting to tear these walls, these blockers, down.

EDWARD P.H: "It was my psychological background that made me feel not good enough—worthless! Therefore, I always felt compelled to

try harder and harder and even then, this wasn't enough. Enough
was never enough. What came out of all of this was fear; the fear of
not being good enough, the fear of failing . . . fear of being recognised
as not being good enough. In the end I realised that nothing and
nobody can put fear into anybody, it was only me who was fearful."

Nobody will become totally free of fear, anger and pride, just as they will
never attain perfect humility and love. However, if we feel these negative isms for a long time, they become so familiar we cannot remember
feeling anything else. By acknowledging, accepting and constructively
confronting and changing our thought patterns—whilst simultaneously
acquiring the willingness and courage to analyse and learn from our
experience and so being able to practically change one's own reactions,
behaviour and attitudes to the situation—we can and will (start to)
make progress.

Important to keep it simple, our personal inventory should be
approached and conducted non-judgementally, with an open mind, without trepidation and with interest as after all it is *your* life, so there should
be no nasty surprises, only a decent and respectable outcome to it all!

2.22 Personal Inventory

Although based on truth, the following personal inventory (Anonymous,
1978) is characterised by representation. At this juncture, it is important
to note, as well as putting down our (rather than 'bad', we shall call
them . . .) weaknesses, it is also *vitally* important that we *also* list all of
our good traits within it; otherwise we can become bogged down and
focused upon just our negative aspects, which isn't recommended. We
must also identify and begin to mitigate our isms with self-analysis and
(the newly found) self-awareness, which is associated against each ism
point, as well as the required self-realisation and self-development which,
in turn, will form the start of our action plan going forward.

Going back as far as can be remembered:

5 to 10 years old.
Remembering Mummy and Daddy arguing all of the time: (Ism/s —)
    Sadness. Fear.
Frustrated that my Mummy and Daddy were divorcing: (Ism/s —)
    Anger. Fear. Self-pity.
I shit my knickers when I didn't make it to the toilet in time at Primary
    School. Everybody laughed at me: **Fear. Self-pity. Embarrassment.**
Clever at school, but lazy: **Sadness. Regret. Sloth.**
Not going to private school: **Ego. Resentment. Jealousy. Self-pity.**
Good trait: **I love and respect** both my parents.
Etcetera . . .
11 to 16 years old.

Father getting remarried and having a baby: **Inferiority. Self-pity. Jealousy. Resentment.**

I don't like my (new) step-mother: **Jealousy. Resentment.**

Left school with little to no qualifications: **Self-pity. Regret. Sloth. Ego and self-esteem** which both took a significant battering.

Eating too much: **Gluttony.**

Good trait: I am **kind** to animals.

Etcetera . . .

17 to 22 years old.

Mother is drinking heavily: **Anger. Fear. Self-pity.**

Boyfriend is cheating on me: **Anger. Sadness. Destructive.**

Took out a bank loan to buy a very expensive car: **Inferiority. Lies** (to myself). **Ego. Greed.**

I don't like my job, this isn't what I wanted to do: **Frustration. Self-pity.**

Cautioned by the police for swearing and spitting in the street: **Anger.**

Good trait: **I regularly give a blood donation.**

Etcetera . . .

22 to 27 years old.

Step-sister going to private school: **Inferiority. Self-pity. Jealousy. Resentment.**

Working long hours: **Resentment. Gluttony** (for money). **Self-pity.**

Hate my manager and my job: **Envy. Resentment. Procrastination.**

Massive encounter/argument with my manager: **Anger. Sarcastic. Defiant. Destructive. Ego-driven.**

Applied for another job but under-qualified: **Self-pity. Regret. Inferiority. Self-esteem.**

Regularly steal work items and 'fiddle' my expenses. **Anger. Defiant.**

Had a physical fight with my best friend: **Inferiority. Anger. Sarcastic. Destructive.**

Mother is STILL drinking heavily: **Anger. Fear. Self-pity.**

Caught an STD:[9] **Anger. Inferiority. Shame. Self-pity.**

Caught using my mobile/cell phone whilst driving: **Anger. Self-pity.**

Good traits: I have an, albeit slightly warped, sense of **humour.**

I signed onto the Anthony Nolan Bone Marrow register.

Etcetera . . .

31 to date

Passed over for promotion AGAIN!: **Resentment. Self-pity. Sarcastic. Envy. Inferiority. Ego.**

Took a week off work feeling 'sick', but wasn't: **Anger. Resentment. Self-pity.**

Car repossessed: **Self-pity. Regret. Inferiority. Ego. Gluttony** (for material possessions).

Boyfriend is regularly abusive to me: **Fear. Inferiority.**

Cannot leave him, because I love him: **Co-dependent.**

Vandalised boyfriend's car: **Anger. Resentment. Fear. Self-esteem.**

Not applying for other jobs—"What's the point?": **Self-pity. Sloth. Ego.**

My mum died: **Regret. Self-pity. Anger.**

Put on nearly 2 stone in weight: **Gluttony. Self-pity. Inferiority. Self-esteem.**

Boyfriend hit me AGAIN: **Fear. Self-pity.**

Called the police on him AGAIN: **Anger.**

Dropped all charges on him, AGAIN: **Collusive/collusion Co-dependent. Regret.**

My best friend just bought a big and beautiful house: **Jealousy. Inferiority.**

Her husband doesn't hit her: **Self-pity.**

I told my director to stick her job RIGHT UP HER ARSE!: **Anger. Regret. Ego.**

Good trait: **I sponsor rescued animals. I wish somebody would rescue me!**

Etcetera. . . .

After your personal inventory is complete, the starting point being is to start to forgive yourself. Then afterwards and eventually over time, you will start to forgive others, however disproportionate the injustice. The following, Table 2.1, is designed to be a summary of all, plus some, of the previous personal inventory isms and self-analysis/self-awareness, which has been further countered with examples of points of self-realisation and self-development which, as previously stated, will form the start of our action plan and healthier outlook.

Even from this very small illustrative sample within Table 2.1, we can quickly infer from this personal inventory summary, that this person has hardened fear, self-pity and resentment, which are manifesting themselves in overall anger issues (which are also coming close to tipping over into resentment) as well as gluttony and slothfulness; which are all masking a deep inferiority complex (which their inflated ego is compensating for), which has resulted in a hardened 'victim' mode. The most common symptoms of emotional insecurity are anger, resentment and self-pity. It is resentment and self-pity which literally 'destroy' people.

To lust for sex, power and prestige. To be envious when the ambitions, or possessions, of others are, or seem to be, realised whilst ours are not. To 'grab' for more of everything which we *think* we will need, fearing that we shall never have enough. "Did I recklessly borrow loads of money—not caring whether I could repay it or not?" "With the prospect of (hard) work do I avoid it and be lazy?" "Does my inferiority complex destroy my confidence?" "Do I try to cover up my feelings of inadequacy by bluffing, cheating, lying and avoiding responsibility?" "Do I loaf and procrastinate or, at best, work begrudgingly and at half of my real ability?" "Do I complain that others have failed to recognise my truly exceptional talent

Table 2.1 Personal inventory summary

The Ism	No. of Counts/ Weighting	Self-Analysis/ Self-Awareness	Self-Realisation/ Self-Development
Fear	42	Anxiety	Natural emotion.
		Victim	Fight or flight?
		Determine triggers?	Breathe.
			Order: live in the moment.
			Courage.
Anger	38	Victim	Natural emotion.
		Determine triggers?	Determine Boundaries.
			Let it go.
Sadness	27	Natural emotion	Natural emotion.
		No mojo	Accept as temporary.
		Determine triggers?	Let it pass.
			One day at a time.
			Cheerfulness.
Self-pity	36	Victim	Practise gratitude.
Resentment	39	Victim	Let it go.
		Assigning blame	Seek forgiveness:
			for self and others.
			Show sincerity.
Jealousy	32	Obsessive	Practise gratitude.
			Tolerance.
Impatience	18	Patience	Courtesy.
			Develop trust.
			Practise order.
Sloth	27	Fear of failure	Courage.
		Anxiety	Faith.
		Not interested	Perseverance.
		No mojo/juice	Progress.
		Time can be productive, abused or desecrated.	Use of time: balance.
Gluttony	26	Greed for more	Balance required.
		Compensating	
Sarcastic	22	Dysfunctional	Apologies: make amends.
		Masking confidence issues	Caution in speech.
		Frustration	
		Anger	
Destructive	24	Dysfunctional	Stop the behaviour.
			Apologies: make amends.
			Have integrity.
Self-esteem	4	Inferiority	Assertiveness.
			Fake it to make it*
Inferiority	29	Victim	Confidence:
		Self-esteem	fake it to make it*
Ego	35	Masking confidence issues	Raise self-esteem.
			Fake it to make it*
Kindness	11	For others	For myself.
Love	16	For others	For myself.
Respect	9	For others	For myself.
Humour	10	Sarcastic	Convert to witticism.

* See Chapter 5, Section 5.9.1 Fake It to Make It

and abilities?" "Do I oversell myself and play the big shot?" "Am I two-faced?" "Do I have a forked tongue?" "Do I double-cross and undercut my family, friends and work colleagues, just to make myself look good?"

When we start to examine the parts that make up our whole, we will see 'as is', just where our strengths and weaknesses lie. What our dominant traits are and possibly where, when and how we acquired them. We cannot change the past, but we have a choice whether to stay there, or to do something about it. The crucial point being, it is the way we deal with the emotion and behaviours that our past experiences have caused us to be what we are *today*. Honesty, openness and willingness together with the required self-analysis and self-awareness, determined through a (completed) searching, fearless and moral personal inventory (Anonymous, 1978), are essential steps forward. It is this which we use as a foundation as a measuring tool for our own recovery and growth—to see just how far we have come, if and when any doubts occur as to "What's the point of it all?" within us.

It is what we start to do from this 'as is' *now*! This moment on, to (start) to root our isms out and remove our inherent and conditioned blockers, which will enable *us* to finally move on to the 'to be', where we are truly meant to be.

Throughout this process the individual learns, gains or (re)gains good feeling and starts to develop a faith that things (i.e. life) will turn out alright for them. However, although faith gives power to the impulse of positive thoughts, faith without positive action is useless!

2.23 Faith and Action

Emmet Fox (1886–1956) became one of the most popular and famous New Thought speakers of the 1930s and '40s. Fox's teachings were ones of humans often learning more from making mistakes rather than from any successful situations, where 'any subsequent suffering is simply the consequence of the error, that weighs heavily upon the conscious mind' (Heindel, 1920) i.e. these thoughts aren't tangible and suffering is purely a manifestation within the individuals' own head (Chesnut, 2011). Fox's key message from this is 'it isn't the external circumstances which destroy the individual, but the way they think about their actions' (Chesnut, 2011). Bill W. and Dr Bob (the founders of Alcoholics Anonymous [AA]) refused to absolutise this viewpoint.

AA refused to say that *all* problems and errors can be entirely removed by simply thinking positive thoughts, as things can and do go wrong, even when the individual is leading a religious, archetypal or a spiritual life (Chesnut, 2011). Instead, AA puts forward the notion that spirituality is simply the means of accepting these situations that are put before us, whilst also facing and dealing with one's own problems by learning to put *everything* into its/their true perspective and responding, not reacting, to them in a positive healthy way. Action is, therefore, required to not only recognise and address our particular isms, but also be aware of what triggers them (e.g. a chain reaction which is caused within us) in the first instance. We then learn to both manage our triggers internally and conduct ourselves externally in a healthy, rather than an unhealthy way.

2.24 Triggers

"What is it that triggers our (unpredictable and volatile) emotions?" (see Chapter 2, Section 2.7, Moods and Feelings). "Is it denial that triggers us?" Which results in making us (ever so) defensive and angry!? Certainly, sometimes, the truth hurts! "Could it be frustration that triggers us?" When things are not going quickly enough for us, or the way we would like them to do and go? Other emotional triggers could be an angry look, the wrong tone of voice. Somebody doing something against our own judgement, values and morals, or simply not liking the words and/or the way which they said them? Perhaps, it is something what they believe in and we, certainly, do not concur. Maybe it's because others can't be persuaded to 'see' things our way because, just like ours, their particular beliefs and values are as deeply anchored within them, as they are within us. Perhaps, it is what team they support. What political beliefs they have—did they vote in, or did they vote out? How do they specifically behave and act which is not the same as our own. They don't do what *we* want them to do, when we want them to do it! More dangerously, they aren't who we want them to be. Basically, they are not living up (or down for that matter) to our expectations. More precisely we allow these characteristics and traits of others to suitably 'wind us up' and internally affect us. These are your emotions acting—without the benefit of intellect. This then triggers an attitude and behaviour within us, an unreasonable emotional reaction to an external stimulus. As individuals we can either (more than likely) immediately *react* (not respond) defensively, nastily and/or violently to the stimuli, or choose to be more mindful (where 'mindful', within this particular spiritual text, is not associated to and so not to be confused in a way with being more 'mindfulness')[10] and do nothing and ignore the provocation. We can also choose to override the negative instinct, acknowledge it and positively *respond* (not react) to the stimuli. In spirituality we learn the importance of suitably responding to stimuli within the moment, not unsuitably reacting to it in the heat of the moment. Most individuals, especially those that are pent up with frustration and rage or even lack self-esteem, if they didn't catch themselves, they would certainly end up reacting and 'exploding' into a confrontational stance and unhealthy situation. Responding is still saying your piece, but this piece is controlled and cooled. It might even be the same words which you would use when you are angry, but it is more the tone of how you say them rather than what you say. Either way, it's considered 'best' when you are getting angry to count to ten and if you are getting really angry, count to 100!

Nothing goes smoothly, either in life or in business. Things inevitably happen and failures undoubtedly occur, which upsets and disrupts both us as individuals and our—the organisation's internal systems and external circumstances in which we/they operate in. Nobody and nothing is immune from this, even spiritual people. The difference is, spiritual individuals recognise this and at best, if the failure is out of their control or not of their doing, they feel the natural feelings associated with this situation, but regard and accept the failure as a temporary defeat so not to be dwelt upon, or obsessed over. At worst (because after all, even spiritual people are only human), they feel the associated feelings and allow those things, situations and failures to upset them. But what really upsets them is that they have allowed these things to upset them and then they get upset that they are upset, so it's then back to the drawing board to work out why they are so upset at being upset!

In this self-directed learning of when things have gone wrong, the spiritual individual takes the initiative and if relevant, takes *their* responsibility for what has occurred. From this they then select, manage and assess their own contribution to the, somewhat, heated situation, together with their own learning requirement and activity, which will increase their tolerance and behaviour for these types of situations happening again in the future. To arrive at this tolerance amounts to discovering what it is that pushes your particular buttons as, after all, there are always going to be certain people and certain situations at certain times which we will get triggered by and yet, we don't understand why we get triggered by them in the first place. Not understanding why we get this transference, and by understanding why we counter-transfer back becomes part of the spiritual individual's work-in-progress. To truly find out what occurs, the individual has to do their own particular soul searching which, incidentally, is different than the previous searching, fearless and moral inventory (Anonymous, 1978 [see Chapter 2, Section 2.22 Personal Inventory]). Where compiling our personal inventory is, pretty much, a one-off event, this triggering determination is a continuous exercise, where the easiest place to start is "What bothers me in particular?" "What bothers me the most?" "What and who, really 'pushes my buttons'?"

Spirituality helps us being around other people, as it allows us to specifically see how we respond to different situations and which triggers we still need to recognise and work on. This is all about being able to trust yourself, and as you start to trust your *self* (see Chapter 2, Section 2.14 Why Find the Spiritual 'It' . . .) and understand why you are reacting to a certain situation, you don't actually need to rise to the bait. You realise that you don't need to be 'dragged' into unpleasant and toxic situations and relationships. Overall, when people are being, or appearing to be obstructive, awkward or just plain horrible, the spiritual individual is more understanding, resistant and tolerant towards this trigger. This doesn't mean to say that the spiritual individual has to spiritually 'love' a provocateur or put up with them, turn the other cheek (especially if, for example, somebody is damaging your property where a polite "Excuse me, could you please stop doing that" would not suffice and so have the desired affect in actually stopping them!) or say nothing (i.e. we keep it zipped), or express agreement with them even if we don't agree. This is a categorically unrealistic, untrue and undesirable misnomer commonly associated with spirituality. Also, on this point, in terms of being physically threatened, any individual is entitled to *do what it takes* to proportionally defend themselves, including the spiritual ones. During any, unfortunate, encounter, *we* certainly do not lead with our chin.[11] However, an individual (especially a spiritual one), in any context, should also be busy trying to sort out what they have done wrong (if anything at all) and determine what's out of balance and start to put right what has gone wrong in themselves and not simply blame *everything* on the other person.

LAURENCE W: "If I just turn round and think of that person as 'You are just an arse hole!' then that's not going to do anything constructive to help the situation and this will not reflect well on myself at all and there will certainly be conflict between us. Instead, I'll be using that opportunity to evaluate what's happening in me. I will be using, first and foremost, the odium [general or widespread hatred or disgust, incurred by someone as a result of their actions] to determine 'What is happening in me?' . . . 'What's been triggered in me?' . . . 'Why am I struggling with this person now?' . . . 'What is actually happening?' . . . and when I start to deal with all of this, then the chances of there being a conflict can either be avoided or be significantly reduced."

Normally, by taking this approach, the individual can then, quickly, move to a resolution through finding a 'good' place between them and the other person, by agreeing to disagree and/or make appropriate apologies/make amends if they are, indeed, in the wrong. By recognising the only part that they can deal with is what *their* own part in the confrontation was, they then mentally 'hand over' (thereby avoiding the verbal blame game) the relevant shortfall/part to the other person for them to (which they may or may not) recognise, learn and/or deal with their particular *ism*, in their own way. This usually means the other (non-spiritual person) feels aggrieved, (more often than not), whether they are right or wrong, and ends up holding a never-ending grudge or resentment against the other, where some sort of revenge is *always* on their mind and on their lips. Sound familiar!? In effect, the spiritual individual learns from the situation and then 'lets it go', with no fallout on their part and so without any associated and ongoing feelings of guilt, resentment or revenge. In this way, our recovery and even the health of others is assured when we place our principles above our personalities, rather than our personalities above our principles.

Many arguments over who is right and wrong ensue but can be avoided, by focusing solely upon principles rather than personalities, as this helps us to reconnect with both ourselves and the other person after we have had a 'big' or difficult discussion, or (unavoidable) argument. Continuing on this particular thread, we also tend to discount a perfectly valid message just because we simply don't like, or get on with, the messenger. "How many careers have been permanently threatened because of a personality clash with one of the managers, even though the person (usually a subordinate) has been right in what they are saying and is adequately skilled to do the required task or function?" Focusing upon only the message and not judging its content by the personality of its deliverer, we grow in *patience, understanding* and *tolerance of others.*

Spirituality positively affects one's own confidence in dealing with people, by feeling that they are saying and doing something helpful, as opposed to making the situation worse. We don't have to understand what others are saying, or like somebody, or everybody, in terms of what they say and do; this is their prerogative, but we can still offer them respect and common courtesy regardless of whether we agree with them or not. This is where spirituality proves to be really helpful, in that it can put us back, as individuals, on an even keel and even if we do get triggered in some way (after all we are only human and are not perfect), we can come back to our default and calibrated settings pretty quickly.

Whilst acknowledging, accepting and coming to terms with ourselves and learning how to *let go* of our isms and past, together with recognising our particular triggering 'push buttons', along with putting principles above personalities, many spiritual people transform themselves from being 'hot headed and rebellious' to individuals who acquire tolerance, patience and understanding. By treating and speaking to other people in the way they want to be treated and spoken to not only enables and manages healthy, connected and interconnected relationships, but spirituality also questions, "Why not just get rid of *your* 'push buttons', completely!?"

2.25 Boundaries

By recognising our trigger stimuli and removing their associated push buttons, spiritual individuals bring as much compassion, understanding, tolerance and patience into both their work and home life as possible. This however leads onto another spiritual misconception, in which the individual is compelled to always find and see the good in people, but to always even *try* to find and see the good in other people is not easy. It makes sense, in this world, that there have to be certain people which we cannot see the good in but, to be sure, there is a little bit of bad in good people and a little bit of good in bad people. "Is it really up to us to find either the good or bad in them?" On that note, spirituality is usually associated with a kind of Biblical, 'love-thy-neighbour'! We have to face facts and be realistic here—this doesn't always work and realistically happen. Spirituality doesn't mean allowing others to treat us like a doormat—letting others walk all over us with 'shitty shoes' on, or turning the other cheek if we are wronged. Instead, we learn to accept that there are certain people . . . individuals who we are never going to get on with. The key here is to accept this and/or mentally and/or physically detach ourselves from them, but without any self-pity, anger or resentment.

'To do unto others, as we would have them do unto us'; 'An eye for an eye and a tooth for a tooth'. There are great emotional and psychological benefits to be had from separating love, care and concern for others from wanting and needing to seek revenge. Although hard to do in our private lives, at work this detachment is considerably harder. At work, if we are functionally divided, it is nigh on impossible to physically detach ourselves and not become directly involved and react (be triggered) to someone else's particular toxicity. We therefore have to learn to mentally detach. Evident to spirituality is individuals' ability to recognise, build and establish healthy boundaries which others must not cross or abuse. By creating healthy boundaries, this ensures that the individual maintains their own safe, psychological and physical, distance (not unlike social distancing) from others. This distancing is where we determine what our practical and healthy boundaries are and what we need to do if somebody crosses them.

Few people really like conflict, but when somebody exhibits some inappropriate behaviours it's either about saying nothing, so 'keeping it zipped' and avoiding confrontation, or saying "You're not allowed to do that" or "I am not comfortable with you doing that." This is about making sure that you are safe around that sort of behaviour whereas beforehand, many people would be aggressive in response to that inappropriate behaviour and then have a good whinge about it to somebody else afterwards. Others would just stuff it down and allow that sort of behaviour to continue, or if it was happening to others (especially friends and respected colleagues), just go up and get involved with things that didn't concern them. In terms of detachment (with love) and boundaries, spiritual individuals take a more observational view of life and as such, through largely coming across more boundaries to adopt, they become more open about what are and what are not their own emotional needs and acceptable behaviours are and are not. To do this we have to learn to express one of those (see Chapter 2, Section 2.18 Nitty Gritty *Isms*) 'awkward' words.

Saying "No!" is one of the hardest words to say. By knowing we have to say things which are extremely uncomfortable to us, but saying them anyway for the greater good of our own sanity, takes a tremendous amount of courage. Knowing when to say "No!" especially without feeling the need to explain or defend ourselves takes even more courage.

2.26 Yes vs No!

"Do we ignore the problem?" "Ignore the answer?" "Divert the original question?" "Procrastinate?" "Even if we don't agree, or are not comfortable, do we execute our/others' decisions anyway?" In order to help in establishing healthy boundaries, "Do we as an individual, or especially as an employee, have the (self)confidence and ability to actually be able to say *No!*?" No is one of those words that we have to say, but find it extremely difficult and hard to do so—as it can easily offend work colleagues, friends and relatives alike and we don't like to do that—do we!? Also saying "No" can be extremely career threatening if we say it to a leader or a manager, even if it is for our and sometimes also for others' and/or the organisation's own benefit. "So how does saying '*no*' (although not grammatically correct, note, there is no capital letter or exclamation mark, which goes back to your tone of voice, rather than the actual word/s that you use) go from being a negative to becoming a benefit?" By asking ourselves the following questions and simply answering either yes or no:

- "Is this request an opportunity for progress?"
- "Is this ask *genuinely* a waste of my time?"
- "Will this add to my life, or take something away from it that I don't want it to?"
- "By doing it will I be of help in any way that is not detrimental to my own well-being, or to someone or something else?"
- "If I say 'Yes', can I achieve what is actually being asked for and within a reasonable time frame?"
- "If I say 'Yes', will I be of value to the overall objective of the purpose and/or to the organisation?"
- "If I say 'Yes', how will this benefit me?"
- "If I say 'Yes', am I being authentic?"

Through asking these questions and assuming that there is a good reason to say "No" (i.e. not just saying it for the sake of it), this displays authenticity because:

- You're being honest with yourself
- You're being honest with the others
- You're staying true to your identity
- You're staying true to your priorities
- You're saying "No" for a genuine reason
- You're saying "Yes" for a genuine reason

SARAH H: "I always try to help my employer no matter what, but it does sometimes work against me, as it's seen as bit of a weakness, as I really don't know how to say 'No' This means that I am in 'danger' of being used and abused occasionally."

When an individual becomes a victim to always saying "Yes" more than they should, then both their personal and professional relationships, together with their work productivity, will and do all inevitably suffer. Instead, when the individual is committed to not always saying "Yes" to anything and everything but rather to providing a "No" response (not a reactive "NO"), this means that they have started to think before they act and have become more assertive in their demeanour. Approaching saying "No" in this way makes for smarter, better, more realistic and wiser decisions and a firm basis to make judgements upon. "Afterall, isn't this what good relations, leadership and management in any shape or form of life, organisational or otherwise, ideally consist of?"

Spirituality is having the courage to set aside emotions whilst making hard decisions and by believing in something strongly enough that the individual will not turn back, regardless of the circumstances. "Isn't this also what being in business means—to be assertive and to be able to make hard, difficult and unpopular decisions and then take an appropriate and firm course of action?" If we want to do this within a business environment, doesn't it make sense therefore, to construct our *own* personal and professional framework of action, consisting of what our defined authority and responsibilities are?

2.27 Example of a Personal and Professional Actionable Framework

For my*self* . . .

a. Ambition: To determine what *I want* in life and to seek the necessary help and support to realise it. Requires: Honesty. Intellect. Courage. Effort. Time.
b. "Have I honestly faced myself, or have I ignored myself through my various isms, to become less than I want to be?"
c. To carry out my daily duties and realistically fulfil them, to ensure peace of mind and progress.
d. To put first things first.
e. To live one day at a time.
f. To accept what must be accepted.
g. To not accept what doesn't need to be accepted.
h. To positively look forward in life, instead of negatively facing in the wrong direction.
i. Have a change of attitude from "I can't take this anymore" to "For this day I can take this and a lot more besides."
j. To accept a 'Thank you' graciously.
k. To give a genuine 'Thank you'.
l. To make timely apologies and make appropriate amends when we are wrong.

m. To accept love and not just sex.
n. To recognise and practise gratitude, for even the smallest of things.
o. To remove myself, or remove the toxic situation from myself.
p. "Do I set an example to others through my various roles, responsibilities, disposition and relationships?"
q. "Have I cheated, or been dishonest to myself and others?"
r. "Frankly, do I consider myself or others worthy, or am I just free-loading wherever and from whoever I can?"
s. To have courage and integrity, in all that I undertake to do.

(Anonymous, 1978)

Within my place of work . . .

a. To seek a work-life balance.
b. If I am lazy, put more effort into my job.
c. To establish order to my working life.
d. To seek work and opportunities which are aligned with my capabilities, but never to the exclusion of my personal obligations and family.
e. To positively utilise my abilities, but never to the exclusion of personal and family obligations.
f. Not to chase and desire money for money's sake.
g. Not to seek power (position) or prestige, or personal acclaim.
h. To deal with all people, morally and ethically.
i. To be less demanding and more productive; business is always looking for the better person.
j. Asking myself, "Am I doing the same standard of job as I would expect if someone was working for me?"
k. "Has my relationship with my organisation, my manager and work colleagues been on an honest level, or has it been filled with ego, pride, resentments, pettiness and deceit?"
l. "Have I carried out my duties, roles and responsibilities to the best of my abilities?"
m. "Are there any ethical or moral considerations in my work that clash with my own, or do I make excuses on the basis it is 'only business'?"

(Anonymous, 1978)

To others . . .

a. "Do I look for my wants and needs to be fulfilled by others?"
b. "Do I detach with love from unhealthy/toxic relationships?"
c. "Do I leave others to get on with their lives and not interfere in it, in any way?"
d. "Do I accept others as to who they are and not try to change them?"
e. "If somebody isn't right for me, do I remove them or remove myself from them?"

f.   "If they are right for me, do I appreciate and cherish the relationship as being true and trusted—appreciating that friends and good relationships are hard to come by?"

g.   "Have I gained and kept the love and respect of my children?"

h.   "Do I want my children to turn out like me?"

i.   "Have I gained and kept the love and respect of my family and friends?"

j.   "Do I dictate to others, or have I created trust through being interested and leading by example?"

k.   "Do I cultivate friends, or manipulate people for what I can get out of them?"

(Anonymous, 1978)

Breakthrough results cannot be realised by continuing to use traditional or old ways of thinking, or looking at and doing the same things in the same old way. The problem is nobody can make the use of an opportunity if they cannot see it, or don't recognise it as being real and possible. Certainly, there is an air of fear around uncertainty and the unknown as, after all, fear stops us from leaving a toxic relationship or situation, through fear of the consequences which are often unknown, or projections that are based upon our previous emotional conditioning, which all prevent us from doing what we really want to do in our life. Fear has the power to stop us trying something new, mainly through the fear of the unknown and potential failure.

Spirituality helps us to see things differently. It provides us with ways to accept, adjust and overcome our fears and allows us to get on with living our lives in a healthy and more positive, meaningful and purposeful way. Spirituality helps us to focus in on bringing more of our inner selves to the surface by keeping an open mind, looking for and finding the opportunities that are available and then taking a leap of faith together with the appropriate action. This opens up new possibilities and horizons for us to explore. Awakened to these fresh opportunities, the individual will perceive and gain new meaning to their life, to events and situations, to numbers, to words and interactions and relationships with other people.

Doubts are inevitable. An individual could be forgiven for challenging spiritual examples and testimonials, however accurate and well-meaning, on how easy, or coincidental, things can appear to be. Ranging from the dear reader and/or the sceptic thinking: "This is all crazy stuff!" to "They (the Author and book participants) are just making it all fit?" or "Is there something quite strong in all of this that, perhaps, requires further considerations?" Trying to deal with a range of complex and contradictory phenomena (e.g. different kinds of histories, beliefs, convictions, and home and work lives together with individual and collective thoughts and experiences—as if they all somehow fit and balance under the same umbrella) is a key part of the overall spiritual problem. A combination of statements, ideas or features that support one another are all well and good, but in terms of fairness and balance, "How can these contradictions, be reconciled?"

2.28 Contradictions

Contradictions in everyday life are regarded as tensions to be resisted, accepted or solved. Contradictions within organisational life are regarded as tensions to be resisted, accepted or solved. Contradictions within spirituality are regarded as tensions to be resisted, accepted or solved. Where there are lots of different people working in the same environment, they may come from different backgrounds, have different religions and cultures so it is understandable and no wonder that we all have different thoughts and behaviours. "How boring would it be, if we were all the same?" Trying to deal with this extensive range of complex and contradictory social phenomena (different kinds of values, beliefs, convictions, histories and communities) as if they all somehow fit under the same (organisational) roof, is (another) key part of the ongoing problem of spirituality.

It has so far been determined that the focus of understanding has to be on the self and that being selfish is the primary spiritual objective behind, first and foremost and above all others, taking care of yourself. This is considered to be fundamental to our growth. But suffice to say, "Isn't being selfish, that is, looking after one's own well-being, welfare and securing growth also true in business?"

CO-EXISTENCE A: What seem to be phenomena which can exist together are, in reality, phenomena which cannot exist together (Davis, 1971). Although spirituality has accepted business into its realms, there is still a way to go before spirituality is accepted into a business organisation.

CO-EXISTENCE B: What seems to be phenomena which cannot exist together (i.e. business organisations and spirituality) are, in reality, phenomena which can exist together (Davis, 1971). Reminding ourselves of work absenteeism number two: The suffering of stress, depression and anxiety, spirituality and spiritual support groups have helped millions upon millions of, very stressed, people worldwide achieve recovery and well-being. As typically testified by . . .

JOANNA B: "I do believe that as my spirituality has improved, so has my physical and mental well-being increased to the same extent, so I am not off poorly from work anymore and my general attendance has greatly improved."

How many times within an organisation have you heard "Just make a decision!"? Or similarly, "I wish they would just make a decision" and no decision is ever made!? A leader or a manager, when suitably challenged and expected to make tough decisions but instead goes and 'hides' in the safety of hierarchy, bureaucracy and authority, is either a coward, inept or so politicised they have become 'paralysed' in both their career and minds. To be fair today's leaders and managers are literally afraid—fearful of making a real actionable decision within their organisation. If they get any action wrong, it seems like their career is suddenly all over, with little or no forgiveness forthcoming, for making, sometimes, only one mistake, permanently side-lining them or where they are eventually 'managed' out of the business. As a result, it increasingly appears that a leader or manager who makes no 'real' decisions, or is (deliberate and intentionally) completely 'inefficient' at making them (Parkinson & Lancaster, 1958), or even makes no decisions at all, is considered to be 'better off' and more highly regarded than one who makes a few bad decisions but has all the best intentions to, at least, try and progress the initiative. This is probably why so many organisations like to contract in consultants to make all of the decisions, so if it goes wrong this 'outsider' gets the blame, but if it all goes right then the key stakeholder is commended for bringing them in, in the first instance. Really!? Surely not!? Striving for competitive advantage in the global market, "Is this what these key people are being paid to do?" "To procrastinate, pass the buck, avoid responsibility and decision-making and/or ignore what is actually happening?" To be earning decent amounts of money, but be so afraid of making a decision that the business doesn't just stand still or grow, it starts to go backwards! Let's just say, consultancy fees and earnings are going through the roof. Today, being innovative means not only having the ability to staying where we are, we have to be even more innovative and imaginative just to move forward! However interestingly, in a paradoxical way and from a spiritual perspective, this negative stance and stand-off can work the other way around to become very much a positive one. Anything worth doing is worth doing badly, is a skewed version of an old saying, and most people have a view that to help somebody, or to fix a problem, you need to actually *do* something. Through your own self-development, initiating *your own* activities for an improved life also includes knowing that doing nothing and/or accepting the situation 'as is', is also an active and positive choice. This is where, rather than getting embroiled in the 'save and fix' unhealthy cycles of somebody else's life, we realise that we are not solving the issue, we are actually contributing to it—possibly making it even worse. Here, it helps to know that consciously not doing something is the right thing to do.

EDWARD P. H: "Understanding that consciously not doing something is actually an active choice and to know that there is nothing I can do in certain situations and for other people and by not doing anything is actually the right course of action to take, is one of the hardest things I have had to learn from spirituality."

'To accept the things *I* cannot change, courage to change the things *I* can and have the wisdom to know the difference'.

HANNAH H: "Knowing that I've got an active choice; when the right and wrong time is to do something and as my spirituality has evolved over time, taking the right decisions . . . taking control, has become my second nature."

HEATHER P: "My spirituality makes me quite ballsy at work, whereas the other directors are not there yet. I find that they are more nervous about decision-making than I am. I will make a decision and that's it, as I know that nothing terrible is going to happen, either way, whereas the others will agonise over decisions and their behaviour for days and days after they have done whatever it is they have done. I am hoping they are going to get there one day, instead of trying to keep pulling me back in."

JANNINE B: "My spiritual beliefs and values have enabled me to cope a lot better at work; to make better decisions, to think about things more calmly."

Today's world cries out for people who can lead with a global perspective. We now need leaders and managers who understand that decisions made affect not just the smallest of organisations, but effect the entire global community. This extends into how leaders and mangers make decisions which promote, engage and deliver sustainable value creation. From the previous testimonials and preceding workings, spiritual values stretch into how individuals grow themselves into making assertive and right, relevant and timely decisions, rather than simply following the 'safe' and same old status quo. Having this ability will place *any* individual right in the middle of the organisation, to enable (creative) flow and leadership in the decision-making process, which truly delivers not only sustainable and shared value creation, but also well-being.

CO-RELATION A: What seem to be unrelated (independent) phenomena are, in reality, correlated (interdependent) phenomena (Davis, 1971). With the levels of domestic violence, together with addictions of all kinds increasing, and when an individual's home life consists of stress and suffering, their work life (which makes sense) also suffers and is stressful as well. Vice versa, with the levels of work-related stress and suffering rising, together with work addiction increasing and when an individual's work life suffers and is stressful, then their home life (which also makes sense) also suffers and is stressful as well.

STEVEN I: "From first-hand experience, I can see by the amount of people who are going through treatment centres who are suffering from workplace stress, addictive problems, personality and relationship problems and so on has gotten worse in the past 25 years, that I have closely been following the Fellowships."[12]

CO-RELATION B: What seem to be related interdependent phenomena are, in reality, uncorrelated independent phenomena. For a workaholic, compulsive working is addictive and chronic as the individual seeks to alleviate personal psychological stress through compulsion and addiction to the adrenaline and/or other hormones which they produce and so continue to seek from their work. However, known as process addiction, those who suffer from unmanageable work procrastination (which can also be termed as work aversion) are also categorised as being stressed and chronic workaholics, where many of these individuals will also seek to alleviate personal psychological stress through compulsion and addiction. Suffering and stress are associated with time off sick from work, but compulsion, addiction, suffering, stress and problems at home are generally not associated with work-related issues, such as the individual having low employment prospects.

Social theorists have highlighted the absence of correlation among phenomena thought to be correlated less often than the presence of correlation among phenomena thought to be uncorrelated. Interesting propositions of Co-relation B (Davis, 1971), are rarer than interesting propositions of Co-relation A (Davis, 1971), because social theorists assume social phenomena to be uncorrelated more often than they assume social phenomena to be correlated. Therefore, what seems to be phenomena which cannot exist together (i.e. organisations and spirituality) suffering and stress are, in reality, phenomena which can exist together.

It is not suggested that this form of spirituality is easy and it isn't the intention (as it hasn't been so far) to skirt around any issues and challenges around the subject of spirituality. As with any initiative or innovation, spiritual or otherwise, these issues and challenges need to be faced up to, dealt with and overcome.

2.29 Issues and Challenges

The only power, control *and love* that a person does have is with *oneself*. This, in essence, is the construct of the *self* and *selfishness* and as such, is of principle importance in spirituality. Although everybody has some control of their own lives, nobody should be at the extreme end of the spectrum where, at one end, they cannot manage everything that happens to them and at the other end, they are trying to manage and control other individuals. We might try and orchestrate and change things by trying to make our life go the way that we want it to go, but we cannot determine the actual outcome from our (sometimes well-intentioned) actions. Essentially, with regards to other people we cannot do anything to orchestrate and change them, as they have their own lives to lead. We are powerless over anyone, apart from ourselves. Trying not to change people is one of the biggest and hardest lessons which we have to learn in our spirituality. You can't force people to change, you can only help them not if, but when they want you to help them. But, importantly, even when they ask for help, it isn't your 'job' or position in life to rescue or fix them. Few people recognise this truth.

DENIAL: Is one of the biggest obstacles to overcome in spirituality.
DENIAL: *Is one of the biggest obstacles to overcome in spirituality.*
DENIAL: Is one of the biggest obstacles to overcome in spirituality.

HANNAH H: "I have worked for over 20 years and I have found that everybody kind of goes all soft, squashy and mushy. They have got this kind of 'looking at everything through rose-tinted glasses' where everything is 'Amazing!' Or 'Amazeballs!' Eventually they begin to realise that it isn't all like that at all and then they start to become all prickly and defensive about their situations. Mainly to protect themselves against reality. Of what is actually going on around them!"

"It's not *me*, it's *them*!" "I am so unlucky." "It's not *my* fault." "No no, that's not what's happening at all!" "There is certainly—Nothing wrong with me!" Denial is a coping mechanism which is designed to protect ourselves from being confronted with unpleasant situations; it also means that we refuse to accept the truth about something that's happening in either our or other people's lives, especially those that are close to us. Denial disrupts our the ability to tackle challenges and change. We go defensive. We get angry. We go into steadfast denial. This is the crux of the problem, where you cannot escape from a cage unless you know that you are in one. Overcoming denial means being completely honest with yourself, by facing up to your own issues and failures.

Conquering our denial means humility. In this context it means being humble; it is not as many assume a state of weakness, but of strength. It does not mean inferiority, kowtowing or submission to anybody; instead the individual reduces their associated ego and so starts to gain self-esteem and confidence. Cunning adversaries even admitting that both denial and powerlessness with regards to ourselves, other people and situations (especially in business) is extremely hard. Although we all like and so seek a challenge in our lives (and spirituality certainly encourages this, as well as individuals taking risks in doing so), phrases that 'give away' our denial and acceptance of being powerless, especially when it comes to other people and what they are (choosing to do) . . . doing are, for example, "I am going to fight them/this." I won't let *them* win." "I will beat them/this, even if it kills me." "Don't they realise . . . can't they see . . . I will show them!?" These are all indications of being involved in a power struggle with another person. Spirituality is not about winning this 'battle' of the wills, or winning an argument, or rescuing others, or either making them happy or sad, or trying to change them into what *you* think they should be and should be doing. Neither is it running to their aid if and when they ('they' as in adults—not children) do something stupid and/or are in a 'situation' and hence need the aforementioned rescuing. Overcoming denial means acknowledging and totally accepting that, despite your own best efforts, nothing and no one has and can be changed. At best, situations (but not our mental state, it may have even gotten worse) have stayed the same; at worst by helping and caring for somebody in an unhealthy (co-dependent) way has enabled them/things to go even worse, which also doesn't help our mental state; in fact, it will probably accelerate us to reaching our rock bottom! These constant break and fix cycles then lead to (even more) chaos, conflict, resentment, anger and frustration where other people, together with situations and emotions, begin to dominate both our thoughts and our lives. We lose, or already have lost, the sense of the self. In essence, we have to accept that we are entirely powerless over most things (apart from ourselves) and this is extremely hard to recognise and to acknowledge as this means admitting defeat, which also isn't easy to do. This admittance requires humility. Otherwise with the alternative being constant frustration, unhappiness and perpetual suffering, when compared to these unhealthy prospects, admitting defeat should suddenly become more palatable.

Although in the recent past there has been a growing interest in spirituality, what *it* actually means and how people and businesses view *it* and apply *it*, is a different thing.

SHELTON D: "The people I work with don't know hardly anything about spirituality and that sort of thing. One day, I was describing it to them and they were all laughing at me and making fun but I didn't mind, that's up to them—I know how it benefits me."

LAUREN C: "I was once talking to my friend about my spirituality and what it all means and he 'laughed his socks off' at me. What made this worse he was also doing all the 'whoooooooooooooah—whoooooooooooooah' ghost stuff at me. Sometime later he asked what book I was reading (as I always keep one in my handbag) and what he could do and where he could go to help both himself and the situation which he was in. Amazing how what comes round goes round!"

PAUL J: "I speak quite freely about my spirituality and some people like it and some people don't . . . but that's something that's okay for me."

RACHAEL D.-S: "People at work think that 'I am a little bit odd' [laugh], because I do see the world differently. But I'm okay with that!"

Table 2.2 Issues and challenges to the application of spirituality

Issue 1	Issue 2	Issue 3	Challenge 1	Challenge 2	Challenge 3	Challenge 4	Challenge 5
Spirituality is often confused with religion. Servant leadership: It's all about being selfless and altruistic. Spirituality is actually all about being selfish. It's all about individualism—it's all in the mind.	Horrendous suffering and trauma bring individuals to spirituality. Spirituality advocates free will.	Stuck in the status quo. Action required not words.	No definition of spirituality.* No measure of spirituality.* No conceptual framework of spirituality.** Spiritual immaturity and maturity. Life is in the now. Denial! To be free from isms and addictive behaviours.	Motivation: desperation. Managers and leaders: bullying and ineptitude. Leaders and managers, paralysed in making decisions.	To have a belief in something 'higher'.	Admit to being powerless. It is hard to let go. Doing nothing is the right thing to do.	Often confused with spiritualism. People think that spirituality is 'a waste of time' and 'just a load of rubbish'. "Am I just making it all fit?" There is such a long way to go for spirituality to be accepted in business.

* Covered and rectified within Chapter 3, Section 3.2 A Fully Considered Spiritual Definition and Section 3.7 A Fully Considered Spiritual measure...
** Covered and rectified within Chapter 2, Section 2.19 The 5S's and Chapter 6, Section 6.3 Transforming Leadership

NICK G: "For many spirituality is a new thing, so there are a lot of people who think that it's 'all a waste of time and that it's all rubbish', that's because they don't really understand it."

SANDRA C: "When I talk about my spirituality some people regard me as either being mad, bad or completely insane!"

This mechanical view and ridicule of spiritual people and the very subject of spirituality is both ignorant and obsolete. However, spirituality aside, many employees today and for different reasons often feel psychological separation and isolation at their place of work. This separation and isolation flows from being judged and ridiculed—the alienation of their very own employees from their colleagues and the organisation alike—the very people whom they depend upon for success. Recognising this reality, any economic and social system is only as good as the people within it.

SARAH H: "In many corporate organisations, there is such a long way to go for spirituality to be accepted into the business world . . . *but it certainly has to start somewhere.*"

Amongst the issues and challenges, identified by study (Broadhurst, 2019), of spirituality within the workplace as they stand, certainly on face value, in relation to the acceptance and integration of spirituality in any business, these issues and challenges, contained within Table 2.2, would not provide any degree of confidence in driving organisational change. However, rest assured, they are nothing that cannot be overcome.

As the alienation between spirituality—individuals—businesses and their employees becomes evermore apparent and as they depend upon each other for success, much more still needs to be discovered regarding what acceptable forms there are and how spirituality can be made a seamless part of the organisation and the life of the individuals within it. Spirituality provides clarity, courage, faith and hope, where risks are encouraged and any fear, failure and changes are met with positivity. Any hurdles can be overcome, but where the biggest fear now is the individual, the employee, business leadership and management all having a closed mind.

Notes

1 By way of suppositories, or 'plugging', as the anus has a lot of veins in it, which quickly facilitates absorption into the bloodstream.
2 Rubbing such as heroin into the lining of their vaginas, or dispensing a heroin solution from a syringe directly into their vaginas.
3 Eyeballing: consuming alcohol by pouring it into the eye sockets, where it is then absorbed through the mucous membranes of the region into the bloodstream.

4 When something is said to 'come with all the trimmings', it means that it has many extra things added to it to make it more special.

5 A gesture of respect, such as a bow. The state of being revered. One held in reverence—more commonly used as a title for a clergyman.

6 Saying someone or something is 'back in business' means it has returned to normal activity after a period of time when it was not possible due to a malfunction, repair or other bad conditions.

7 Act in an excessively subservient manner.

8 Adapted by the learned as well as the vulgar, and as such, it expresses a truth that can be distinguished from any counterfeits.

9 Sexually transmitted diseases are infections that are passed from one person to another through sexual contact. There are more than 20 types of STDs, the causes of which are bacteria, parasites and viruses.

10 Mindful: The state of being conscious or aware of something.

Mindfulness, used as a therapeutic technique: A mental state achieved by focusing one's awareness on the present moment, while calmly acknowledging and accepting one's feelings, thoughts and bodily sensations.

11 Leading with your chin: Known in boxing to approach an opponent with your chin thrust forward, so making it easier to be hit. The term also alludes to being unprotected and so vulnerable.

12 Doctors are seeing a rise in people reporting severe mental health difficulties. www.bbc.co.uk/news/health-53742121.

3 Not Starting the Spiritual Journey

Spirituality as a positive action has, perhaps, been one of the most misused and misconstrued concepts where, over the years, it has acquired diverse and somewhat conflicting meanings.

Despite the vast amount of literature given over to the subject of spirituality, little progress has been made towards the establishment of a widely accepted definition of the term, or even the affective measure of it. They simply, currently, do not exist. This can be further expanded upon by specifying that any organic growth, appertaining to both individuals and business, without either a structure or framework of some kind is in a state of *chaos*. As the overall subject of spirituality doesn't, **yet** (see Chapter 3, Section 3.2 A Fully Considered Spiritual Definition . . . and Section 3.7 A Fully Considered Spiritual Measure . . .) have either a definition or measure spirituality can also be considered to be, therefore, in a current state of *chaos*. Like the majority of us are! Like the majority of organisations are! Going forward and along with fresh and creative thinking, spirituality needs to be clearly conceptualised to include a new definition and a new measure, together with a new construct which are all supported by a more inclusive terminology, which both encompasses and bridges the gap between spirituality and the individual/s (as employee[s]) and business leadership and management. This, in turn, will bring with it fresh opportunities and growth—for all. Therefore, "Let's not louse it up with Freudian complexes and things that are only interesting to the scientific mind" (Bob, 1980).

Keeping it simple: Critical thinking requires open-mindedness in examining diverse ideas, persistence in seeking answers to crucial questions, prudence and assertiveness in making judgements and decisions and reaching conclusions, all before taking the appropriate course of action. Action consists of having a growth mindset where everything brightens . . . it expands, it creates energy and possibilities.

Growth: a process of developing, physically and/or mentally. A process of increasing in amount; an economic activity or importance. To grow: of a living thing; to undergo natural development, by increasing in size and changing. To become larger or greater over a period of time. Develop or expand something, especially a business. Of a person; to come to think and feel something over time. This capture of grow and growth, therefore, begins with the belief of our human potential and development, but it does *not* start with a/our spiritual journey!

3.1 The End of the Spiritual 'Journey'

A journey is defined as either a trip or a tour, meaning to travel from one place to another. A journey also means travelling a long distance, over some time and often in dangerous circumstances. A trip is a shorter journey. A tour is used to describe a journey which has numerous stops in it. Both a trip and a tour end at the place where they began.

Spiritual changes aren't dangerous but maintaining the way things are, considerably, could be. Neither does spirituality mean going a long distance to get to either it or there, but once undertaken we can go a 'long way' in a short amount of time. Spirituality will never take you back to where you started from. Only you can do that! Nor will it take you to or through dangerous places, to get to where you need to go. However, spirituality will take you to a different 'safe' place within yourself. Suffice to say, an individual with desire, faith and persistence can reach great heights by eliminating negative energy, thoughts and behaviours, by focusing on their greater aims in life. Therefore, spirituality is neither a journey, trip nor a tour, *it* is an attitude that acts as a progressive guiding principle to conduct our actions against, within all aspects of our everyday lives. *It* is also a multi-cultural philosophy, free and open to anybody who wants it. A philosophy is a pathway to lead your life by.

3.2 A Fully Considered Spiritual Definition . . .

Pathway: a way or track laid down for steady walking; a course of action. The direction in which a person or thing is moving and progressing; a way of achieving a specified result. This specified result is for *us* becoming an authentic human being. Therefore, based upon all what has been discussed and determined so far throughout the preceding chapters, the following considered and so new definition of spirituality is procured:

> Spirituality is an awareness that you are on a pathway that is expanding and that you are moving into different areas of yourself, so it is really becoming aware of who you are and what all of your potential is.
>
> (Broadhurst, 2019, p. 86)

A pathway is described as a way to get somewhere; thus by acquiring an interdisciplinary, spiritual outlook and application (which also bridges and encompasses different and isolated streams of thinking and research) a pathway as a terminology is suitably applicable as it does form the important and relevant, healthy relational behavioural and affective link/s between and beginning from the 'I' (the individual), to the you (the real you), to the we (the connected, but not in a co-dependent way), to the us (the recognised interconnected individual*ism*), to the group (but not emmeshed) collectiv*ism*, to all come back to the *I*, the free-willed Individual—the *Self*. It then begins all over again with the *Self* to lead, through example and attraction, another individual, the 'I', to start the cycle over again, in a continuous improvement loop.

A pathway can also be described as a route to get somewhere. Furthermore, a route can also be formed by a chain of nerve cells, along which impulses travel. Neural pathways are a sequence of reactions in a living organism, a series of connected nerves along which electrical impulses travel in the body. A neural pathway is a bundle of axons, which connect two or more different neurons, which enable a signal to be sent from one region of the nervous system to another. There are 100 trillion atoms per neuron. Ten trillion, trillion atoms make up all of the neurons in your brain. "So what?" I hear you ask!

Many believe that we are what we are because of the vibrations of thought which we pick up and register, through both negative and positive vibration . . . a frequency—a stimuli of our daily environment. This, thus, becomes the law of *you*.

3.3   The Law of *You*

A nucleus is the centre core of an atom. The nucleus itself is an organelle, which is derived from *organ*. Just as our organs support the body, organelles support an individual cell. This organelle is also the most important, as it has a very specific function or job to do within this cell. This is because it contains the genetic material, the DNA which is responsible for controlling and directing all the activities of that cell. Breaking the nucleus apart—or combining two nuclei together releases large amounts of energy. Nuclear weapons use this energy to *trigger* and create an explosion.

KATIE D: "If someone is, *you know* . . . being confrontational and I find myself starting to become engaged and embroiled in that conflict, my triggering process starts and I then become activated. Where I can literally feel the momentum . . . the energy . . . a huge powerful energy rising up along my spine—expanding and rushing all around within me. Now, in an ideal scenario I would breathe . . . really connecting my breath and listen and be present in the moment; because if I didn't catch myself I just end up reacting and it all *explodes, you know*, into a full-blown, no holds barred, confrontational situation of energy and destruction" (see Chapter 2, Section 2.24 Triggers).

Building upon our Spiritual *5S*'s model (see Chapter 2, Section 2.20, Figure 2.7 The spiritual *5S*'s), it is therefore offered, as concept, that it is *you*, *the self* who is the nucleus—the organelle, at the centre of your own life atom, because you are important and have a specific function to do in your everyday life. The surrounding 'electrons' therefore represent life, one which consists of both good (positive) times and undeniable (negative) trials and tribulations, which (both) constantly test your isms as well as your well-meaning behaviours and intentions. Surrounded by both of these positive and negative isms in your life, it is therefore your 'job' to control (minimise/remove) the internal negative ism ones and direct your positive isms, thoughts and behaviours, without either/any of them colliding and thereafter 'exploding' into confrontation. This is achieved through connected and interconnected awareness right through from the 'I' to the *I* in a continuous loop and, when and where required, *we* seek the appropriate support that will enable us to grow and become an—more all-round, authentic individual (see Figure 3.1).

Atoms within every molecule are always vibrating and each bond between atoms vibrates at a certain frequency and in a certain direction. Everything in the universe moves and vibrates—nothing is at rest, including you! When different vibrating things/processes come into close

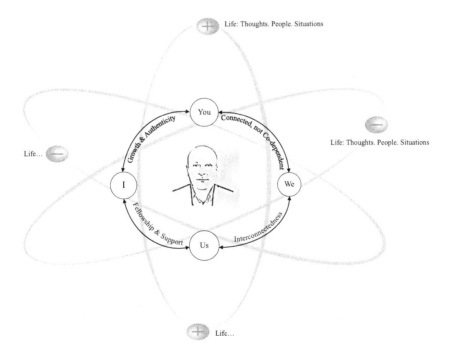

Figure 3.1 The nuclear individual.

proximity, an interesting phenomenon occurs; they will start to vibrate together and at the same frequency. They synchronise in ways which can seem mysterious to us. Through self-reflection we start to understand both our negative and positive drivers and how they are affecting us; together with what/they/we are attracting in terms of certain, good and bad, people and pleasant/unpleasant situations, into our lives.

3.4 All Sorts Attract All Sorts

Magnets work at an atomic level. By creating an invisible area of magnetism all around it, this magnetic field can either do nothing, repel, attract, or not attract something. Doing nothing is well! Doing nothing, everything just stays the same. Opposites attract where often individuals who have different characters either become friends, join gangs or groups and/or become sexually involved with each other. These relationships can be regarded as being edgy, dynamic, risky, challenging and exciting. However, after this glitter has faded, this intensity can also lead to severe tensions and challenges. What's more, the stronger the relationship, *the magnetic* attraction between the individuals, the harder it is to pull away. This is especially pertinent given the inclination, which seems to be present within most of us, to regard the way that we are and the way that we do things as being the 'right' way (my way, or the highway—if only either of these were true, wouldn't the world be so much better off and great for everybody!?) and so we set about (trying) to influence the other 'wrong' person to become more like we are, which is the right way, as in co-dependency (see Chapter 2, Section 2.9 Co-dependency: Servant Leadership and Altruism). Like attracts like and by the individual attracting into their life the experiences, situations, events and people which 'match the frequency' of their thoughts and feelings, which at first glance looks ideal, however, those individuals who are insecure and self-abandoning attract each other, whilst those who love and value themselves also attract each other.

At this point, the questions which need to be considered are these: "Is our particular 'frequency' attracting something or someone who is making us feel *dis-eased* (see Chapter 2, Section 2.14 Why Find the Spiritual 'It' . . .), that is, suffering, miserable and unhappy?" "Do we really want to attract someone/others who are like, or who are not like us?" If you are attracted to particular people or to a particular organisation you have to ask yourself "Why is that?" Incidentally, circa 5% of interviewers stated that they made a decision about a candidate's suitability for a role, within their organisation, within the first minute of meeting them. Twenty-five percent decided within the first five minutes. Overall, 59.9% of decisions, made on their suitability, were made within the first 15 minutes of meeting them. "How long does it take the candidate to decide that they want to work for the organisation?" Milliseconds!? Mainly because they just want a job. Offer accepted!

Human beings consist of a bundle of negative and positive emotions, which make up our rational thought, feelings and responses. Spirituality heavily influences the ending of both the purely irrational and the purely rational and instigates a new beginning where both the emotional irrational and rational are taken into account and catered for. Through providing this emotional perspective and balance, spirituality encourages the reduction of our highs and the raising of our emotional lows (see Chapter 2, Section 2.7 Moods and Feelings; Figure 2.1 Emotional variation) by harmonising of all of our emotions. It therefore follows that an overall sense of wellness will not be achieved without having a balance between all of our attributes. Attributes: a quality or feature regarded as a characteristic, or an inherent part of someone, or something. An attribute has been stated as one that cannot be measured, but can be assessed using a number of indicators or manifested variables. However even when allowing for some (emotional) variation this is a fine balance, but one which will have a huge impact on life: the individual, their friends, families and colleagues and the productivity of a business. "But what to measure?"

3.5 What to Measure . . .

Measure: to ascertain the size, amount or degree of (something) by using an instrument or device marked in standard units.

Quality: a distinctive attribute or characteristic; possessed by someone or something . . . the totality of features and characteristics which refers to the set of inherent properties which allows the satisfying of stated or implied needs . . . how good something is compared to other similar things. Within business: to improve quality; constantly and forever, to be fit for purpose, to be of value. Profit (see Chapter 2, Section 2.1 What Is Business?): to fund the costs of operating, as well as to maximise profits.

Within (for some) 'spirituality' has other meanings such as bodhisattva.[1] Zen: slang for feeling peaceful and relaxed. Enlightenment: understanding and interpreting reality, according to certain principles and truths. Transcendence: existence or experience beyond the normal or physical level. The Spiritual Well-Being Scale (TSWBS or SWBS). Well-being. The 12-Steps. Achieving a spiritual awakening. Growth. Hedonism. Success. Happiness. All these describe some kind of measure, a way of knowing where we started and a knowing where we are at any point in time and 'if' we are suitably getting 'there', or, indeed, have reached where we would like to be.

Spirituality provides a way and means of getting *you* from where *you* are *now* to the 'there' . . . as in somewhere . . . the there where *you* are *meant* to be. Where your progress will be dependent upon the effort that *you* put in, in relation to where your particular 'there' is. Vague? Perhaps! But, as we are all different with different lives, this kind of makes sense! Besides (but honestly not offered as a cop out of any kind), as spirituality is all about progress (not perfection), we will always be *here* and in the

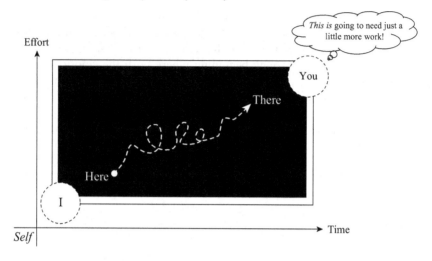

Figure 3.2 From here, to there.

now, at some and any given point in time; by that, it is meant because we will always be works-in-progress, we will never actually reach 'there' anyway (Figure 3.2).

It is happiness that, perhaps, is our main goal . . . the driving force—the measure behind so much of our lives and what we do within it! The word 'happiness' is a derivation of 'happening' and what happens in our life is, certainly, not always happy. Happiness is also widely known to be, at best, only temporary, at worst subject to the law of diminishing returns.[2] Certainly, we live in a consumer, materialistic and hedonistic society, which is both 'sold' as and geared towards the individual 'purchasing' and so 'achieving' happiness, in some way, shape or form. Within this has also come the prominent thinking that happiness comes in accomplishments, recognition, material possessions and comfort. Having such strong desires for these, the individual is prepared to work long and unsociable hours (which literally means having less *self*-time) while they may also be racking up lots of debt to 'purchase' and support this 'achieving' of the desired lifestyle! We have come to believe the mistaken (and according to the Bible—Satan promoted!) notion that if we just acquire and do certain things, then we can and will be truly happy and secure in the details of our lives. As a consequence, individuals tend to develop their own agendas, both honest and/or dishonest methods and ways by which they seek to achieve success, together with this elusive and fleeting happiness (Figure 3.3).

Okay! Maybe not Satan promoted, but then again . . . who knows—let's put that one down to the spiritualism debate, shall we!?

Figure 3.3 The Devil is in the detail of happiness.

People say that they are "happy" to be cancer-free. Partaking in their favourite sport or hobby. Meeting up with and speaking to good friends and (maybe) having a laugh or two. Going to their favourite place. Having carnal knowledge. Having their favourite meal and/or a glass of wine, or two. . . . Winning something. Finding something. Watching the sun go down, or up. (Maybe) having children—watching them grow up. Getting married. Some people even cry (especially, as they say, at weddings) when they are happy. Although these are all different emotional situations and states, we still use the term 'happiness' for all of these occasions. The multi-dimensions of what happiness is considered to be is further coloured, glossed and even measured against having lots of money, fun and free time. These *pleasurable and enjoyable* experiences are more hedonic in our character where, unfortunately, this pleasurable and enjoyable life doesn't last for very long. We can also, safely, assume different individuals experience happiness, pleasure and enjoyment in many varieties and very different ways. Whatever the variety and difference, life is certainly *not* made up of a never-ending demand and supply of 'syrupy sweet' happiness and definitely *does not* deliver continuous hedonic experiences. The pursuit of happiness through external sensory pleasures, of which the hedonist chases after, does not bring the sustained satisfaction. This is attained through self-actualisation. Self-actualisation is what the eudaemonist pursues, where their highest goal is the experiencing and achieving of meaning and purpose. However, spirituality is a combination of good times (whilst also accepting bad times, but minimising them as much as possible), together with hedonism and eudaemonist experiences, which all contribute towards our overall well-being, which we seek.

Happiness was much discussed amongst the Greeks under the term well-being. In his *Nicomachean Ethics* (written circa 350 BC), Aristotle

(385 BC–323 BC) put forward the proposition that eudaimonia means 'doing and living well' . . . which also subscribes to such things as being virtuous, having and giving love, having good friends, experiencing happiness and pleasure, where the individual feels they are in their *own perfect* state of well-being. Even though happiness is an integral part of our personal well-being, it doesn't stand alone. It also includes other criteria such as fulfilling long-term goals, having a sense of purpose and how much you feel in control of your life. To this, the Spiritual Well-Being Scale (SWBS) was developed as a tool for self-assessment around these aspects of general and perceived well-being.

3.5.1 The Spiritual Well-Being Scale

One 'companion' or aid to assessing whether somebody is spiritual or not is the Spiritual Well-Being Scale (SWBS [Paloutzian & Ellison, 1982]). The SWBS provides an outcome—an indicator of how well a person 'is doing', in the face of whatever the individual is confronting. Ironically SWBS is not synonymous with spirituality, neither is it to mental or physical health. SWBS implies one's subjective perception of well-being, in relation to the religious and God (i.e. having a personal and meaningful (connected) relationship with God) and the existential (i.e. I don't know who I am, where I came from, or where I am going!) To 'answer' these two dimensions the SWBS is self-assessment tool, which consists of a Likert-type scale ranging from 1 = strongly disagree, 2 = mostly agree, 3 = disagree, 4 = agree, 5 = moderately agree and 6 = strongly agree. Amongst all of this it is fair to ask "What's going on there then?" Suffice to say the SWBS has both its supporters and critics alike. However the Spiritual Well-Being Scale does reason that a good and well life can be explained by looking at all three components of material, psychological and spiritual well-being, but despite the 1–6 scale and the ambiguity surrounding this Likert scale measurement *and* that of both well-being *and* that of spirituality the problem of measuring spirituality still remains.

3.5.2 Well-Being

Well-being: the state of being comfortable; the experience of health, happiness and prosperity. Well-being includes having good mental health, a high life satisfaction, a sense of meaning and purpose, the ability to manage stress. More generally and simply, well-being is just—feeling well! Even though happiness is an integral part of your personal wellness, it also includes other things such as the fulfilment of long-term goals, your sense of purpose and how in control you feel and are of your life. Nothing in nature is reproduced, every single snowflake is different and it's the same with human beings. This, in turn, creates a *perception*—an air of mystery that, can be and is, interpreted differently across all countries and cultures of the world. Until we choose to accept that we are all totally different, "How can we focus upon our similarities?" Whilst also creating a one approach which answers the question "How do (all of these) individuals have their different needs met and well-being satisfied within their place of work?"

Alcoholics Anonymous (AA) is a spiritual support group, which found that through its 12-Steps, Concepts, Traditions and Principles, it is certainly possible to create a one approach, which is also bespoke enough to cover all of these previous variations. AA, still today, also represents and provides a successful model of how an organisation can grow to a very large size and yet still reach millions of individuals on a world-wide scale, whilst also fully supporting an individuals' well-being, human dignity and equality on a local level.

3.6 Spiritual Support Groups: Fellowships

Spiritual support groups consist of an interconnected network of people who provide emotional and practical help to others who are in serious difficulty. These support groups are more commonly referred to and known as 'Fellowships'. The founders of Alcoholics Anonymous, Bill W., and Dr Bob, developed a set of guiding principles, consisting of 12 separate steps which each outline a course of action for recovery from addiction, compulsion and/or other behavioural problems. Shortly afterwards Bill W.'s wife (who was suffering herself), Lois W., started a spin-off from AA, Al-Anon: a Fellowship group set up, specifically, for the family and friends of alcoholics. Today there are many (but importantly, their format isn't different to AA, but due to the subject matter there are/has to be differences around the theme) spin-off *12-Step support programmes*, which exist to support abstinence from a multitude of addictions. These variations of Fellowships include: Workaholics Anonymous (the name speaks for itself) and CoDa—a spiritual support programme for co-dependents (see Chapter 2, Section 2.9 Co-dependency: Servant Leadership and Altruism). However amongst all of these various Fellowships (over 50 at the last count), Al-Anon could be considered to be unique as, in the main,[3] its members do not suffer from addiction per se, but these individuals have suffered and or do suffer (especially if they are a newcomer) as a result (or again as a spin-off) from those individuals who are alcohol dependent. Whereas other support groups use, as their main measure, the number of years the individual has stayed clean and/or sober (even giving them a 'medal' at set frequencies, in terms of the length of time they have stayed clean and sober), and although Al-Anon follows (as all of these support groups do, so they are not different in this respect) the same format and methodology, Steps, Concepts, Traditions and Principles which are contained with the AA programme, Al-Anon doesn't recognise this sober and clean measure (or even give medals out and there are plenty of people in Al-Anon who deserve one—ha!); instead they are seeking some form and way of achieving (and without being flippant) *sanity*—as do all of these Fellowships *set out to* do. "How's that measured then!?" Nevertheless, many have found that these spiritual support programmes are not merely a way to stop their particular compulsions, but become a guide towards a new way of life, in all areas of their lives.

3.6.1 The 12-Steps

Although the 12-Steps in their very name suggest a measure, the issue for measuring from this perspective of spirituality is that the 12-Steps, although they appear to do so, are not practised in a linear fashion and neither are they time specific or bound. Instead they continually flow back and forth, stopping (or pausing) at any one *Step* where the individual feels that they need to be and so use at that particular moment and in *their* time. In effect this becomes an infinite process, which further supports spirituality as being all about progress, not perfection. Neither is the individual required to reach a specified standard and/or quality against each of these Steps, in order to have been judged and deemed worthy as having completed each and every one of the Steps, before they proceed to the next/ another Step. Such is also the case with the Spiritual 5S's lens model (see Chapter 2, Section 2.20 The Spiritual 5S's), which is why, upon taking this point, it has been constructed as a series of related interconnected 'bubbles' rather than a compartmentalised linear fashion. However and in particular, the 'last' 12th Step of AA et al. is an interesting one. As contained, stated and stipulated within Step 12: 'Having had a spiritual awakening as the result of these steps, we tried to carry this message to others and to practice these principles in all our affairs' (Anonymous, 1952), "Does this really mean reaching and achieving this 12th and 'final' Step is the ultimate measure?" If so, is the individual 'rewarded' with a 'spiritual awakening', having finally reached and completed all of the previous 11 Steps?

3.6.2 The 12-Steps: A Spiritual Awakening?

Back when Bill W., the co-founder of Alcoholics Anonymous, was hospitalised for treatment, depressed and delirious, he witnessed 'a blinding light and felt an ecstatic sense of freedom and peace'. When Bill told his physician Dr Silkworth about the event, the doctor replied, "Something has happened to you that I don't understand, but whatever it is that you have had you had better hang on to it." This 'awakening' experience ultimately led Bill W. to abstain from alcohol for the remaining 36 years of his life. Belladonna is known to cause hallucinations, but in the day it was widely touted as a cure for alcoholism. "Was Bill W's spiritual awakening the effect of a belladonna hallucination, or did something else happen to him which cannot be explained?"

Dr Bob is the other co-founder of AA and he never had a spiritual awakening in terms of a sudden and blinding flash of light, but he did have proclaimed spiritual growth and achieved inner peace and importantly he too stayed sober for the rest of his life. The 12th Step does, upon the reading of it, give the distinct impression—even a guarantee—of a spiritual awakening after 'working' the previous 11 Steps; however, if we look at the actual wording and together with the factoring in of Dr Bob's experience, 'having had' is past tense. In other words, each sum of the parts (not exactly to a standard) is 'working' it and so progressing every step in terms of what *you* need to achieve from it is 'an awakening', within in its own right. Where the 12th Step is not the final step it is simply the sum of its previous parts.[4]

3.6.3 The 12-Steps: The Message to Be Carried

Back to the 'message' part of the 12th Step (also bringing in the 'parts and sum' of the equation), which we are asked to 'carry' in our affairs. "What does this 'message' part mean?" and "Does it also mean 'carrying' it to our work?" "What words do we use within this message because it doesn't (directly) tell us what to say?" Starting with the relatively easy part. This capture *all* 'in *all* our affairs' is certainly written clearly enough, with no ambiguity surrounding it. We have to take it, as this is exactly what it means, 'in *all* of *our* affairs', so this obviously includes *our* work. So far so good. But still, "What is the message to be carried and the words to be used within it?"

Upon 'reaching' the 12th Step (because we cannot just jump to it straightaway without working, at least, some 'part'/'parts' of the other 11 Steps), in theory *and* in practice we then have a *reasonable idea*, an amount of knowledge and experience, of what (maybe only one/some of the part/s of the sum) the previous 11 Steps are about (note it says 'about' and not 'all about' because we will never know it all—this is progress, not perfection) and what it and they, singularly and/or collectively can do, did do, have done and are still doing/producing for *us*.

Taking *our* 'reasonable idea' of the Step/s, etc. (because we only know what *our* knowledge and experience is), we can then *only* talk about our *own* knowledge and experience of the Step/s, together with the/our programme and spirituality. So we are *only* able to describe this in our own words, so it is these/our words which we put into, what is in effect, *our own message*. Therefore, it is this/our message we then use (which will, obviously, be different than somebody else's, as their knowledge and experience/words will be different than ours and so their message will be different than our message), hence the reason why there is no standard, directly given, a prescriptive text to 'a message'. In turn, we are then able . . .

. . . To carry a message to others . . . and through using our own words . . . to help people who are looking for some answers. Who are looking for a change in their life—to move from suffering, to being *well*! The main focus is to carry the/our message, that life doesn't have to be the way it is for them. From suffering and despair there is a way out. To give whatever is needed to *help* those people to have *hope*! Thus, this is our/a message which we carry. Phew again. Simple!?

Across all distances and barriers, laymen[5] are ready to co-operate with all people of goodwill, whatever their creed or nationality. Although this reads as being somewhat evangelical or zealous (in advocating or support-ing a particular cause), it certainly isn't meant to be. The key words here being 'co-operate with', not standing in the street trying to stop people. Spiritual attraction rather than religious promotion is the difference here.

PAUL J: "Some people are okay with it [spirituality] and some are not—but that is perfectly okay, as that's just part of it—that is up to them, not for me to try and convince them otherwise."

JAMES P: "I don't think you do any harm just to talk about spiritual stuff. When I'm at work, sometimes, I can sense when people want to lis-ten and talk and I can sense when they don't want to talk and listen. Sometimes people just do want to talk but not listen, as they mainly just want to offload stuff."

SANDRA C: "I'm not going to force my spirituality onto anybody and say 'You sit there and listen to me'. It's only if *they* enquire, when they open up a conversation, I would share my thoughts and experi-ences, but I am finding that, as I go along, more and more people are becoming interested in this subject [of spirituality] and how it may help them, in *their* affairs."

Affair: anything done, or to be done. Anything requiring action, or effort; a business or concern. An affair of great importance. Affairs: mat-ters of commercial, private or public interest, or concern; the transactions of public or private business finance; a special function, business or duty. *What's none of your affair* is a situation or matter which someone should not interfere in by saying, doing or asking anything about; an event, inci-dent or happening which occasions, or arouses, notoriety and dispute.

Most of us also dwell in the past—replaying good and bad events and situations, perhaps wishing "If only we had done something differently." Or "Not done something at all." This is a dangerous 'what if', 'if only' and 'should have done' game we play in our heads. Dangerous!? Because this 'game' is what keeps us anchored firmly in the past, perhaps, miserable and unhappy—unable to move on and get on with the flow of life, in our *now* moment. Living one day at a time refers to our mental and emotional lives and means. Having vision is not the same as projecting into the future. This projecting is 'hellish' as there is a distinct probability we will use our past to convince us as to what our futures are, in terms of 'the inevitable doom and gloom, which lies (and lies in wait like a liar) before us'. Then we start to dwell on this foregone conclusion of what seems like the inevitable fate that will befall us. This is where all of our hopes and dreams disintegrate, because we think that the future will just be a replay of our, disappointing and demoralising, past events. The very same events which have all ended in the way *we* didn't want them to. We therefore convince ourselves that disappointment is distinctly and unequivocally foretold. So, "Why bother to have hopes and dreams in the first place, if they are not going to amount to anything!?" We have, in effect, given up hope! Our past *does not dictate or determine our future. You do!* This is why there is no such thing as associating anchors with spirituality, as anchors are exactly that—they anchor! Anchors hold things and you back! The need to break free from our anchor and link chain consisting of our previous disintegrated dreams and their continuous disappointments is paramount to our progress and growth. To coin a phrase, which is not yet a cliché, 'yesterday is history—tomorrow is a mystery'. In spiritual terms, we have to learn to let the past/things go; to break the chain links that are anchoring the 'I'—which is holding *us* back from 'surfacing' into living a quality of life and enjoying well-being, whilst also having faith that both the future and the *I* will be alright (see Figure 3.4).

Figure 3.4 Can we honestly never break the chain?

Many people live their lives as if the next moment (as in, where they want to get to) is much more important than this moment. Where actually your life will never be the same in the next moment but is always in the moment of now. As human beings, we do have a considerable capability of foresight, and having vision is having the ability to make good estimates and we should use this. However sometimes people have very high expectations of themselves and they feel very disappointed . . . very upset—they feel very low if they haven't achieved what they are/were trying to achieve within the time frame that either they or others expect of themselves/them.

We cannot change the past, the past is gone and neither can we confidently, accurately or really predict the future. The only thing we have that is real is, indeed, the now. Being in the now provides an opportunity for saying: "You know what! Don't expect too much from yourself. Look at what you have achieved so far and you still have time to improve on that, so let's just take it a step at a time (which is always better than going from zero to 100% in one go). Let's just sort this bit out first and move on." It helps to have this common-sense approach and to reassure and remind ourselves (by not staring at where *we* have come from, but just pausing, every now again, to reflect upon what we once were and as such, just how far we have come since then) and other people (ditto, but how far *they* have come) . . . to the progress which both we and they have made, up until that day—one day at a time.

As with everything, you always need a solid foundation to keep building upon as we cannot say on day one things have changed, because our state of mind doesn't change on day one.

This is important as it shows spirituality as being a steady path which is being tread, one day (or even one hour for some individuals) at a time. With no deadlines or end, spirituality is a steady path of progress, which gradually reveals more and more of our true self, together with our valuable attributes, where every step we take is an evolution, maybe even a (industrial) revolution!?

3.7 A Fully Considered Spiritual Measure . . .

A proposed attribute is often one that cannot be measured directly, but can be assessed using a number of indicators, or manifested variables. Reminding ourselves, once again, of work absenteeism reason number two, the suffering of stress, depression and anxiety, this unplanned sickness absence costs UK businesses alone, circa £8.4 billion a year. Spiritual individuals, both collectively and individually unequivocally state that, because of their spirituality their overall well-being had improved and so they were/are less prone to stress and anxiety. This, in turn, meant less sickness and so less unplanned time off work. Within all instances, spiritual individuals speak directly about their calmness, peace and being more relaxed and relatively untroubled in their life.

THERESA F: "It has got to be something that is consistent, because if I can
    manage to be consistent, if I can apply what I actually think to be true

all of the time, it gives me a great sense of peace . . . it gives me the feeling of calm . . . of serenity . . . of things being right; where I am and feel comfortable and that is something that I want in my life."

RUSSELL W: "For me, it's everything to maintain my serenity, because it also helps me to maintain my dignity."

Building upon the previous sections and testimonial's, we soon start to realise the various dominant negative, one dimensional, isms (see Chapter 2, Section 2.18 Nitty Gritty *Isms*, Figure 2.6 The one-dimensional windmill of emotional isms) together with the links (see Figure 3.4 Can we honestly never break the chain?) that are anchoring us down in life. This is the point where we begin to begin and continue to be a 'fourth dimensional' human individual—a human being consisting of dominant positive traits, instead of negative shadowy ones (see Figure 3.5).

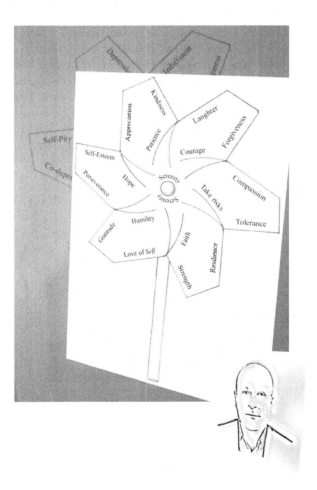

Figure 3.5 The fourth dimensional windmill of emotions.

Serenity is an illustration of everybody's well-being. It makes perfect sense, therefore, *serenity* thus becomes the offered and realistic spiritual benchmark to which we can measure both our progress and growth against (Broadhurst, 2019, pp. 81–87). By accepting (whilst not allowing them to dominate, i.e. putting them into the background, in an effort to minimise and ideally remove) our negative emotions and by discovering, mitigating and overriding them against achieving more positive emotions, serenity becomes both our *constant* reference point and default position, which we can quickly bounce back to if and when we become out of sorts in anyway.

3.8 Benefits

Potential benefits exist in the possibility of a 'something' being capable of being developed into actuality. The benefit of something is the help that you receive which enables you to get from the 'here' to 'there' and realising the advantage of such by the results from the effort that is put in to all that you do, which is proportional to the result that is actually achieved. In other words, if you make a half-arsed attempt at something, you will get a half-arsed 'result' out of it. It therefore makes sense the more that you put in, the more you will get out of something. The gift of serenity is priceless, so achieving it is relative to how you approach it, the advantage being once undertaken you will soon start to feel it, so in this instance the 'there', together with the *Self,* is always in the now (Figure 3.6).

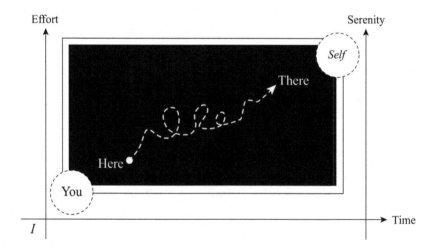

Figure 3.6 Achieving the priceless gift of serenity!

Although there is still a misconception that the spiritual key to productivity and efficiency is from a social and moral angle rather than a financial one, there is a relationship between spirituality and job satisfaction, as well the successful achievement of business goals.

The positive connection between spirituality within the workplace and enhanced job performance, financial success, decreased absenteeism and stress reduction lies within overall wellness and organisational morale.

GEMMA I.—MANAGING DIRECTOR: "It's always about going the extra mile with the customer. They are the main people, the main body of what we do. I also think about our stakeholders, how they would feel if we did this or that and how we can delight and surprise—go beyond *everybody's* expectations and deliver something that you know they want, but they never even asked for it and wow! It's suddenly there! Brilliant!"

ROWENA N.—RETAIL MANAGER IN A LOCAL STORE: "I try to help people. To give *my* customer a positive experience when they come in, where a smile is worth 'a hundred pounds'. It's always to let people think 'Oh, I enjoyed going in there and I'll go back again'. It's all part of the culture. Because if people simply don't like what they come into, then they won't come back again. It's very easy to run a business down, but it's very difficult to build one up again."

A prime benefit for applying spirituality within business organisations is its contribution in the development of both the self and others. Individuals displaying their spiritual values and behaviours—subjectively and so unintentionally—positively affects those people around them.

FFRANCON W: "When I'm at work I love to bond with people, customers and colleagues, just to get a connection going."

SANDRA C: "My awareness is the connection to everything; where nothing stands in isolation and everything has a ripple effect. This means that I conduct myself and respond to people and situations in a positive way, rather than a negative one. This makes for better relationships for not only myself but also for all others who I come across as well."

The multiplier effect: the social multiplier effect is a term used in sociology and public health based upon the principle that high levels of one attribute amongst one's peers can have a ricochet effect on other individuals.

How does all of this help? Perspective! Knowing, that actually, you can do something about both yourself and a particular situation, by having a different attitude and way of thinking in a different perspective, gives you a much wider scope on how you deal with different and sometimes difficult situations.

FFRANCON W: "We have a number of challenges which come in from our customers, who are waiting for various bits and pieces from our department and some members of my team don't deal with these customers, issues and challenges, terribly well. Because of my spiritual beliefs I have more of a calming influence on both the customer and my team. I often get feedback from them saying, 'How on earth do you manage to be so calm amongst, *you know*, all of these difficult and stressful situations?' But I really don't see them as being stressful, because I kind of look at things from a different perspective and this behaviour, this approach and attitude, seems to be starting to rub off on my team."

Everybody hears, sees and views things and situations in a different way. Sharing and listening to other people is important in order to gain clarity and/or confirmation that they are seeing/hearing the same things which we are. Labouring upon this point, sometimes, what we write and others read can be two completely different things. Equally what we say and what others hear can also be completely different. Everybody has a different perspective on any event, situation and/or circumstance, etc.

SUE P: "I like to listen to every person's perspective, I value all perspectives, because how could I possibly know what their perspective is until I ask and they tell me what it is?"

Finding and adopting spirituality breaks the vicious[6] cycle of unhappiness and negative stress, and additionally through learning, self-help and appropriate support, spiritual individuals indicate that they have managed to change their own lives—to both their own and to others' considerable betterment. Individuals, as a result of their spiritual values, beliefs and actions, commonly express that they have created virtuous cycles, acquired greater psychological benefits, greater job satisfaction, enhanced empowerment, a better work/home life balance and less stress and anxiety. This personal and professional well-being (both physical and psychological) is an all-important attribute of this contemporary spirituality, which is supplemented by the establishment of healthy boundaries and having no fear, stress and/or conflict. Although the spiritual individual brings as much compassion into their work as possible, none would (any longer) tolerate, and as testified by both Jo C. and Yvonne T., being "Treated like a doormat."

Constructed to deflate the ego and raise the self-esteem, this form of spirituality provides a balance between self-examination and associated positive action, and by facing each day with a positive outlook, the individual is very much influencing hope, whilst also having faith that the future will turn out for the better. Hope is an energising force, which arouses an individual towards action. It is action itself (including the action of doing nothing) which brings about a change. Vision and faith provide direction for these actions, as well as the sense of conviction and tenacity to persist, even when the going gets tough. Action changes who we are and what we believe is worth doing.

JAMES P: "If I'm stressed about something, or if I'm angry or afraid, I now realise that I am operating from a thought process which isn't working and by recognising this I can now look at the situation from another more positive perspective."

MICHELLE O: "I'll go round all of the workplaces and talk to all these stressed people. They'll ask me 'What I'm on?' I'm not on anything [laughs]. I was . . . I was and it was making me worse! Medication! Antidepressants! Forget it! Just put things into perspective. How important is it? . . ." [Long pause.]

Counteracting the issues and challenges within Table 2.2 (see Chapter 2, Section 2.29 Issues and Challenges) to the application of spirituality, by not immediately judging them on face value and in not doing so, and in keeping an open mind, the benefits of a positive spiritual resources and through applying spirituality within an organisation far outweigh the problems of the current status quo that organisations currently face. These benefits are conveniently summarised within the following, Table 3.1.

Greed and exploitation, together with mistakes and flaws, have all been abundantly witnessed and experienced within a multitude of businesses. In the face of economic downturn and global competition for organisations (as well as us) to survive into this century, *this is the time* where they/we can no longer afford to ignore or compromise on human values and virtues. Growth doesn't require a radical personality or professional makeover, just incremental changes in the way we carry ourselves, the way we communicate and conduct ourselves and the way we interact with others—which all often make a world of difference in how affectively we lead, either through example and/or as what's considered to be an authoritative figure. The question still remains, however, "How far can our/the spiritual message be carried (see Chapter 3, Section 3.6.3 The 12-Steps: The Message to Be Carried) whilst keeping all of the benefits—the value and profit at the central core and reason of the organisation's very existence?" Importantly, we have to ask ourselves, "Why are we currently failing to do this—what is it that is actually stopping us from doing this?" By determining the answers to these questions, we can then move onto putting the appropriate solutions in place.

Table 3.1 Benefits of applying spirituality

Benefit 1	Benefit 2	Benefit 3	Benefit 4	Benefit 5	Benefit 6	Benefit 7
Spirituality removes suffering and stress. The spiritual individual has less time off work due to unplanned sickness.	Spirituality isn't religious: It's a (multi-cultural) philosophy. *It is a free,* self-help programme. Spirituality advocates authenticity.	There is an acceptance of both the self and others. *It establishes* functional and healthy relationships, both at work and at home. Spirituality suitably avoids fear, stress and conflict.	Spirituality advocates and links together both individual*ism* and collectiv*ism*. Spirituality develops both the *self* and others, via the multiplier/ricochet effect. Spirituality develops assertiveness and robust decision-making processes.	Spirituality now has a *new* real definition, together with a *new*, universal and realistic measure.	Spirituality now has a *new* '5S's' conceptual model that can be realistically followed.	Spiritual individuals are commercially astute.

Notes

1 Bodhisattva: a state of mind which has a clear understanding of the true nature of the mind, not the relative nature that we live in most of the time, but a mind that transcends that relative state into a point of unconditional wisdom.
2 In this context, this phrase is used to refer to a point at which the level of happiness starts to decline and becomes less than the amount of energy and or money which is invested to try and achieve it.
3 The only requirement is to have a family or friend who is an alcoholic. Many addicts have such relations and so are free to join the meeting, as long as they are clean and sober when doing so.
4 Sum of its parts (plural: sums of their parts): a concept in holism related to the idea that the total effectiveness of a group of things each interacting with one another is different or greater than their effectiveness when acting in isolation from one another.
5 In case you have forgotten, because this is important!
6 The terms virtuous circle and vicious circle, also known respectively as virtuous cycle and vicious cycle, refer to complex chains of events that reinforce themselves through a feedback loop. A virtuous circle has favourable results, while a vicious circle has detrimental results.

4 Culturing Cells

The main reasons why businesses fail: the lack of leadership ability. Poor capability and management skills. The lack of uniqueness, value or authenticity. Not being in touch with the customers' needs. An unforeseen crisis. A lack of trust between employers, employees and customers. An unprofitable strategy and business model. Poor financial management. Rapid growth and over-expansion.

Work, in the main, isn't an individual experience, as somebody always works for somebody else, either as a direct employee or for a customer/client facing service role such as a Gardner, Window Cleaner, Hair Dresser, Housekeeper/Nanny or Business Consultant, etc. where, more often than not, the 'employer' (whatever their guise[1]) seems intent on forming a one-way relationship of dominance, command and control within an environment of servitude which either directly, indirectly or subliminally conveys a message that says "Your work survival is dependent upon ME!" The majority of our time is spent at work. At best, work offers the ability to earn money and so we are able to either just 'get through' life, or live a 'comfortable' life. Work may also provide an opportunity to learn about co-operating, collaborating and communicating affectively as one. However (as more commonly experienced), at work the individual can be subjected and exposed to the brutality of other human beings; a growing number of dissatisfied workers are increasingly complaining of bullying, harassment and poor relations. This behaviour often reflects the 'power' structure, the 'artificial' even 'real' culture of the organisation, and although these negative acts usually come from someone who holds a more senior position (i.e. the formal and 'real' managerial 'power' within the organisation), these poor relations can also come from an informal and 'artificial power' structure (i.e. one's co-workers).

4.1 Culture

Whether it be at a local or regional organisational level, business leadership can be considered, at best, to be challenging. Together, with the added complexity for those who operate at a global level, this will stretch even the very best leadership and managerial capabilities and abilities. At worst, it will break them.

GENERALISATION A: What seems to be a local phenomenon is, in reality, a general global phenomenon (Davis, 1971).
GENERALISATION B: What seems to be a general global phenomenon is, in reality, a local phenomenon (Davis, 1971).

Culture consists of the ideas, customs and social behaviour of people, or society. Distinguishing between global, cultural globalisation and organisational culture, global culture is a set of shared experiences, norms, symbols and ideas which exist at the national, regional, city, town and village level whilst also uniting them at the global level. This 'uniting level' includes, for example, businesses and professions, sport, art, music, holidays and beliefs. Cultural globalisation is the transmitting of ideas, meanings and values around the world in such a way as to extend and intensify both connected and interconnected relationships. Organisational culture is the behaviour of people within an organisation and the meaning those individuals attach to these behaviours. There is a general assumption that it is best, right and proper for everyone within a workplace to have, share and follow the same 'global—one-size-fits-all' organisation culture. In reality there are numerous and different 'local' cultures, *perceived* to be either real and/or artificial, within an organisation.

A macro-culture is the dominant culture. A macro-culture occupies a position of prestige, privilege and power. Macro-cultures are considered to be the (global phenomenon) majority groups whose norms are very visible, dominant and overarching and can be seen across historical timelines, which means they are often imposing and long lasting. Often confused with a sub-culture, a micro-culture is a very small (niche) culture, which has a unique identity within the macro-culture, but still functions as a part, even dynamically complementing the interconnected relationship of the dominate culture. The macro-culture, together with the various micro-cultures and multitudinous sub-cultures, contain many interconnected individuals within them, yet they are being led and managed by a 'professional', 'corporate cultured' (perhaps brainwashed) few.

The level of interaction and communication between the cultures determines whether they are divided, or diversified. It only takes a small group of employees to form a (local phenomenon) micro-culture, where a number of these micro-groups can, in turn, form a sub-culture. A sub-culture is in contrast to and is separate from both the micro and the dominant macro culture. Sub-cultures are formed and based upon difference and variance in terms of 'we' (note 'we' plural not 'I' singular) are better than *you* and *you* are worse than 'us'. From this, these sub-culture groups *choose* to exploit their differences by acting irrationally and uncooperatively against the 'official'—dominant—business group culture (i.e. the 'you'). The individual 'members' (the aforementioned 'I') of these sub-cultures are predominantly more concerned about conforming within their own group, the 'we', instead of thinking and acting for themselves—in this case the *I*, meaning themselves. In effect, these weaker individuals are acting through a 'powerful' *we* group, rather than acting alone, and through the 'we'—meaning being together—they are *all* rebelling against the very fabric of and (often valid and good) cultural values of the organisational itself. By creating their own deadly 'us and them' work circle, attitude, behaviour and situation, this situation is very much aimed towards the *them* who they consider to be different than the us, in some way, shape or form. Us and them: them and us—"Who is the us and who is the them?" A valid, but very difficult, quiz. "But can it be answered?" (See Chapter 4, Section 4.1.1 A, Difficult, Quiz.)

However (as a significant clue), this us versus them alone expresses a sense of division within any group of people. This us and them: them and us also brings with it a disease, or a *dis-ease* (see Chapter 2, Section 2.14 Why Find the Spiritual '*It*' . . .).

4.1.1 A, Difficult, Quiz

A petri dish is a shallow transparent lidded dish used to grow and develop culture cells such as bacteria or fungi which, if let free, cause diseases. *Dis-eases!* (see Figure 4.1).

Figure 4.1 Petri dish of 'culture' cells.

Quiz from Figure 4.1, from the organisational petri dish: "Can you identify who the *us* is and who the *them* is?" Vice versa, "Can you identify who the *them* is and who the *us* is?" "How many micro-cultures are there?" "Can you pinpoint the sub-groups?" "Can you spot/find the customer?" "Who is the leader amongst all of these cultural cells?" "Who are the mangers, who are effectively managing amongst all of this *diseased* culture?" Lastly, "Which one of these individuals in this growing cultural organisational petri dish is *you*?" Finally and more importantly, "Are you going to be 'droplet'—the 'antibiotic' who starts and begins to change things for the better and so cause and affect the 'multiplier effect'?" (see Chapter 3, Section 3.8 Benefits).

4.1.2 *'Us and Them' Now Becomes 'Us' vs 'Them'*

In sociology and social psychology, the 'us' (also known as the 'in-group') is a group to which an individual belongs and in which they feel a sense of identity. The central hypothesis of social identity theory is where group members of an 'us' group will seek to find negative aspects of the 'them' group, thus enhancing their own self-image and self-esteem. The 'them' (or 'out-group') is a group with which an individual does not identify with, does not belong to and so feels a sense of (sometimes unhealthy) competitiveness against and/or hostility and resentment towards. This us and them isn't just the obvious (i.e. us versus (vs) management), but also peer vs peer, night shift vs day shift and team A vs team B but, perhaps surprisingly, such mentality also extends and encompasses, for example, IT versus automation, the educated vs the not so, the haves vs the haven't/can't affords, doers vs thinkers and old timers vs the young blood. These various groups also apply vice versa where, confusingly, the us becomes the them and the them becomes the us. Perhaps worst of all, amongst all of these versus, is the organisation vs customer and of course, vice versa customer vs organisation, where even customers (try to) leverage better terms, trade and lower prices on the pretext of 'taking their business elsewhere'. From this us and them—organisation vs customer and customer vs organisation—cultural organisational viewpoint, the customer, amazingly, becomes just a 'faceless, outside, loose cog', 'lost' within the general scheme, purpose and meaning of things within that business. This is where the business has, simply, not just lost sight and focus of their, faceless, customer, but also is forced, at best, to grind along because internally everybody is so busy politicking, competing with one another and/or 'jockeying' for power; at worst it jams the very mechanism of achieving its overall purpose and function, in effect leaving it—everybody with not knowing either which way to turn or with nowhere to turn (Figure 4.2).

Figure 4.2 Which way to turn: Nowhere to turn!?

This us versus them mindset, attitude and behaviour is alive and well in organisations of all different sizes whether they be domestic, international and/or global; this mindset is one of the root causes of employee disengagement. Highly destructive, this is a (maybe not so) subtle form of workplace bias that prevents inclusion, promotes non-collaboration, destroys meaningful and affective communication, is unprofitable and severely slows down progress and growth, for not just the few but, for the all! Over time this us versus them becomes ingrained as being a 'normal', everyday occurrence. It becomes real and accepted for all who operate within it. An environment in which confrontation and silent sabotage is fostered, instead of constructive dialogue and positive action. As individuals this us and them is a dangerous and unhealthy culture, as it shows that people bond on weaknesses not on strengths to achieve the common bad. Ironically and conversely, although, within spiritual support groups these people also bond on weakness and not on strength—but in a healthy and productive way, to achieve the common good.

Organisations cannot change their culture unless individuals on all sides change their behaviour, and changing one's own behaviour, as we have so far established, isn't easy. Consequently each 'us and them' now becomes 'us' versus 'them' where the 'us' are anchored in as deeply and as equally in wanting and waiting for the 'them' to change and of course, vice versa!

4.2 Organisational Culture

Culture encompasses values, together with what constitutes both acceptable and unacceptable behaviours, those that are approved of and those that are not. Organisational culture is a system of statements and permissions which can include the business vision and mission with its, particular, values, norms, systems, assumptions, environmental intentions and targets. Employees are obliged to subscribe to their company's history, brand and beliefs which all contribute to the (intended) meaning and purpose of that business and . . . "Why shouldn't they – if they are valid and decent?" Although leaders state what kind of culture that *they* want, they cannot create it. The problem lies therein.

Viewing culture from a micro-level outward, where numerous and various 'atoms' add up to make a part, these parts then make up the whole (the macro-level) and as such are unproblematic. However, if any of the parts are imperfect (as humans are) or missing, then these 'faulty' and/or 'missing' parts will add up to make a different whole which in the main, is problematic. Although atoms are made of the same three basic particles, protons, neutrons and electrons, these basic particles also provide different combinations, where each combination results in a whole multitude of possible interactions, including having the ability to collide with one another to cause an explosion. This can also be applied to both the individual and in life, where each combination of individuals results in a whole multitude of possible interactions with other individuals, including having the ability to collide with one another to trigger and cause an explosion (see Chapter 2, Section 2.24 Triggers).

Viewing culture from the macro-human level inwards, although basically we all share the same need for food, water and sleep, we are all made up of multiple combinations which occur at our (micro-level) individual atomic/DNA level of detail. Therefore, we are all naturally different on a macro-level. With the added complexities and contradictions of an individual's *own* social experience, when our different social experiences are 'mixed' in with our own (faulty) atoms/DNA (singular and plural), on some level we (have got to have and so . . .) will *all* have a 'fault', or even two! Combining ourselves with other 'faulty' individuals (singular and plural), it makes sense that no dominant culture can exist as there has to be, by its very nature, some kind of a 'fault' on *every* conceivable level and combination of that culture/environment. These faults then increase exponentially the more individuals there are in one place, so any expectations of achieving a full agreement, compliance and adherence to an overall organisational culture by the masses has got to be unrealistic. Therefore, any 'capture all' culture cannot be implemented and affectively led and managed by forcing complex and 'faulty' individual/human nature into what is an artificial form of a 'perfect' culture.

Despite all of these inherent faults, organisations, through its leaders and managers, still persist in (trying to) 'shape' both the individual and others, or even endeavour to force them to conform to their own cultural traits and requirements accordingly. Hence developing, leading and motivating employees to be committed to the organisation together with its vision, mission, goals and values is a major challenge. This is where servant leadership also falls down, because against all of this previous (faulty) backdrop, the leader or manager cannot promote and enforce the company culture and its values whilst also putting the interests of each and all of their followers above either his or her own, or that of the organisation, as more than likely there will be some parts which are incompatible with each other.

Just as opposites attract and like attracts like (see Chapter 3, Section 3.4 All Sorts Attract All Sorts), some people naturally get on with others and some people don't, and as a result, there have to be, by default, pockets of resistance occurring somewhere within the overall mix of things. This resistance, in turn, then leads to a desire to unintentionally or intentionally form the aforementioned 'us and them'—'us' vs 'them' and sub-group situation (see Chapter 4, Section 4.1.2 'Us and Them' Now Becomes 'Us' vs 'Them'), but the stronger the resistance between the 'us' versus 'them', the more chance there is of something 'breaking', especially when we try and (really and intentionally) force (and the more we force something the greater the chances of it breaking) something to do what it doesn't want to do. We can even break something unintentionally, either realising or not realising it. But within this context, "What is meant by 'resistance', 'breaking' and 'intentionally?'

4.3 Sabotage

Sabotage is a deliberate action aimed at weakening an intended effort or organisation through subversion, obstruction, disruption or destruction. Sabotage can also be achieved through tampering, meddling, tinkering or malicious hacking. Saboteurs conceal their identities through fear of being detected and so (try to avoid) receiving any resulting reprisals and consequences for their destructive actions. Not to put too finer a point on it, these individuals are cowards! The two main methods of sabotage are physical destruction and the human element. While physical destruction is self-explanatory, the human element is based on opportunities to either make faulty decisions, to adopt a non-cooperative attitude or to induce others to follow this flawed suit.

Most individuals derive a sense of who they are through affiliation and so associate themselves closely to others. A 'tribe' is a group of people or a community who share similar values and/or interests and who tend to accept 'all the glory', but have had little or nothing to do with actually achieving it. A group is a number of people or things all together in one place at one time. With all these people having the same interests and/ or aims, they organise themselves to 'work' and act together. Another (termed) group is generally comprised of young people (especially men), often fighting with other groups and generally behaving badly. Collectively these factions can be regarded as a mob: a large crowd of people, one that is disorderly and intent on causing trouble and where their resulting behaviour often leads them to lose their inhibitions. This, in turn, leads them to carry out destructive actions which, sooner or later, they come to regret. Enmeshed within this mob the individual is eventually stifled, losing any hope and ambitions which they may have had. This isn't just 'street talk' as these 'mobs' are also prevalent within organisations. This is because organisations, inadvertently, provide their employees with the opportunity to 'join' and 'belong' to a mob, which is more commonly known as a sub-group. A sub-group consists of the kind of people who are consequently employed to provide a quality function and value and in return, are paid reasonable salaries, kept warm and safe . . . but who are totally de-motivated and ignorant to the point where even if their salaries were doubled, they would still 'kick out' and rebel against 'the system'.

These sub-groups are all counteractive and counterproductive and they can become, in some cases, even more 'powerful' and (covertly) influential than the business organisation itself. Ironically, the individual, once in, is stuck in this sub-culture and so 'fights' the organisational system, in a system they cannot leave. Whether this is through fear and/or lack of courage, either way, the mob is quick to squash the very thought and action, by quickly 'reminding' the individual of the consequences of trying to leave their particular faction. Workplace gang and mob members commonly engage in harassment, the goal of which is to exclude, humiliate, intimidate or even drive a colleague from the workplace.

4.3.1 Silent Sabotage

Such is this threat of these consequences, the need to conform within these sub-cultures is extremely strong. In effect, the cultural requirement of the business is replaced with their own mob version of *directly* enforced values and uniformity which, ironically, goes on to constrain the individuals' free will, identity and individual*ism*, far stronger than the very organisational culture and its (overt) values against which they so rebel. Any ounce of ambition and desire for advancement at work by the mob member is also frowned upon by these sub-cultures, and totally discouraged—those who want to 'get on' are met and blocked with threats, ridicule and contempt. This 'let's have and do it our way, or have and do nothing at all' is mistakenly powered by a visionless driving resentment. Nothing hinders (good) leadership than opposition for opposition's sake. As part of mob/sub-group collusion, *they* protest by way of damaging disruption, where even carefully made decisions—even the well-intended ones—may be sabotaged, undermined or ignored by these particular stakeholder factions. Many individuals who belong to these sub-groups don't have either the courage or confidence to vent their own objections individually and directly (so building and forming a connection) to their leaders or managers in a reasonable way. Ironically these individuals, if they are that unhappy, won't go and find another job or just leave the organisation which they are so set against. Instead, as cowardly individuals, they take 'strength and courage' by identifying with and becoming part of a mob rule and so choose to take on their particular bad attitudes and indecent/unacceptable behaviours, whilst still expecting to be paid for what they do, or even what they don't do.

Groups can be tremendously supportive, but they can also come with a downside where, from a sub-group perspective, the cost of uniformity of thought and behaviour is ultimately at the expense of the individual's own perception of what (and knowing deep down) is right and what is wrong. They, the individual/mob, perform without any real conscious involvement in their work. They become detached, with no engagement

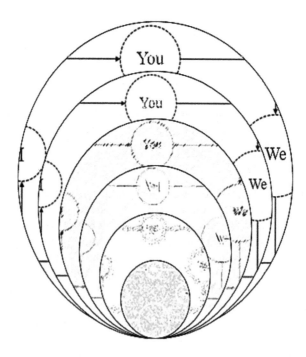

Figure 4.3 The toxic law of cultural quicksand.

or interest to the work at hand. At best these employees perform on autopilot, bringing far less than their greatest capabilities to the task. At worst they become and regard themselves as 'rebellious slaves' who consciously or unconsciously, but certainly silently (for again fear of being caught), sabotage the work which they are supposed to do while being paid to complete a fit-for-purpose standard. These particular employees/individuals genuinely feel they are simply owed a living by 'them', for doing as little as possible. Whenever and in whomever this brand of arrogance develops, it brings with it aggression and an agreement where 'us or else' is demanded. Where it then becomes very easy for both leadership/management and sub-groups, even those (others outside of the work environment) with destructive convictions and tendencies, to assume that their way is *the truth*, for all what happens and needs to happen, within an organisation (and their home lives). The ultimate truth, however, is that leaders, managers and operators as employees and as individuals all become all 'sucked' in and so lose their *identity*, their individual*ism* and their *self* to this nonentity 'toxic cultural quicksand' (Figure 4.3).

This is dogma,[2] where 'the only good is moral good and the only bad is moral bad'.

4.4 Organisational Behaviour

Despite the growing interest, there is still a lack of progressive empirical research on the subject of organisational behaviour, where research models have shown a degree of inadequacy in explaining and predicting both business performance and organisational behaviour. Together with a sparse development of new leadership models, contemporary leadership is still identified and recognised by a measured linear and materialistic growth. This, it could be said, has led to a tremendous amount of self-interest, which has 'encouraged' a winning-at-all-costs attitude and behaviour. Organisational behaviour theory is the study of human behaviour within an organisational environment, by asking questions around "Why do individuals behave the way they do, within their place of work?" As previously discussed, organisational culture greatly influences employee behaviour where bullying, harassment and poor relations with leaders and managers and even their peers often leave employees dissatisfied and uncertain of their role and future within the organisation.

4.5 Leaders and Managers

In big corporate organisations, there is often a lack of a humanistic type of view and approach. The more responsibility you hold, the greater shadow you cast. That's perhaps why individuals who are said to be the next great leaders don't have anybody actually saying to them when they finally get 'there', "Well—you're now just being a complete arse!" Before

Hannah H. started her own company, she had previously worked for some big corporate companies like AOL, Mirror Group Newspapers and IPT (a big online company).

HANNAH H: "They were all the total and complete opposite to me. They all had hierarchical systems and because I was successful at what I did . . . because I applied myself every day, I always found myself being promoted to senior positions and I have to say I was really uncomfortable with that. I didn't like being the leader in that kind of environment . . . I never kind of had that, *you know*, that domineering asset, so I always had that feeling, which I was always trying to avoid, which is feeling that I was not doing very well at my job. What made this even worse was those above me telling me what to do, when they clearly weren't doing what they were telling me to do themselves."

One of the biggest difficulties/struggles that individuals have is when leaders and managers tend to say one thing but their behaviours, actions and business aims are suggesting another.

Rachel M. said about her management's view,

RACHEL M: "They weren't aiming for the same thing. They may have been saying they were aiming for the same thing but, in reality, their actions spoke louder than words and they were only in it for the money and I found that extremely difficult to understand."

YVONNE T: "They [directors and managers] are all words and certainly no actions. They also never-ever asked me how I was. Or showed any interest in what was doing or what I had done, to successfully achieve my work."

ALISON R: ". . . This all left me feeling a deep sense of never wanting to make *anybody* feel the way that they [the directors] had made me feel. Working with these people who were very, very driven but the way they drove other people was mainly through fear. I just didn't like that and I made a promise to myself, that I would never make anybody who ever worked for me . . . I was *never* going to try to drive anybody forward in that way, because I knew how horrible it felt for me. I knew how de-motivating it was for not just me but also my colleagues as well, which is not progressive or productive for anyone, within any organisation."

Insightfully:

JAYNE B: "They are all just doing it that way, because that 'way' was 'shown' and taught to them by others, because this is what they think has worked for them in the past, that got them to where they are today, which is pretty much in a position of nowhere."

The brutal reality is that the only way to change an organisation is to change its management. As long as a toxic manager remains in (their) place, there is no hope that the business can recover from its current standing.

4.6 Leaders and Management Objectives vs Employee Performance Appraisals

Globally, organisations spend billions of their budgets on external consultants, leadership recruitment and development, yet most of these continue to report an acute shortage of good leaders and managers and still achieve no startling improvement in their business performance. Adopting a strategy of continuous growth at any cost is promoted, trained and delivered by business schools, consultants and business academics alike. The likes of operational excellence (opex) comes in the forms of business process re-engineering and lean and Target Operating Models (TOMs)—in other words, it is all about doing more of the same, only faster and with fewer people. These initiatives are nearly always combined with fixed and hardened (where some of these 'dashboards' were constructed decades ago and yet, there still seems to be an unwillingness to change them, and they are probably only looked at, referred to and actually used by a minority anyway. Just call *me* cynical!) financial performance measures together with (what were previously labelled as 'personal' but now deemed as) professional appraisals, which support these less-than-successful opex improvement initiatives. These financial measures and (bi)annual appraisals, may therefore be accused of creating behaviour and activities in line with a 'blinkered vision'. This is because the individual loses all sense or reasonability (as they are employed and so 'blinded' as an employee, who is told what to do so they just do it) and, as such, who only solely focuses upon their objectives, which *must* be carried out, usually at the detriment of other areas of the business. This inevitably means numerous other 'pressing points' are left outside of their remit and so go 'conveniently/intentionally' unnoticed and as a consequence, these pressing points are not recognised and are ignored. When eventually realised, probably because the organisation is experiencing a multitude of problems and customer complaints, these pressing points then rapidly rise to the top of the organisation's priority list and so become the 'flavour of the month'. This 'new focus' then inevitably overtakes and overshadows the employees' *pre-written* objectives, so when appraisal time comes, these original objectives will not, or only partially, have been achieved and as such, comes the inevitable 'blame storming' (unfortunately, a more common occurrence than 'brain storming') and bollockings all round—and don't even think about a pay rise, or a bonus! In turn, the new priorities become this year's new and particular 'focused' objectives. The cycle thus continues. Putting all of this another way, when senior management sets specific (usually) quantitative targets and attaches an employee's job/performance/pay rise and/or bonus to it, which all depend upon meet-ing *their* objectives, this creates self-interest, so back to being an individual rather than an employee. Now acting as the individual who now has their eye on the money rather than the 'blinded' employee who can't think for themselves, they will more than likely meet their set targets—even if they have to neglect, even 'destroy' other individuals'/employees' objectives and even the rest of the business to do so. In achieving *my* goal but not my aim, I then do stupid things in the name of reaching my goals and achieving *my* pay rise and bonus but, at the same time, it is *me* who consequently stops the overall aims of the organisation from being achieved.

YVONNE T: "Working non-stop 12 hours a day, I was bringing in about 30 grand a month and I was doing absolutely everything and I could tell by the numbers that *she* [the manager] was falling short in all what she was supposed to be doing. Not only that *she was horrible . . . a hor-rible person*! A bully in the first degree and although I didn't think that it was possible, my/her director was an even bigger bully than she was. Continuously thinking about both the unfairity[3] and conduct of my so-called leaders and the pressure of satisfying my customers, through hav-ing stupid out-of-date objectives which couldn't be satisfied, I felt like I was on a constant merry-go-round of stress, pressure and unhappiness. If I honestly wasn't insane, I was definitely getting, very close it."

JO C: "I was running around like a headless chicken! Horrendous times! *I was crazy! A wreck!*"

JIM N: "I was being driven in the job that I was in, but absolutely not enjoying it. I went from a highly results-orientated, focused, goal-driven gotta get it done, gotta get it done, gottagetitdone—and if I hadn't got it done, then my director would say, 'Why haven't you got it done? Whatyergonnadoabout it?' [all said very rapidly] back to me . . . me being a highly driven person . . . , so *you* [meaning I] had better get it done then . . . However, if I look at why I was driven like that, I was fundamentally driven by fear, which is not unusual in any organisation. Which led nicely into the whole thing of me becoming a workaholic and actually being, very *successful* [meaning inversely successfully bad] at being one."

PAUL J: "My boss, at that point in time, was in the USA [United States of America] and he was always calling net meetings at 8 o'clock at night, because this was 2 o'clock in the afternoon to him. I'd be at work, in the office from 7 am in the morning and I was still going at midnight and regularly going home after 1 am. Then it becomes really clear—I became and was a workaholic. Travelling over 150 nights a year, where I could be anywhere and everywhere in the world, working for a boss who was 'making' me think that it's okay to work over 12 hours a day where, unconsciously, I was being forced to do it—that's what you feel like internally . . . that you have to do all of that. I was just doing more and more and more. I was trying to do everything and doing everything is not possible. Then I was left wondering—why I was wondering why I was always feeling absolutely exhausted by it all."

There is an emerging awareness there is more to life than working for a mechanical entity (incidentally, 'mechanical' organisations are built upon the command-and-control structure which originated from the Roman Army, which all started off well enough, but didn't end too greatly for them), which makes you feel like you are just part of the machinery. However, although it is accepted that machines break down and are promptly fixed, yet when the human element breaks down there is little or no desire, or even the ability by the employer, to 'fix' either the person or the situation to prevent it from happening again. Put simply, employees are not machines with simple push buttons. For most people, work lacks leadership, inspiration, integrity, meaning, purpose and authenticity. "Could this be true?" "Or is it because goal driven opex objectives only motivate/make the leader and/or manager desperate to cut (even) more corners?" This cutting of corners, in turn, may involve and be the reason why everybody is being forced to settle for lower moral and ethical standards, as a result of the consequential pressure and stress of delivering these required opex results.

Many organisations are unlikely to talk about, admit to using or even acknowledge the 'carrot and stick' approach. If current business methodologies are analysed, truth is we will, most likely, find a high amount of scientific 'stick' which is being used by today's leaders and managers, rather than any positive 'carrot' incentives.

4.7 The Employee's View of an Organisation

"Do employees question their leaders and managers' authority or do they question their morals and ethics?" Employees can also feel stuck in some big, huge corporate organisation, with results at all costs, where everything is forever at a pace which is unrealistic, often within the organisation's structures that don't want to listen—where the boss says something and everybody else just follows and the ability to actually question, the ability to actually think for oneself, becomes quite limited.

On one hand, it could be said our own moral and personal ethics are being . . . not so much challenged as subverted. These leaders and managers make it more difficult for us, as individuals, to be *ourselves*; they ask us to do things at work which don't feel right, which don't morally and ethically sit comfortably with us or more simply, we just don't agree with. Hence the feeling that, perhaps, our own values are being squeezed, ignored and disregarded in order to achieve the organisation's goal. Couple this with the stresses and strains that are commonly being forced onto the employee through arbitrary numerical targets, performance numeration and performance appraisals, together with what seems to be the never-ending drive towards maximising shareholder values and/or improvement to the bottom line; this always seems to be at the 'expense' of the people who are carrying out the actual work. However, on the other hand, as employees and/or individuals, "Are we really in a 'squeaky-clean' position, mindset and attitude which allows us to balk at such unethical and morally wrong enforced organisational requirements?" Aside from being paid to carry out our duties, and we are certainly not being forced to work where we work, are we truly selling our good souls for the greater bad, "Or is there some hypocrisy going on?"

When questioned on their morals and values, employees admitted to lying about sickness, stealing and taking credit for other people's work. While younger staff lied more often than their elders, they were more willing to stand up for colleagues rather than their managers and leaders. Men were almost twice as likely as women to say they would accept praise from a manager for work that someone else had done. Almost a third of those surveyed[4] admitted to stealing work supplies. Four out of ten workers admitted to fiddling their expense claims. Two out of five adults admitted if they needed some time off from their work they took 'fake' sick days. It was also revealed employees can be influenced by their leaders and managers' behaviour. If the leader is seen 'dragging themselves in' feeling poorly, whilst also not taking breaks and eating lunch at their desk, this tends to reinforce 'the message' that it is not okay for anybody to either take a legitimate break, or to be off work sick.

Always giving mixed messages, these leaders and managers are unfortunately regarded as the type of people who say one thing, but their actions and the words don't go together. That's what many employees struggle with—where the behaviours of others haven't adhered anywhere near to the behaviours that you'd expect from either an organisation, or religious or professional individual. Trumpeting what they think other people want to hear them say—what they think is the 'right' thing to say—most individuals (especially leaders, managers and politicians) have been taught and are expected to put out a false persona to others, including their workforce. This way is neither progressive or productive for anyone.

Working long hours and living in a toxic relationship (including a personal one at home perhaps) with your manager and/or work colleagues is both physically and psychologically draining. Many of us at work are thrown into a situation where we literally have no choice as to who we are working with and for. You accepted your job offer in a millisecond and are all excited, and on the first day of joining the company they say, "Right, you're working here—with them" and you find yourself sitting next to, or working for somebody, who might be a complete and utter idiot. "Who wants to see someone flapping around all the time, waving their arms about and/or shouting, even swearing—talking about others and running people down?" This is when we need to take a step back and listen to the reasoning in our heads. "Is what they are saying and doing right?" "No! Of course, it isn't." But you can't always reply and say what you really want to say, because you've got to protect yourself and that's the hardest part—showing restraint, particularly within a work environment. Then we feel that we are left with a choice: leave, or stick it out. Work then becomes all about just having a job where, at best, you are certainly not enjoying it—but making the most of it, to purely earn money. At worst we could eventually join the mob and become silent saboteurs. Either way, as individuals, we get to a point where we just start to lose interest, or burn out, losing any sense of hope and faith from it all. We become stuck in a mundane rut. We become stuck, in the horrors of the rat race!

4.8 Case Studies: Horror Stories

The next generation of leaders and managers will have strong convictions and courage, will put principles above personalities and put plans and policies into dedicated and affective action. People will be motivated enough to want to both support and work for them and achieve the overall aims of the organisation. "But how far off from this, are we?"

SHELTON D: "My manager, he doesn't really open up much about things. He goes home stressed and rather than talk he drinks instead. He's got a big belly and he's a very very angry guy."

Paul J., had a boss who 'was psychologically flawed in his own right'.

PAUL J: "I suspect, challenged inasmuch, as he was an even bigger people pleaser and perfectionist than I was. He over-compensated for this by working himself crazy and working everybody else crazy as well around his agenda and only his agenda, and he just didn't and wouldn't listen to anything, or anybody else."

Yvette T., was bullied by her director, who also 'belittled her in front of other people'.

YVETTE T: "I was on a sinking ship: He just wasn't interested. He never ever looked at me, or anybody else in the eye for that matter. He always looked down at the floor when he was speaking to *you*. One day, he asked me, 'How many members of staff have you got in your office?' and I would say 'Fourteen' and he drew 14 stick people on this piece of paper. I thought, 'Something up here [pointing to her head] is telling me you're not even listening to me and that he didn't know what he was doing'. Then he asked me, 'Who do you manage?' I said, 'Those fourteen stick people there that you've just drawn'. I have learned to box quite clever over the years, especially when I'm dealing with *twats and bitches*, what seems like, all of the time."

SANDRA C: "My manager said, 'He's [the MD] really upset with you, because you discussed money in a meeting', and I said, 'Can I just say that he discusses all sorts of things and it's mainly about sex, which has got nothing to do with business'. Even though (according to the numbers) I was doing really well in my job, I only lasted just over six weeks, before they had to find some way to 'get rid' of me. Then came the day when he [the MD] said to me 'You haven't really got the company's attitude, what we really like and want, so I am going to have to let you go' . . . so I just got up and went . . . [laughs]."

ROZALIN F: "One day, I questioned my CEO and he said, 'Are you questioning my authority?' and I said, 'No, I'm just questioning your morals actually!' [laughter]. Very soon afterwards, I got dismissed for wearing a black bra under a white shirt. I didn't even possess a black bra! It was then that I realised that I didn't want to work with these sorts of people anymore so this was the last time I worked in a corporate environment."

SARAH H: "When someone is being a complete and utter dick! I meet many people, in my profession who are not very nice, *you know*, they're idiots—aggressive and very, very competitive and it's only getting worse as time goes by."

Rowena N., gets really 'fed up' with people, specifically managers.

ROWENA N: "You get some of them who come in who are so rude—it's unbelievable! I just try and think to myself 'Well! There's no point in me getting annoyed with them, because that's just counterproductive'. I then go into the back office and I say a few expletives to myself, then I come out and have to deal with my next customer, with a smile on my face. I just really try hard at work to keep a very positive attitude and then go home . . . shut the door . . . have a large glass of wine and just let them and the rest of the world get on with it . . . twats and arse-holes, the lot of them, and that's before I have had a wine!"

VICTORIA W: "It's horrifying, especially in work. When you are dealing with other people's egos—great big massive egos where they think they can speak to you like you're ab-sol-ute-ly, nothing."

JANICE D: "I was taught by my parents to keep my eyes and ears open and my mouth shut! So, I listened to and watched all the directors and managers just swanning around, all 'playing the big I am' and I was thinking, 'They might have a fancy degree and I may be just "Jo Blogs" with next to no qualifications, but if I can put all this together and get all of this business in I cannot be as daft as they make me feel that I am!"

STEVEN I: "The future for any organisation is not boding well at all. There is a distinct lack of kinder—softer values in the workplace, where everything is geared towards the opposite. This is mainly due to the stresses and strains being forced onto people by hardnosed, figure-orientated and target-driven, pressurised structures, processes and systems."

This is supported by Karen A.

KAREN A: "The reason why people are getting stuck on these issues, is because at any level of the organisation there are no intellectual capabilities and soft skills at all."

JO C: "At work we all have somebody who we have to answer to, I did, I was answerable to no end of people and you say to yourself 'Why do you have to answer to all of these people? What and where, is the sense in that?' But of course, you have to do as your told by any one of them, however ridiculous!"

STEPHANIE W: "Bosses are just human, aren't they!? They're only like us!? We're all the same, whether you clean the toilets, or you're the bloody Chairman of ICI! All the same and at the end of the day, we're all going out the same way as well!"

4.9 Organisational View of the Employee

The prevailing view, amongst many economists and business academics alike, is that corporate directors only have a fiduciary responsibility to maximise profits for shareholders, the success or otherwise being entirely measured through monetary value. This somewhat distorted view provides the idea that human beings are just artificial constructions, created by individuals for the benefit of stakeholders and their sole desire for money.

CHRIS H.—MANAGING DIRECTOR: "I heard nothing from this guy for over two years and one day, out of the blue, I got an email from him and it was a terrible, terrible rant about how I, was supposed to have, deliberately limited his ability to get another job. It was just unbelievable what I was supposed to have said and done and what actions I'd taken to stop him. I had previously employed this person on three separate occasions, so it certainly wasn't me who wanted him not to be in employment. Through my spiritual programme, I knew that I didn't have to respond. I just read it out and I then I was just able to 'let it go', because I realised that the person who needed the most help was him—not me!"

PAULINE H.—MANAGING DIRECTOR: "Once, I had to lay somebody off at work as he was lazy and cost the business a lot of money. But I didn't have to dislike him for it. He's human and as a human he was alright."

Pauline was good to him, let him serve his notice so that he wouldn't be short of money and on his last day she took him out for lunch. "You always have to see the good in people and that's as good as it gets, it means that I am on track!"

Where the human element of the organisation was previously discussed as being 'viewed as a nuisance, a resource of uncertainty and variation to be reduced by science' (Shenhav, 1995 [see Chapter 1, Section 1.2 Science, the Proclaimed Panacea?]), the question is "Why bother with all this spiritual stuff and why now as, after all, we have all seen plenty of predictions that science, via technology (AI and robots), is coming to terminate *all* of our jobs and put *everyone* out of work!?" Blue collar workers are considered to be particularly vulnerable to automation, with predictions of apocalyptic job losses resulting from an explosion in robotics. Although it may not feel like it, these aren't new revelations; in fact, this takeover and hysteria has been predicted for over 200 years, where advances in technology have always fired up fears of mass unemployment.

The foundations for the Luddite movement began in 1779, when a group of English textile workers in Manchester rebelled against the introduction of machinery, which threatened their particular craft. However, the first noticeable riots began in Nottinghamshire in 1811, where workers sent threatening letters to employers and broke into cotton and woollen mills and destroyed the new machinery. Since then, in every single decade until the present—although not as (directly) confrontational as the Luddites rebellion—mass unemployment hysteria has always surrounded the coming of robots, automation, computers and AI.

Robots 'killing' jobs is (still) an exaggeration. In nine out of the ten occasions when robots are purchased and located within an organisation, although they do help to increase production, they do not take people's livelihoods away. Suffice to say, even robots break down, and although they are described as 'intelligent' they are not intellectual, versatile, adaptable or flexible. As such and in addition, we are seeing more and more new job titles and descriptions for roles that did not previously exist even a few years ago. Ironically, even today, employers are still complaining about a shortage of skilled workers, where nearly every organisation is experiencing a labour shortage. But here's the twist, they are having a harder time filling blue collar positions rather than professional ones which 'require' a university/business school education. Suffice to say robots, Arnie and/or job annihilators, are not the future of impending doom on our employment prospects, the role of humans will always be back, in some shape or form (Figure 4.4).

Figure 4.4 The job annihilator: Fiction and fantasy.

"But surely one of the benefits of globalisation has meant an increased access to talent and skills beyond local, regional and even country pools?" Well—yes, it does! However, on the flip side to this, organisations also face increased competition for those (what have now become) scarce resources (i.e. skilled individuals, who can now look for employment on a global scale, as a result of this easier access to it). Therefore, these organisations must keep ahead of the business talent curve—although it could be considered to be imperative, albeit difficult, in attracting and recruiting 'decent talent' to their organisations—companies have histori-cally left their greatest and best resource untapped: the initiative and the productive drive that lies within and is readily available in every indi-vidual who already works there!

4.10 Case Studies: Success Stories

Human beings are all different and although they (but only to some extent) respond to the 'carrot and stick' approach of management, they also respond to ambition, decency, unfairness, boredom and self-doubt. Remember Paul J., (see Chapter 4, Section 4.6 Leaders and Management

Objectives vs Employee Performance Appraisals), who previously stated that he was in the office from 7 am until after midnight? "It was early on, near the start of my spirituality, when I learned and started to gain the confidence to be able to say 'No!'" (see Chapter 2, Section 2.26 Yes vs No!).

PAUL J: "With this, I also began to learn to be able to start to balance *me* into everything that I do. In the end, I had a conversation with my boss. I said, 'I am not doing this anymore'. I said, 'I am working from 8 until 5 pm and unless it is a real emergency, I am not going to be on call before 8 am and after 5 pm!' I didn't ask him, I just told him! He just said, 'Oh okay'. It was amazing! What was really interesting, as I started to dramatically reduce my work time, my performance appraisals didn't get worse, in fact they went up! I was busting my guts off (and I am getting paradoxical here), working and really trying hard and there I was feeling guilty, by thinking I am not doing anywhere near as much as I used to do, but actually the feedback I was getting was showing a tremendous improvement! So, I thought, 'Okay, there's a learning lesson to be had here'."

Although it helps to have values in a company and to know that they are both good and of worth, there is also the requirement of leading and managing people on both a team and on an individual level. It is possible to develop things like empathy, understanding, compassion and to know when your behaviour is good or bad, whilst also appreciating that other people have bad days and make mistakes as well.

CHRIS H: "Knowing this helps me to keep it all real and helps my staff to know that I'm human too! I won't hide behind the company name, neither will I ignore either its or my spiritual values. I never speak down to anybody. I treat everybody as an equal. . . . I don't want to be seen as an ego, as having an ego can never be satisfied."

YVETTE T: "I can remember being totally—totally deflated! I always seemed to draw all of the short straws, so this meant they [the managers] always gave me all the really shit jobs to do. I realise now this was a form of bullying. I thought long and hard and then one day I said, 'Right that's it!' and banged my things on the desk. My manager said, 'Where are you going?' I said, 'I'm going to HR and I'm going to tell them that I'm off'. HR said, 'Can you just help us out for a couple of weeks?' I couldn't believe it. . . . I said, 'You want me to fill in, until you find somebody else? . . . After the way I have been treated, not a chance! You sort it all out—just like I've been doing for the past four months'. Through my spirituality I have started to believe in myself, *you know*, I won't let . . . I vowed that I wouldn't ever be bullied and be put in that position at work ever again."

NICK G: "I treat everybody equally and I treat everybody fairly. Although I am the manager and I do expect things to be done, but I don't force either my role or my spirituality on anybody. I won't demand for anything to be done and I don't say, 'You must do this, or you must do that, to any one of my team'. If my director ever tries to boss me about like that, I immediately have to say 'No!' (see Chapter 2, Section 2.26 Yes vs No!). 'Please do not speak to me like that, I can't be doing with it and I certainly don't appreciate it, so if we are going to sort it just ask me and we'll do it together.' It's the same with my team, I will simply *ask* them to do something and if they say they can't do it, for whatever reason, I'll go and help them to do it. I've got their respect and they've got my respect, so when I *ask* them to do something, they'll bend over backwards to help *me*, cos they know I'll bend over backwards to help *them*. To treat everybody equally and with respect, is a massive, massive plus on anybody's side."

Stipulated by both Syd B. and by Alison R . . .

SYD B. AND ALISON R: "I have learned through my spiritual beliefs, by treating everybody equally means you get more respect and more work out of them, which means better productivity, plus everybody goes home happy!"

John W., leads the team, but also leads the company.

JOHN W: "I've always said, even before I started working is, 'Whatever I do . . . whatever I apply myself to, I have to feel a sense of achievement' and my spirituality helps me in giving me the confidence to stand by that."

Although leaders need to have excellent judgement and morals, it has to be accepted that no leader is remote, impersonal or perfect. When a leader is a 'power-driver', there will be resistance; when they just 'bark' orders, trying to command and control and exercise no judgement of their own they are not a leader. A good leader knows that a good plan or idea can come from anyone and gives credit where credit is due. These true leaders are rare! This is because finding the right combination of required skills, personality and ambition which are essential to this type of leadership is difficult to find, develop, exhibit and practise.

HEATHER P.—MANAGING DIRECTOR: "Things like gossiping! Where previously I would say loud narky snarky comments, but now my thoughts match my . . . at first it was just my actions which were good . . . but in my head I would still be saying 'You bitch, or you bastard' or whatever. But now my actions and comments and the thoughts in my head are just . . . are all in tune with each other."

Motivating others to want to achieve shared aspirations, which creates a common, all-encompassing vision of a successful future, whilst also providing challenging, interesting, different, meaningful and purposeful work through a sense of "Why we are *all* here?", "What do we *all* need?" and "What do we *all* want to do and be?" will, at least in theoretical terms, deliver a culture that enjoys shared core values and ethical systems.

JULIA T: "*My* spirituality has definitely helped *me* to improve my tolerance, compassion and understanding of *others*."

JO C: "I didn't ever think I could calm down and listen, cos I was too bossy and trying to organise everybody else, rather than organise myself. People now say to me and my staff, 'How do you cope with that?' I'm not a slave driver—I'm not a woman who likes to walk in and say 'Right! Do this, do that'. No! If they've done all of their duties, they can sit with me and have a cup of tea and they just say, 'Everything you say and do is just so lovely and calming'. At the end of the day everything goes like clockwork and they go out of work feeling peaceful and I go home feeling peaceful."

Working together, collaboratively, co-operatively and communicating healthily, underpinned with first class interconnected healthy traits, together with common sense and decency, ensures the wheels of life—the cogs of any organisation are well oiled and so move, turn and run together in sync, balance and, accurately, tick in time, for the benefit of not just the few, not even the many, but for the all. "What, who or which organisation, and customer for that matter, wouldn't want that?" (Figure 4.5).

As individuals we allow a lot of our power and energy to be diminished, or to be 'taken away' from us through either fear, lack of self-esteem and/or feeling insecure of ourselves. This mental state can trigger and be particularly activated when we are dealing with very (perceived to be) 'powerful' individuals, who we either come across in our personal lives or encounter within the organisation we are working in. This inside feeling can, in turn, manifest itself on the outside, where we can go into a sort of "Excuse me, Sir" subservient mode and mentality. Victoria W. provides the following example.

VICTORIA W: "I then have to work really hard to get back into flowing on equal terms with others, otherwise I tend to go into an over-compensation of . . . it's almost like how can I say it . . . 'Crawling up someone's arse!' By that, I mean, I can feel the energy rising up in me and I get confused

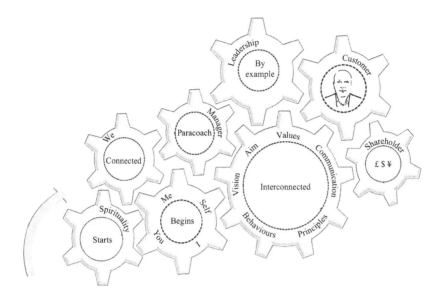

Figure 4.5 Tick Takt, it goes like clockwork.

and I have to, like, *remember who I am* . . . but not like having *power over them*, but just get back into *my* own sense of balance and power. I can then start to flow naturally with someone—but I have to work really hard at reconnecting with being good enough and being valued, on the same terms as they are."

How does all of this help? As an individual it is important that we must not forget, we are more than capable of *changing things for ourselves*. However it doesn't matter if you're stuck with a salary of £10,000 a year or £1,000,000 a year, or if you're stuck in a relationship which has all but ended, or with a house (not a home) that you don't really like or love, or stuck in dead-end job . . . stuck is stuck and we all get stuck at times. However, a majority of individuals make the mistake of blaming being stuck on the pressures and expectations of modern living and the *need* to 'appear' successful; it is this 'appearing' to be successful which we feel the need to project, which makes it difficult for many of us to cope and so not to be able to move on through the stigma of then appearing to be less successful, than what we want to project, to the outside world. Couple this with an inherent fear of the unknown, or delusions of failure, of losing it all, then this state of affairs is not a healthy position to be in—and 'ending it' becomes a distinct consideration. Thereon in lies a problem, when we have a problem with the solution.

If you have a problem and like the solution to it then that's okay—but if you have a problem but don't like the solution to it—then that is an entirely different kettle of fish![5]

CHRISTINE S: "I fled an abusive relationship in the middle of the night. I left a 5 bedroomed farmhouse, with a fabulous materialistic lifestyle that went with it, too literally go and live in a freezing cold tent in the middle of a field. I had no money so I basically had to steal to survive and at one point I had to root around in bins to try and find food. I honestly remember having a stand-off with a dog over a sandwich that I had found in the street. It was either this or go back and be raped and severely beaten by my husband again. Through knowing I had a choice, although I didn't find leaving a difficult one, it took me a long time to—not so much make the decision but have the courage to do so, but I know plenty of people who just stay in those types of relationships because they don't like the prospect of the unknown and the 'less, materialistic, well-off' alternative. Today, I have met somebody new and I am doing okay. You have to have courage to make tough decisions in life and then have hope and faith that things will turn out better, however the difficulty and unpleasantness that you may need to initially face.

LINDA R: "I made the decision to make my son leave my house. I was sick of him coming back drunk and out of his head on drugs—constantly lying and being violent towards me and having to call The Police every other day to him. I now really, really, worry about him living on the streets, but I would rather have that worry than the one where he comes home and steals from me, smashes things up and has drug dealers knocking on my door." A lot of my friends ask me "How can you see your only son living on the streets?" "How do you 'live' with yourself?" I admit this is a pretty shit choice to have to make, but it was the right one for me. Anyway, if they they [my 'friends'] feel that strongly about it, I don't see a queue asking him to go and live with them!"

SHELTON D: "I really, REALLY, hate my job and I don't enjoy my job—sometimes it is a real struggle to just get out of bed and go in a morning, it's far easier to just call in sick every now and again: basically, I am just in it for the money. People ask me "Why don't I just leave? I guess it is a case of because, because, because . . ."

Spirituality gives the individual a sense of empowerment knowing that, actually, they can do something about their situation and they are not just a victim of life and circumstance. A change of attitude, or way of thinking in a different perspective gives us a much wider scope on how we deal with situations.

4.11 Empowerment

JO C: "Running around 24/7 in a 24/7 business. No! I won't do it. (See Chapter 2, Section 2.26 Yes vs No!) I did do it and it nearly killed me and I will not do it anymore."

MAGGIE C: "The first element in all of this has to be me—it is what can I do, to change things."

YVONNE T: "After 25 years I finally said to my business partner, 'I want to split the business', mainly because she was a really lazy bitch. She immediately said, 'Oh! Well! I will have to speak to Rob [their accountant] about that!' I said, 'You fucking[6] well won't—I'm telling you—I want to split it and I want to split it now and I will also *tell you* what I am having!' I didn't give her any choice. I thought, 'No! I need to do this—I need to do it for my sanity'" (see Chapter 2, Section 2.26 Yes vs No!).

A further example of where an individual knows that they are empowered to make choices and where previously, Yvonne T. took the action of splitting with her professional business partner, she also took the action of *doing nothing* in her personal life.

YVONNE T: "Yes! My spirituality has definitely given me strength. At one time I wouldn't have said 'Boo to a goose' and everybody used to walk all over me, including my alcoholic husband. But he doesn't anymore and neither does anybody else, because he/they know that it just won't happen; because I now know that I can simply walk away. . . . I can walk away and just take myself wherever I decide to go. Just by knowing and accepting my freedom of choice means my life has now got significantly easier and a damn sight better. I now listen to what I want to do for myself—for me and that's the spiritual thing."

This spiritual 'thing' is not all light and fluffy—light up the incense, put on your music and away you go! Some things in life aren't easy and being in business isn't easy and spirituality isn't easy and neither has this book pretended that spirituality, or any of these things, is easy. However nowhere within this book or spirituality does it say "You have to be perfect!", "Love thy neighbour" or "You have to be a 'servant'" or "Like and love everything and everybody" and you certainly don't have to be, or need to do any of these things. However, there is a need to serve yourself by liking and loving your *self*. Because if you don't, "How can you expect others to like and/or love you?" Spirituality takes you from the pits to the pinnacle, whilst never seeking perfection from either you or others. But always, to *just* progress!

This spiritual approach offers and creates a vision and value congruence and assertive empowerment right down to an 'atomic' individual level, whilst also catering for, encompassing and influencing through attraction, other people. Within any organisation and everyday living this ultimately fosters higher levels of commitment and productivity. Therefore, a strategy—an action plan of recognising the value of your *self* and other people—is required, to enable spirituality to become an integral part of the 'real' business culture, and every day living.

By real we need to remember both *we* and others are human beings and everything that *you* do has a cause and effect. Nothing is separate. Work and home aren't separate and home and work aren't separate, especially when we are suffering and miserable. Everything that you do has a consequence. Everything! Some people are just lazy. Some people can't be bothered to take responsibility. It's so much easier to blame somebody else, or look for excuses, or just take a 'drink', or a pill, isn't it!? Rather than do the 'work' that's required to get yourself out of *it*, whatever *it* is to which you are in!? If you don't like the people, places or the situations which you are in and the things which are happening to you, there is no point in looking in the mirror and saying "I don't like what I am seeing." You have to go back to the projector which is *yourself* and look at what you are thinking and what you are feeling and how you are helping to create these goings-on and on-goings in your life. But it's also *knowing that you* are an empowered being and it is only you who can shift—transfigure and change things—and spirituality helps you to do exactly that.

CLAIRE S: "The evolution for me from being in a spiritual programme and applying spirituality to my life is seeing my own part in things and the more I do this the more I can see and that I can only be as truthful as I am self-aware."

Notes

1 Guise: Refers to the outward appearance or form of someone or something, which is often temporary or different.
2 Dogmatic goes back to the Greek word 'dogma', which basically means 'what one thinks is true'. To be dogmatic is to follow a doctrine relating to morals, a set of beliefs that are never questioned.
3 You say "Unfairty" a) to really bring out the argument and your side of the discussion. b) Not getting what you want and crying about it to no avail.
4 Com Res survey for the BBC. www.bbc.co.uk/news/business-50486921.
5 The expression 'a kettle of fish' means a real mess, a muddle or awkward state of affairs'.
6 Yep! Even spiritual people are allowed to and can swear!

5 Inventing the Wheel for the Global Era

As we become more of a trading world, what is evidently required is the need for a strategy and network of understanding, approach and balance, which contribute to and establish 'healthy' and successful workplaces, in which individuals (as their employees) and profit are given equal consideration and weight. "However, if this is the answer, what is the question?" "Is it possible to create a one approach, where spirituality is not only considered to be a realistic and relevant business option, but also remains bespoke enough to cover all of the employers' and employees' needs?" (Note 'needs', not necessarily wants like, for example, I *want* a massive pay rise and a, top-of-the range, company car for free!). The short answer is *yes, it is!* The problem is because spirituality was first translated within the 5th century (see Chapter 1, Section 1.3 An Historical Account of Spirituality), it has since become so cheesy, saturated and fragmented and as such, generally misunderstood amongst the masses (see Chapter 1, Section 1.4 What Spirituality *Isn't* All About . . .), as opposed to what spirituality is actually all about (see Chapter 3, Section 3.2 A Fully Considered Spiritual Definition and Section 3.7 A Fully Considered Spiritual Measure . . .), so simply dusting 'it' off (again, like it has been) and repackaging and relabelling spirituality will not serve the purpose of introducing, accepting and progressing spirituality within the workplace, or for the benefit of the individual as an employee or employer, so the only thing that we can do based upon this new definition and measure is to go on and invent the spiritual wheel for this global era.

At this point, it is important to distinguish the difference between wants and needs. Materialism: personal and professional growth and the need to live life; to enjoy it and prosper from it is certainly not lost within this particular spiritual script. It is positively encouraged. Although spirituality does address and recognise the material needs of humanity, it doesn't promote the individual's wants. To clarify and to put this in to perspective, needs are something that you must have in order to live and, as such, represent life's necessities. Wants are viewed as objects, only in relation to an individual's own desires, which purely feed the ego.

5.1 Globalisation

Globalisation together with interconnected markets and interconnected relationships brings about undisputed opportunities and benefits whilst, at the same time, raises some new, inescapable and difficult challenges. These new and difficult challenges present well—just that—challenges! New and difficult challenges are created for leaders particularly in designing, building, establishing and executing strategic *goals*, in a way which creates sustainable value and competitive advantage, on a considerable scale. To become affective in managing within the complexity of globalisation and interconnected markets and interconnected relationships, leaders now, more than ever, need practical tools for engaging and managing the multitudinous dimensions of human values and morals, in order to accomplish the extended strategic, global, business *aims*. The practical value of applying spirituality within turbulent interconnected markets and interconnected relationships is related to a need to further understand human resource behaviour in a wider and moral context in order to leverage assertive decision-making abilities. To move from being confused and insecure about their strategies and tactics, to succeeding and contributing to their own well-being and that of their organisations and its employees, we need leaders who can address and manage problems on not just an integrated local level, but also with a holistic perspective. But "How far can these *new* requirements be practically interpreted and engaged with, whilst also keeping the business financials as its central core?"

Leadership that wants to link their business strategy together with its vision and values must be able to build into it a holistic system which integrates a diverse culture which appertains to a multitude—a plethora of personal and professional values, including their own. Endeavouring to synchronise all of those values and behaviours, to be all things to all people/employees, leaders have three choices. The first one, simply do nothing. The second, progress by groping along; or third, do something else. The answer to the first two choices being self-explanatory, the latter answer to the 'do something else' may be that well-known negotiating tactic of creating a win/win situation.

5.2 Values

As human beings we all have our own values, beliefs and attitudes which we have collected and developed throughout our lives. Where each one of these contributes to our sense of who we are and how we view the world. Our values influence the majority of the judgements we make, and give us the ability to have both a positive and negative impact on other individuals. Human values can also shape both conscious and unconscious perception and interpretation of events and experiences, so they may be open to subjectivity rather than objectivity. In any respect we need to be aware of our own personal and professional values, beliefs and attitudes and be prepared to impart but not (which is a fundamental mistake, which is made by a great many individuals) impose them onto others. Importantly, from a spiritual perspective, having values is also being prepared to, personally, regularly review them and if and when required, make the appropriate adjustments and compromises in order to make progress for ourselves in all aspects of our life.

A value is commonly formed by a particular belief which is related to the worth of an idea, or a type of behaviour. Behavioural values reflect an individual's, or an organisation's, sense of right and wrong. These values can come from our surroundings, for example our families, our peers, our education, our religion and our work environments, but unfortunately what we consider to be generally okay, right, good and proper behaviours (in terms of being a nice person and being polite in society and particularly within a work environment), sadly, more often than not, are generally seen and regarded as being weaknesses in the people who have and display them.

Values are principles, standards and qualities which an individual or group of people hold in high regard. These values guide the way we live our lives and the decisions that we make. A value may be defined as 'something which we hold dear to us' (i.e. those things and qualities which we consider to be of worth). For some it is the designer label thing, or having an expensive watch or car. It's almost like we've been programmed to buy self-worth, in the absence of having it. This mentality of what value is seems to be steeped in our culture. However, connecting to one's values is part of assessing and determining, as expressed by Heather P., "Who am I, together with who I actually am!? But valuing oneself in this way can be quite a challenge, from where I have come from anyway." In spiritual terms an individual's net self-worth has got to be more valuable than their *gross* ('gross'—in every sense of the word—i.e. very obvious and unacceptable wrongdoing, with regard to income, profit or interest) worth.

Spiritual core values may be expressed in words such as: truth, trust, respect, diversity, impartiality, integrity and freedom. Organisational core values may lie in creativity, co-operation, collaboration and communication, as well as employees' having pride in delivering quality and value for money to their customers. The customer is really, actually and objectively 'at the heart' of everything that the organisation does, rather than being steeped in subjective meaning and surrounded by complex (mainly financial) models which try to reflect and even try to explain this subjectivity and relationship. From this perspective, work also constitutes a significant challenge for subjectivity for the employee, one that either enhances that subjectivity through self-fulfilment, or destroys it through a negative mindset. Negativity hides the true 'what is', by influencing *you* to protect yourself which means pulling back, avoiding and separating yourself, from reality. Positivity 'tells' you that it is safe to recognise that you are not separate from reality, after all.

The answer therefore lies in clarifying and resolving value conflicts and developing a sustainable strategy which bridges the gap between the current status quo and *everybody's* aspirational values. The problem therein lies in treating individuals (both singular and plural) in their entirety. This entirety means understanding and responding to both the individuals' (ditto) material and immaterial needs, and no individual can coerce (spiritually or otherwise) another individual into accepting, or believing, or doing something immaterially and/or materially against their own free will. Suffice to say all co-operation, collaboration and communication has to be voluntary, or the initiative simply won't work.

To find out what people are wanting, what they're needing, what they're feeling, where they are in their hearts and minds *right now* and given how they are feeling, the organisation should ask, however impractical/difficult, "What do these people, their employees *actually really want*?" and more importantly, "What do they *actually need*?" Amongst all of this, we also have to consider there cannot be any values 'belonging' to an individual/employee which are either right or wrong, or true or false, within an organisation, other than what are shared values, and as we have so far uncovered, this isn't an easy task.

Although spirituality does involve a decrease (note, not a complete removal) in the importance of having conventional materialistic values, *it* also encourages and advocates individuals adopting *additional* values; these are reflected in an increase of a (contained, as in not perfect) immaterial attitude, as well as a virtuous approach and an economic quality of life, where work and home and home and work are, also, considered to be more inclusive and important in value and as such are both equally valid in relation to each other. Together with the effect and affect that *all* of these (sometimes newly acquired) traits, (shared) values and personal and professional domains have on us, both as an employee and an individual in our overall lives, this all-inclusive approach to spirituality is more centred and balanced, by taking into account the individual's own aspirations and both their own and shared values within this (global trading) world. Through this centring and balancing of aspirations, (shared) . . . values and (individual and group) efforts, these become the ones which forms the important and relevant, *healthy*, interconnected and connected relational and behavioural links. This truly forms a (business) *pathway* between and beginning with and from the 'I' (the individual), to the you (who you actually are), to the we (the connected, but non-co-dependent), to the us (the interconnected) and finally back to the I—the *Self*. To then all begin again in a continuous improvement loop; through the *I*—the *Self* leading by example and/or being supportive to the 'I'—the individual, where the cycle thus begins and starts again.

So far, we have ascertained—although this all *begins* with the 'I', the individual—this (continuous loop) all actually *starts* with the *Self* and the knowing of oneself. The *Self* means one's own person known through self-analysis (i.e. the analysis of oneself, in particular one's motives and character, is the acid test). Therefore, with this in mind, let us now move onto the *Self* in relation to "What work means to *you*?", together with what our particular drivers and motivators.

5.3 Work: Spiritual Drivers and Motivators

Figure 5.1 has been constructed to consider, reflect and classify the meaning and purpose of work according to: intrinsic reward, extrinsic reward, psychological altruism and psychological egoism together with their associated intersections.

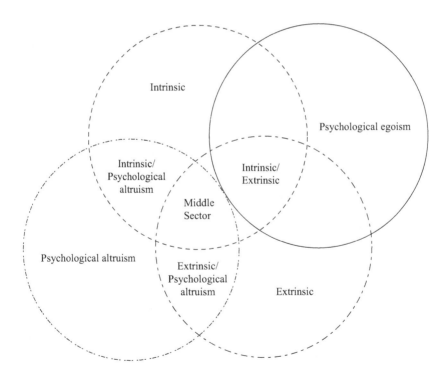

Figure 5.1 The meaning and purpose of work.

Key

> Intrinsic motivation takes the form of personal satisfaction (i.e. work itself is the reward).
>
> Extrinsic motivation rewards any work done.
>
> Psychological altruism is a motivational state with the goal of increasing another's welfare.
>
> Psychological egoism is the polar opposite of psychological altruism, which refers to the motivation to increase one's own welfare (Sills, 1968).

The following provides a sector-by-sector/intersection perspective, together with some suggested and associated meanings, purposes and motivational traits.

5.3.1 Intrinsic Sector

Never connecting work with and for money. "Being paid for who I am." Where work is something that enriches, but doesn't define *me* as a person. Where work shouldn't be *my* only thing in my life, but it's something which I should find both fulfilling and be passionate about. Where *I* put something in and I get something out of it as well. Whatever the goal is, or what the objective is, *I* have to feel a sense of achievement that *I* have done some good that day and that's the main thing that drives *me*.

5.3.2 Extrinsic/Intrinsic Intersection

I consider work to be both important and incredibly valuable; it gives some structure to my life, in terms of work being a social experience. This can be described as a 'very rich' environment, as work provides *me*, as an individual, with a lot of self-satisfaction, which is achieved mainly through my interactions with other people. *I* have an element of pride in *my* work. Work can also be an expression of *who I am*! However, I am not just my job and I am not defined by my job, but even if I didn't have to work, I would still work for the sense of (my)self and the satisfaction just from doing a good job. In other words, if I am in, or get a job that I like and enjoy, I work more and I work harder. This is typified by . . .

ROWENA N: "I don't really want to climb the greasy ladder, I don't want to be more important in that respect as I am happy doing the job I am doing and I am not looking for promotion, or anything like that."

Money is also cited as a factor within this intersection, where work pays the bills and enables the individual to look after their families. An extension of this, work/money also tends to provide the financial means to enable the individual to fulfil some life goals. Work is about, *me*, having an aim in life, to provide a way of living where it is considered: I have to work to survive, but I can't just work to live and I can't just live to work, I need a balance—a happy medium, somewhere in between!

5.3.3 Extrinsic Sector

Work is just about making money. *I* don't enjoy my job: *I* am just in it for the money.

5.3.4 Intrinsic/Psychological Altruism Intersection

Previously where work is just about earning money, within this intersection, it is now considered to be so much more. Work now becomes all about doing something which gives meaning to *my* life. "The need to feel that I am putting some good into the world." Also, within this intersection, a guiding principle is considered to be just trying and doing the right thing and in doing so these individuals feel good within themselves. In essence, it could be considered that, *my* work duties/environments 'feel right' and that they ideally reflect *my* own, ethics and values. People, within this intersection, may not necessarily work in a highly paid job, but they consider it *to be much more authentic to what and who I am.* Self-esteem, recognition, pride and helping others, even being in a position where they are providing other people with a job. Work is now no longer work, as they now seek to enjoy themselves, through helping others. *If it's work-work—I simply don't do it!* "I want to get out of bed in the morning knowing that I am going to be helping somebody, rather than going to a job where I am 'just watching the clock' and wondering when my next lunch break, or holiday is coming . . . *I want to be my own person!*"

5.3.5 Psychological Altruism Sector

I want to be of service to others. Work means labour and labour is something that one does in order to earn enough money to live and eat by. Individuals within this intersection *don't do any of that.* "I am paid to do things for other people which I don't regard as being work;" instead they 'love' using the term 'calling' for what they do.

5.3.6 Middle Sector

I work to pay bills and to eat, whilst also enjoying helping other people. Work also tends to fulfil a need in these individuals, as it gives them something productive to do and so, perhaps, fills a gap in their lives. It is also suggested work stretches their mind, as *"I like to keep my brain active."* Individuals within this sector also tend to be self-supporting, earning their 'own way' in life, whilst also proving themselves, through work and wanting to progress, and to be part of the local community. Seeking constant challenges, they, perhaps, also endeavour to improve their qualifications as, when combined with work, "This provides me with a constant challenge which keeps me alert." It could also be considered they are paid less than most people, but equally they are less stressed than most, so yes! *I* could even be considered to be happier than most.

5.3.7 Psychological Altruism/Extrinsic Intersection

Where individuals want to help others, to grow in both their psychological and their functional competences, by helping them to identify and remove barriers and/or blockers, which are stopping them from maximising their business/career opportunities and/or their own personal growth. By the same token, "As *I* help others to achieve growth, *I* also develop and grow, in myself."

5.3.8   Psychological Egoism

I just want to be prosperous and feel good about *myself.*

   In the spirit of spirituality, in taking stock of ourselves and it being all about the self and knowing one-self, the purpose of this book cannot be to either advise or tell you which particular sector/intersection to be in. This is obviously up to your good self. Further to this and both surprisingly and interestingly, at the same time, it couldn't tell you anyways. As, the author's past research suggests, spiritual individuals are shown to be randomly 'spread' across all of the previous sections and intersections contained within Figure 5.1 (see Chapter 5, Section 5.3 Work: Spiritual Drivers and Motivators), with no discernible pattern to decipher the 'best' (spiritual) profile and so fit to what appertains to a 'typical' spiritual individual (Broadhurst, 2019). The optimum 'fit' therefore has to suit the meaning, purpose and motivations of being spiritual with the profile of the individual who is practising *their* spirituality, as being an agreement that they make with themselves as a reflection of *your self*. In effect, there is no right or wrong answer to this; therefore, the point of this section is to enable the thinking, food for thought, of where *you* presently are and more importantly where *you* want to be through *your* choice either now, or for the future!

5.4 The Exit to a New Start: Sexit!

Many individuals change jobs because of the attitude and behaviours of their leaders and managers. They may also leave due to a lack of recognition for their efforts, abilities and skills, or to earn more money, to relocate due to family commitments/circumstances, or to find better career prospects, or to

Figure 5.2 Sexit!

take on fresh challenges. Perhaps they have been forced to find another role, due to being either fired (or being given the 'sack' as they say here in the UK but, for some strange reason, giving another individual 'the sack' means something else within the USA![1]) or made redundant. Maybe a fresh start with a new partner, was and is, the compelling event. Others who want to work but are fed up with the 'rat race' go out and seek a role which gives them a reasonable work-life balance. Perhaps the most damaging reason (apart from being fired, that is—or being given 'the sack' for that matter—where plenty of people have had to 'move on' due to this, shall we say, 'indiscretion!') is the resulting and tragic loss of wisdom and experience from those who consequently felt like they had no choice but to leave the organisation.

Spirituality provides courage and confidence to withdraw from old lives and ways of thinking and behaviours, to start afresh with new and exciting (usually unknown) challenges, with the positivity—hope and faith of the prospect of a brighter future for *ourselves*—to coin a paraphrase—spirituality = to start afresh, by exiting our old ways, where, this means, in this instance, Sexit! (Figure 5.2).

Part of this 'Sexit' and being spiritual is having the ability to objectively evaluate your own life. Articulated by . . .

KIRSTY R: "It was the first time I stopped and really thought, rather than how much money can I earn and how successful can I be seen to be, what do I actually want?"

A change of attitude and unlocking old ways of thinking and behaviour can act as a new and powerful stimulus. Spirituality intellectually empowers individuals to equip themselves to be able to tackle unique challenges. However, it is only through taking appropriate action that brings about a change in circumstances, as any action changes who we are and anything what we truly believe in is worth doing.

5.5 Transfiguration

It is only *possible* to transfigure yourself from your present standing to another sector/intersection by taking positive action. The 'possible' part of this transfiguration is based upon one which either reflects and accommodates for your present mindset and situation, or for your future speculations and ambitions, otherwise you are just going to end up wasting your time. This required shifting of your thinking is regarded as being both pragmatic and relativistic,[2] as the level of motivation and ability are two factors which can only be influenced through free-thinking and progressive practices.

Through self-actualisation (the drive or need that is present in everyone) and self-realisation (the motivation to influence one's own potential), the individual combines these two factors with hope, faith and trust and together with their (newly found) attitudes and activities will provide a (positive) outcome, which will produce a step towards achieving a more meaningful purpose and quality of life. It is at this point where courage comes into play again, as previously we needed to summon it to explore and confront our *ism's* (see Chapter 2, Section 2.18 Nitty Gritty Isms). This required courage, at this point, is twofold firstly because learning, by definition, starts with unnatural and often superficial behaviours, which are all about trial and error from which we learn and grow. Secondly, this transfiguration also entails a fundamental reconstruction, (re)testing and (re)adjustment of our core beliefs and values.

5.6 History Repeats; Behaviour Repeats; Testing Repeats = Repetition Repeats

"The definition of insanity?" Doing the same, absurd, things over and over again and expecting different results. A history of (unhealthy) repeated (intentionally done) futile efforts and attempts, which all inevitably end in a pattern of our wasted endeavours. This is the point where *we* have tried "Absolutely everything!" Everything! We have tried this and we have tried that and we are at our wits' end. Everything we have tried—but to no avail. *Everything!* As such we have nowhere, no one and nothing else to turn to— we have exhausted everything! When asking someone at this juncture (who has tried 'absolutely everything'), "Have you tried spirituality?" more than likely (betting money on it) you will be met with an (somewhat scoffingly) immediate and sound response of "That won't work!" Which, to be fair, is a standard knee-jerk response to many a good suggestion. Credited to Herbert Spencer (1820–1903) although others cite William Paley (1743–1805), this scoffing and rejection is 'contempt prior to investigation'. This contempt prior to investigation, basically, means that a person or a thing is beneath consideration, worthless or deserving scorn, before the individual has had all of the facts. Upon 'jumping' to this contempt, we then have three choices but, foremost, we have to recognise and accept this 'contempt' as a form of denial, a blocker and so remove it from our minds.

Thereafter our choices are to carry on doing the same *insane* thing(s), secondly do nothing, or thirdly do something—different! This 'different' is the difference between the then and the now.

By overcoming the past, eventually, spiritual individuals realise that their previous failures were not fatal, but rather regard them as being a time which taught them that they can come through, overcome and survive any adversity. Other blockers are fear and failure. By overcoming our triggers around both fear and failure, they start to dissolve from our mind and our attitude. Fear is to be accepted, adjusted and so be overcome by viewing fear as an opportunity to take exciting risks. By the same token, failure is regarded as being just temporary defeat. To further avoid the repeat of the feelings of fear and failure, keep an open mind. Go forward with an open mind with fewer assumptions and lower managed expectations as to what the outcome might actually bring (i.e. by planning the plan but not the *end* result, we can remain positive, reminding ourselves we get what we need, not what we necessarily want), so knowing whatever the outcome we will be alright, without feeling any exaggerated disappointment but only (as we are only human), just a tad disappointed, which we can quickly get over.

Humanistic ideas place importance on thinking and reason, in ways in which people can be fulfilled. Coherent repeated (healthy) patterns of this kind provide the individual with ongoing choices they can make, which serves as a stimulus around which (further) thought and positive actions grow. This is all part of testing an initiative, or continuous improvement of any kind. However, it is important to understand, the outcome of testing is never proof. It can either support a hypothesis, or reject it. Thereafter, we—the individual—can test (with courage) the validity of the possibilities that have been revealed to us from our spirituality with positive and associated actions. These are the building blocks for the construction of the *self*. As expressed by . . .

IAN P: "Spirituality is a personal code—it's a personal belief system, which has given me fresh values and a new attitude in my life. My values and attitudes now influence all of my decisions; this then provides me with the motivation that, in turn, drives my behaviour for taking [further positive] action."

However, not much in life ever runs as smoothly as this.

Old habits and attitudes die hard. When we have been conditioned to thinking, behaving and doing things in a certain way over a long period of time, they become ingrained within our subconscious; in effect, they become second nature to us and we react to situations and others, through the triggering of our isms. As previously discussed, (see Chapter 2, Section 2.18 Nitty Gritty *Isms*), our isms are entrenched and our view and way become the right view and the right way! This, aspect of, denial is difficult and stubborn and a major obstacle to overcome but it can be, with a little perseverance and effort.

Whenever you face trials of any kind consider them as nothing but in a positive way, because you know this testing produces endurance and by letting endurance have its full affect, you may start to become mature and complete—lacking in nothing.

(Adopted and adapted from James 1:2–4 [NRSV])

Spirituality is all about 'progress not perfection' (Al-Anon Family Group UK & Eire, 1992, 1997; Wilson, 1988), so by approaching life one day at a time, if you 'slip' from time to time (this type of spirituality tests and retests your new-found beliefs until you get 'there'—please don't ever feel despondent; instead, rest assured, that the process is truly working) you can very quickly correct yourself and get back onto your pathway and so an even keel.

This, both yours and mine, consists of a mixture of process and compromise, adjustment and trade-off between the individual's wants and needs, together with the *actual* given (and received) elements resulting from our experiences where we find any positive associated actions lead to a tendency to be repetitive. A repetitive experience is a process of *saturation*, which leads to, positive, reinforcing cycles within the human synoptics. In other words, they start to not only become second nature to us, but also shape and define our character and identity, for the better. The good news is this overall process leads to your own brand of recognised authenticity. Authentic: original—not a copy!

HEATHER P.—MANAGING DIRECTOR: "I have deconstructed and built up myself as a different person, by throwing away all the things that, deep down, didn't make me feel good about myself. I'm now a calm and fair person, all, again, from this spiritual moral code that I have built up for myself, that I will stick to—no matter what. I am not a new person. I am not a person that has been formed, or shaped by other people. I am, who I have chosen to be. Through just me and my choices.

This process leads us to authenticity, with spirituality being a unique approach to achieving this authenticity. Where and when spirituality is central to a new organisational framework, this requires a new and unique type of leader i.e. one who will not only be able to, and is not afraid to, discover the reasons behind any turmoil and challenges, but also be able to bring a sufficient amount of order, honesty, integrity and humanity to these challenges. As authenticity and a unique (spiritual) approach is the solution, then a (spiritual) leader who is authentic and unique who will, in turn, bring a unique (spiritual) approach to leadership is, quite obviously then, the answer! "So, rather than just thinking about it, why not just do it?"

5.7 Why Not? Beyond Just Thinking About *It* . . .

The challenges of globalisation go far deeper than the operational capability and performance of the employee. Questions still remain around the limitations of the organisation's current operational strategies and if they are suitable to effectively and affectively operate/compete, within not just a global interconnected market environment and culture but also a 'local' market. The challenge, therefore, is to produce a compelling need for a radical organisational transformation, which is designed to reduce employee cynicism and mistrust and improve the meaning as well as the emotional aspects of work, whilst also delivering against the bottom line.

So far, it may not be clear how spirituality can positively influence the bottom line, but we only have to remind ourselves of the following official statistics:

- One in every six workers experience problems relating to work-related stress
- Within the UK alone over 15.4 million days are lost to work-related stress each year
- Unplanned sickness absences cost UK businesses, alone, circa £8.4 billion a year
- £15.1 billion a year is lost from reduced productivity
- £2.4 billion a year is spent on replacing staff who leave jobs because of mental ill health

Disturbingly, these figures are also increasing by the millions year on year, across the world. This is real time and real money!

Purveyors of spirituality adamantly highlight and make the connections between an increased attention to spirituality within the workplace and enhanced job performance, together with financial success, decreased absenteeism, stress reduction, overall wellness and overall morale. Through identifying common and successful spiritual tools and techniques and by incorporating them within any workplace, such elements can aspire to ensuring low employee turnover, longevity in their attitudes and approaches, efficiency in producing product/service output and affective and greater customer satisfaction, which all lead to realised and sustained profits.

However, attempts to link and integrate various leadership theories have, previously, been made, but a majority of academic literature and business lectures state what a 'good' leader or manager must be and must do.

ALAN T: "I was probably 95% to 98% reactive. If somebody said 'Do!', I did! I tried to learn all the things that I was taught in my (and it cost an absolute fortune) MBA (Masters of Business Administration) and then apply my knowledge as best one could. But I was fighting a losing battle."

Globally, organisations spend £$¥ billions each year on leadership development. Offering quick fixes and solutions over the years, many leadership and management change programmes focus upon providing strategies, technologies, management tools and techniques and focused training which, often, prove to be inadequate. There could be various reasons behind this inadequacy, such as these 'solutions' are not really appropriate for driving meaningful corporate change. Or the organisations aren't fully committed to (the) change, or the organisation does commit to the change but influential employees display passive resistance and/or they just pay lip service to the initiative. "But why this passive resistance and lip service?"

Many, many leaders and managers, actually (and secretly) 'enjoy' working in chaos and all the trappings of 'firefighting', by *actually feeling* that they have done some 'hard and good work' and that they have 'earned' their money through putting all the 'fires' out for that day. Just to start again tomorrow. In denial of anything that is remotely wrong with any of this. Fear: afraid of change. Afraid of the unknown. Afraid of *actually having to* make a decision (see Chapter 2, Section 2.28 Contradictions). Conscious incompetence: afraid to feel and appear to be incompetent, even unconsciously being incompetent, without feeling it. Denial and/ or any of this fear must not be an excuse for sticking with what is this accepted way of (paid) working and the status quo.

Nothing happens without a readiness for change. Aside from individuals who are in denial, there are other warning factors around this lack of 'change readiness' within organisations. Managers may genuinely see and know that they need effective change as part of their strategic programme, but only want certain (usually liked what's in it for them, or relatively easy . . .) change within the, fixed and so forced, realms of their strategic plan, which is, undoubtably, separate and isolated (as we have so far uncovered) from their employees' particular and different wants and needs for change. And of course, vice versa where employees block the organisations' ambitions for change through passive resistance (with the added, compounding, problematic factor from the aforementioned managers simply paying lip service to change) and/or sabotage. Or for those organisations who do not seek affective change, their employees can start to become stagnated if they do want change as part of their working/home life. Then that resource is at risk of leaving through frustration, or, perhaps, at worst, stays and rebels against the machine. . . . It is only where and when there is a clear willingness and desire of the individuals to change—from all parties (where the ones who don't want to change must be let go) within an organisation—will spark the beginning of the beginning.

5.8　The Beginning of the Beginning

Various management styles include: authoritative. Autocratic visionary. Transactional. Servant leadership. Pacesetting. Democratic. Laissez-faire. Persuasive. Consultative. Participative. Inspirational. Results-based. Collaborative. Example-setting. Strategic. Affiliative. Charismatic. All these 'styles', which have long been well documented, together with their various pros and cons, have all been discussed and debated accordingly. Regardless, they have all been adopted and applied either in their purist prescriptive style or in a hybrid form which, maybe at the time, served the organisation well for a while and then dropped off, only to be replaced with the next best/combination, or latest management fad. The truth of the matter is that there are, still, ongoing and increasing reports of waste and lower productivity, together with a poorer quality of work and costly delays to the customer. In addition to the increasing turnover of employees, there are (even more) issues of theft, vandalism and absentee*ism* being reported, all of which ultimately lead to reduced profitability for the organisation and a decreased overall well-being for both the organisation and its employees.

Within this, there are always those who inevitably find fault and apportion blame everywhere and to anyone apart from themselves (blame storming!) but still everybody carries on regardless, with everything and every day painfully predictable and expected. The answer, therefore, lies in clarifying and resolving value conflicts and developing a sustainable strategy which bridges the gap between the current status quo and *nearly* everybody's aspirational values. 'Nearly everybody's', as some individuals are destructive critics and no matter what leadership and management do and say they always face long and continued criticism from these certain types of people. Nothing prevents change and good leadership and management than opposition, for opposition's sake alone.

Culture is defined as the values which form beliefs and behaviours. These values, commonly, characterise different groups. A dominant power promotes behaviours, beliefs and values which are congenial to it, making them (sometimes appear to be) natural, universal, self-evident and even inevitable, whilst disregarding any ideas and alternative ones which might challenge those behaviours, values and beliefs. In the workplace, managers are expected to be role models for those values, beliefs and behaviours which the organisation and its leaders *say* that they want others (i.e. their employees) to adopt and to adhere to for the benefit of the business, but not necessarily what they, the leaders or managers, themselves believe in and adhere to. Words speak more, than their actual action does (see Chapter 2, Section 2.29 Issues and challenges).

There are, as always, choices. We can stay as we are, or we can experiment with new (leadership type) behaviours and activities, in order to find new ways of achieving work and life requirements, especially during these (global) times of turbulence, transition and uncertainty. Inevitably there will be miscalculations of what these experiments and the future may, or may not bring but rather than refusing to think about the future and anything at all, never mind something new, surely it is better to think about potential ideas and solutions, to at least move forward with as much confidence that can be mustered, rather than continuing with a plan—an approach of what, essentially, either hasn't worked before, or isn't fit for purpose for today or tomorrow!?

To most people someone in a 'powerful position of authority' is automatically regarded as a 'leader'. The role of leadership and management (although stating the obvious but still, remains sadly lacking) is to facilitate the accomplishment of a common aim through human endeavour, which shows progress against a real working plan. This occupancy of power leadership and management, sadly, gives the individual the distorted view that this occupancy—this power position—provides them with the legitimate authority, the requirement and means to make others obey them. This is the disconnect which distinguishes between real power and real authority. Although it is true a leader must (try to) convince and motivate others to follow them with what could be a real leadership mission (i.e. one which creates a better and secure—profitable—future for all); to achieve this mission together with the vision is to be able to influence the whole, rather than just a few individuals. Utilising unity and growth in this way, the aim is to achieve a holistic common good, which will manifest itself in overall success. This overall success means advancement, not just for those at the top but for all levels of the organisation. This is consistent in the real capability to link self-awareness and positive purpose with empathy, reason and co-operation. Rather than false communication, (i.e. just words), power and authority.

RAYMOND H: "It's an evolution! In my position [head of . . .], it's [spirituality] an increase of self-awareness and as my self-awareness has improved it has just become a natural way, which I have chosen to interact with others."

CHRIS H: "The whole atmosphere at work has changed for the better, because I am so much more relaxed. If and when there are any problems, I'm able to deal with them differently and the staff have responded to the new way I am, because I've certainly changed and they like the change in me. It doesn't mean that I am any less demanding, but I'm now demanding in a different way, in a way which they prefer and can, *you know*, really get behind."

Keeping an open mind, the moment has now arrived for flexibility, responsiveness and adaptability. This requires being as trusting as you can be (whilst not being naïve), where both interconnected markets (see Chapter 2, Section 2.2 What Is an Interconnected Market?) and interconnected relationships (see Chapter 2, Section 2.3 What Is an Interconnected Relationship?) are based on honesty, where people are not afraid to constructively challenge each other, without any subsequent grudge or resentment. Good leadership isn't about having a 'touchy-feely' spirituality-driven popularity contest, or pandering to every single persons values above and beyond your own (for example servant leadership), where the employee—the individual happily complies and does what others want them to do out of love and/or admiration. Within any organisation, confusion and ineffectiveness

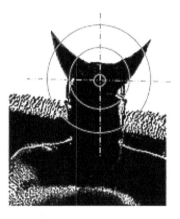

Figure 5.3   . . . Okay! Not in the way.

will be inevitable and no one, no organisation structure can fully guarantee against any damage done through clashing egotistical and conflicting personalities. Spirituality does not attempt to solve or rectify this clashing situation; rather it strongly advocates if an individual, whether it be a leader, manager, operator or office worker, cannot or will not do their job, is disruptive or defiant, they should—and must—be taken out. . . . A nod to and spiritualism aside, the devil/s—the deliberately disruptive and affront individuals amongst us begone, to be exorcised in no uncertain terms! (Figure 5.3).

This approach not only creates and accepts the freedom of each person to either rise or fall in accordance with their own values and innate qualities, which are reflected in their own decisions and actions, but it also opens up the realistic possibility of being freely receptive to other people's values when coming together, under and for a common cause. In other words, the individual might as well pursue their own self-interest (as long as they are not destructive and opposing) along with everybody else's, for the sake of achieving the greater good. This approach will also attract even those spiritual bootlegger individuals who are either not ready or do not want spirituality, but appreciate and want the learning and application that goes with it on a human level. As such *everybody* then benefits. This is attraction, rather than promotion!

SARAH H: "It's a value system . . . a belief system . . . a set of tools that I can apply in everyday life and to cope with life's pressures by. It makes me a nicer person when I interact with other people. It makes me more kind of laid back, even tolerant of other people's viewpoints and opinions."

5.9 Not Workplace Spirituality

This is a typically 'used' and so cited definition (other common definitions tend to contain the same words but are rearranged and, in others, some words are missed out and the odd one replaced with another word altogether; however these types all tend to revolve around the following . . .) of workplace spirituality: 'Workplace spirituality is a framework of organisational values, which are evidenced in a culture which promotes the employees' experience of transcendence through the work process; by facilitating their sense of being connected (note "connected": when *two* things are related, NOT worded as "interconnected," i.e. when a *number* of things are related to others) . . . in a way which provides feelings of (personal) completeness, emotions and joy'. Another definition which is also, commonly, cited and used includes, 'Workplace spirituality speaks to the deeper needs of the human heart . . . this quest (or journey) *is* instrumental in satisfying one's higher order . . . *a mindful inner consciousness in the pursuit of meaningful work* . . . an inner life that is nourished and nurtured by meaningful work'. The last one is, 'Workplace spirituality is about how organisations can better reflect and accommodate, for the whole human being' (Adams & Csiernik, 2002), because the individual is expected to bring their *whole self* (further explored in Section 5.9.2 First Act: Neutral Darkness—Some New Awareness) to work. On that note just a "*Hmmm*" from the author for now, a direct opinion on all these definitions will be saved until below Section 5.9.3 Second Act: Breaking New Ground. In the meantime, "Can you guess what this opinion will be?".

Accommodating for the 'whole' human being has been determined as not only being complicated, but nigh on impossible; besides, even if it was possible, "Why should we bring our whole self to work, or anywhere else for that matter!?" Because, on occasions, we all need to put on a false persona (see Chapter 4, Section 4.7 The Employee's View of an Organisation) to 'fit' the situation and circumstances *and* avoid losing colleagues, family and friends through a frenzied amount of 'poor me' talk and resulting eye-rolling (see Chapter 2, Section 2.4 What Is Work?). In other words, sometime in the main, we also have to fake it—to make it!

5.9.1 *Fake It to Make It*

Fake it until you make it works when you identify something within yourself that is holding you back (see Chapter 2, Section 2.18 Nitty Gritty *Isms* and Section 2.21 Self-Reflection: Root-Cause-Analysis and Section 2.22 Personal Inventory). Behaving like the person who you want to become is about changing the way that you both feel and think, not what others tell you should think and do. This fake it until you make it catch phrase is often associated to 12-Step spiritual support programmes, as an aid for those who feel that they cannot 'get' the programme and may become despondent (expecting instance change results (see Chapter 2, Section 2.10 Want and Need: Now and When) and so, will/may, go back to their old behaviour(s). Fake it to make it suggests, by imitating both confidence and competence and an optimistic mindset, the individual can realise those qualities within their everyday life.

5.9.2 First Act: Neutral Darkness—Some New Awareness

Changing ingrained behaviours and attitudes and having the motivation to do so isn't easy. It takes courage. Although not just paying 'empty lip service' to spirituality is advocated, instead a practical transitional period is actively encouraged and is perfectly legitimate within spirituality. This is where the individual sometimes, nearly always, has to 'fake it to make it', as we cannot do anything very well in this world unless we first of all learn (regard and consider yourself as a student) and start to, rather, clunkily apply *it* to what we need to do. This is neutral darkness. Crucially, this learning is underpinned with a genuine new awareness—a desire to 'get there'—wherever their unknown get there is (see Chapter 3, Section 3.5 What to Measure, Figure 3.2: From here, to there). Continuously practising our newly found behaviours and actions means that we are always endeavouring to progress and realise our (healthy) qualities, becoming better and better with each and every pragmatic application in our lives.

Bringing your whole self to work means bringing all of the components of what makes *you*: your identity, *yourself* and your *self*.

This involves everyone taking *our* 'mask' off to 'reveal' both our true—good and bad—*self*. If indeed we did this, could you imagine the bedlam and the destruction if everybody revealed their bad sides!? This bringing your whole self also involves merging both your work self and home self together. Although spirituality actively encourages an individual to progress and bring their 'essential being' (referred to as the *I—the Self*) to everything which they are involved with, and there is certainly lots of merit in doing so in their place of work, this is a tall order for everybody to be expected to bring <u>all</u> of their components to work and home for that matter. This, aside, some people, frankly, can't or won't want to do so and/or are not, or never will be, ready to be spiritually minded anyway. As such, and either way, we cannot force spirituality on anybody (see Chapter 2, Section 2.14 Why Find the Spiritual '*It*' . . . and Chapter 5, Section 5.11 Inventing the Wheel).

SHIRLEY ANNE P: "I decided to reject the whole idea of going to a (12-Step) spiritual meeting, which happened to be just ten minutes away from the place I was working at, so I went all the way over to Londonderry [about 40 miles away] cos I wasn't brave enough to go to a local meeting, cos I thought I would meet somebody I knew there and I was embarrassed of them knowing my situation and what the bad—the horrendous state, I realise, I was, actually, in."

We all use different 'cloaks' (spiritual or otherwise) and use different 'masks' in order to adapt and to fit into our various life situations and scenarios. It is this 'chameleon' type of ability, which when put to good effect, serves as either an 'oxygen mask' (see Chapter 6, Section 6.4 Culmination, Prior to Suggestion), or as a negative false humility affect (i.e. a mask of a self-lover; see Chapter 2, Section 2.16 Self-Love and Love of Self).

Being a whole person involves utilising our heart, our soul and our mind. These elements are meant to work in an integrated and holistic manner; however they invariably don't all 'work' together and at the same time. As both we as humans and organisational entities are only as strong as our weakest links (see Chapter 2, Section 2.15 The *Self* and Chapter 7, Section 7.6 Is There an App for *It*?), there are always going to be fragments of ourselves which we will feel uncomfortable bringing to our work and to our personal lives. We are reluctant to expose our secrets for all the world to see (as my mum used to say, "Never wash your dirty linen in public our Stephen!") and comment on, for everybody to know everything about us. Although spirituality is about admitting your vulnerability and faults to a trusted individual (i.e. a sponsor) and having courage and honesty to take (exciting) risks, we don't want our noses rubbed in it (i.e. our past and sundry events). Sadly, such is human nature—to use our weaknesses and vulnerabilities against us!

This is why we determine our boundaries and when we feel uncomfortable and out of sorts we can quickly refer back to our *isms*, triggers and/or push buttons to see what is causing our discomfort, or simply realise that we are just having some natural feelings and that they will and do pass. Sometimes (and keeping it simple) when there is no readily explained reason for feeling low we can take a quick dip check and HALT and ask ourselves Are we Hungry? Then of course we eat. Are we Angry? Why? Are we Lonely? Probably, but not isolated or in solitude just temporarily alone (living with oneself, (see Section 5.12, p.159). Are we tired? Which is self-explanatory. When either feeling alone or our boundaries have been crossed and so the issue is much deeper than the HALT remedy, we also now have the option and so know where to go (our group, sponsor or trusted friend) to ask for some (note, not for advice) non-judgemental perspective. We are all complex and work-in-progress human beings, so let's stick (maybe for the moment) to getting ourselves back on an even keel, to being comfortable in feeling uncomfortable and to being able to concentrate on both our own serenity and progress, on the way to being an authentic human being, where attraction rather than promotion has always been and always is the key! On the back of this if and when other individuals come to *us* feeling out of kilter with themselves, we have the time to listen, encourage them and remind them how much progress they have made accordingly.

5.9.3 Second Act: Breaking New Ground

As promised and let's be completely honest, the first paragraph in the, previous, section 5.9 Not Workplace Spirituality around the various definitions of workplace spirituality is (at least, in the opinion of the author) all, complete and utter, bollocks! Isn't it!? Even just reading the content, the wording of these definitions wouldn't convince anybody, never mind a corporate organisation, into remotely thinking about entertaining and implementing any/all of this claptrap! No wonder workplace spirituality 'hasn't received the recognition it deserves'. Crikey! Clearly, from the previous examples, the 'developing' of workplace spirituality theory (and interestingly, but perhaps not surprisingly, after over 100 years in the making, this is *still* a theory) currently suffers from the distinct lack of an understanding of what spirituality is and what real spiritual initiatives actually are. What's more generally stated (throughout a majority of other spiritual subject-related literature) is 'workplace spirituality has not received the recognition it deserves'. "Is there any wonder?"

Also, commonly quoted, 'There is also a need for thorough scientific evidence, in order to establish with scientific certainty a connection between workplace spirituality and positive outcomes, both at the organisational and the individual level' (Schutte, 2016; Gotsis & Kortezi, 2008). However, as previously discussed and determined, 'science does not apply within spirituality, as there is no need to test cause and effect relationships in areas of human experience which rely upon faith, as scientific theoretical models which are accepted upon faith are determined to be fixed, invariant and true' (Fry & Smith, 1987) (see Chapter 1, Section 1.5 The Pursuit of Happiness). Enough said regarding workplace spirituality and science. From all of this seemingly white noise though, it is readily apparent that now is the time to reboot and tune in the whole subject area of spirituality, so let's start by calling it . . . "Spirituality in the Workplace: A Tool for Relations, Sustainability and Growth in Turbulent and Interconnected Markets." A bit of a mouthful so let's, for now, keep it simple and, just call it "Spirituality in the workplace" and henceforth under *nurture*, *nourish*, *transcendence* and '*joy*', etc., together with these rather over egged, old and spurious, definitions and break new ground, once and for all!

5.10 Spirituality in the Workplace

Critics of spirituality focus on the ways in which it could be, selfishly, misused or misappropriated for organisational gain (Lips-Wiersma, Lund Dean, & Fornaciari, 2009). Viewing this laterally, these critics are, in effect, admitting spirituality *would*, indeed, be beneficial to organisations, hence the concern in regard to its use. Further to this, achieving organisational gain is what businesses have been doing from the dawn of the Industrial Revolution, so there cannot be any surprises in which they will, of course, use any purpose and means to leverage any (innovative) competitive advantage. They will also keep on doing this, at least for the foreseeable future! But still, it is right to consider and balance this concern . . .

5.10.1 Part 1: The Truth Is Far Removed

Spirituality has long been regarded as being (ultimately) about having non-materialistic concerns. So, the question/s needing to be asked, "Is it appropriate, therefore, to focus on material gains by integrating spirituality into organisation life, as a means to reap profit from it?" "If so, is not the real meaning of spirituality lost?" Therefore we have to consider the difference and distance between what's often being said and offered as the truth to what actually is the truth and is it far removed?

YVETTE T: "I could not live with that imbalance. I could not live in a falsified situation, because as soon as I saw anything that, I thought, was incompatible with my [spiritual] nature, I'd have to flag it up and of course, I wouldn't be thanked for that; because most businesses are only there to make a profit and that is their only reason for being."

CHARLOTTE D: "If somebody—anybody tries to manipulate me . . . *I can't be.* . . . I'm not easily manipulated, because I used to be The Great Manipulator, so I can see it coming a mile off. Which is good, both in business and as an employer."

There are lots of spiritual people who work in jobs, but it's very difficult to say, as expressed by Linda O.

LINDA O: "Right, I'm just going to take the 'spiritual cloak off' and then to go to work and be a 'normal' person. By that, I mean, spirituality permeates throughout all of my life and so I cannot just 'switch it off', or deny it during working hours, because work values and my values are totally, totally different."

This is further supported by Charlotte D.

CHARLOTTE D: "I would find it very difficult, because most businesses don't operate on a spiritual awareness basis and therefore, I would be living a lie. Spirituality is my life and so I can't separate it out from work. I couldn't go and say, 'Right, I'll go and work my shifts at Tesco's and then I'm going to go home and do the spiritual stuff'. I would also be doing it in Tesco's as well, which is probably why they wouldn't ever give me a job there."

5.10.2 Part 2: The Truth, Is It so Far Removed?

As previously discussed, 'the developing of workplace spirituality theory has been over 100 years in the making', but the practical application of this theory is to, still, no avail. It is fair to say, we are now at the point where the subject of spirituality both needs to and wants to move on.

Reframing the previous question/s accordingly . . . 'spirituality has long been regarded' as being all about non-materialistic concerns and as such "Is it appropriate to focus on material gains, by integrating spirituality into organisation life and as a means to attain organisation profit?" "Is not the real meaning of spirituality lost?" "The difference and distance between what's being said and offered as the truth to what actually is the truth, *is it* so far removed?" The truth is—no! It isn't.

The Step-12 method, 'We tried to carry this message to others and to practice these principles in all our affairs' (see Chapter 3, Section 3.6.2 The 12-Steps: A Spiritual Awakening?), leads to a viable consideration of achieving corporate advantage by influencing spiritual behaviours and values towards 'creating a win/win situation' (see Chapter 5, Section 5.1 Globalisation). If we consider this in line with Figure 5.1 (see Chapter 5, Section 5.3 Work: Spiritual Drivers and Motivators), this makes considerable sense. As most people acquire (unless inherited or stolen) their material possessions through working, now is the time to balance and accept both materialistic and spiritual aspirations and integrate them both into the *business world*. This business world should also comprise a set of *interpretive* moral and material practices that are visible and so realistic for all. After 100 years plus in the making, this 'what's in it for me and what's in it for you' era has got to be and is a major consideration for progressing spirituality in the workplace, and as such, it has to start somewhere, but also where to begin?

Altruism, or selflessness, is defined as 'an individual performing an action or actions, at a cost to themselves through losing, for example, pleasure and quality of life, time, the probability of survival, or reproduction, but benefits, either directly or indirectly, another third party, without the expectation of reciprocity, or compensation for that cost'. "But how does this stack up?"

KAREN A: "I am willing and utilising my spiritual values and beliefs and they are certainly valid in my job and used to good effect. However, they [her spiritual beliefs] are starting to be 'really used and abused' by my organisation and to some extent, although my efforts are being appreciated, they are certainly not being reciprocated by my managers. I am now finding their demands on me are constantly increasing and they are also pushing more and more upon my goodwill. This has all reached a point, now, where these demands and 'pushing' on me has gone far enough. They [her managers] are also trying to encroach more into my personal time which *I* consider to be completely and utterly non-negotiable."

EDWARD P. H: "Within my previous role I was very much 'giving' and helping people using my spiritual values and behaviours, to recognised success. The 360-degree feedback I received from everybody was both fantastic and very humbling at the same time. However I left in the end, because, although the organisation was 'happy' for me to approach my role in this way, I wasn't allowed to balance my own personal spiritual values, behaviours and aspirations with my own time by either my manager and/or director, so it became very much all giving, rather than receiving."

PAUL J: "Once my role had started to become more and more confined was when I decided, enough was enough!"

JOHN S: "What my spirituality means to me . . . is being able to be much more selective on who I'm going to do business with. The [contract] job that I am going to start next week I am very happy with; because the more I speak and get to know them. This organisation, the more excited and looking forward to working with these people I become. Not only that, I also know we will have a sensible conversation and dialogue and as such we have also established a fairly, informal, reciprocal agreement, so I now know when we agree to do something it will get done. There are other organisations if somebody rang me up and said 'I want you to help me', I'd just say 'No!' Or there would need to be a very strong contract—a reciprocal agreement that says 'If this is what we agree—this is what we do' because otherwise I am just going to end up wasting both *mine and their* time."

LEE K: "When I have ever asked for anything from my bosses, they have always been quick to say 'Yes!' To me, so I always wanted to be just as quick to say 'Yes!' To them. My boss did once say to me, 'You know, we do appreciate all what you do, but we are not surprised as we know you do like to work in this way'."

KATHRYN W: "I apply what I actually think to be true all of the time. When I'm at work, this gives me a great sense of peace, of serenity, it gives me the feeling of calm . . . of things being right . . . of being comfortable and this is something that I want in my life. Because of this, I have always found a give and take situation with my employer, so I am more than happy to do what is asked of me, because I know they will be more than happy to give back to me."

PAULA B: "I have been very lucky [note 'lucky' not expected or standard practice] where the people I have worked for, my employers, have always operated this way where people will give and take so freely."

PETER J: "Working on a one-to-one basis, they view me as somebody who is always consistent and reliable. If somebody asks me to cover [duties at work, not in a criminal or being in a battle sense, but then again who knows?] for them, *you know*, there is no problem, I will do that, cos I know they would cover for me."

MICK P: "This is the result of everything about me, the way I would approach people from a spiritual point of view . . . but also in pragmatic terms. This is the best way that I would go about all things . . . to have the generosity of spirit. This doesn't mean that they . . . *they* cannot walk all over *you* . . . but by approaching them, and everything in this way, is wanting the best for both of us and I have always 'worked' in that same way."

A reciprocal agreement is duty bound. It is an (informal or formal) contract between one individual to another, or one organisation to another. etc. Where one party will perform a certain act if the other performs a specified act as well and vice versa. Where any obligations are assumed and imposed by the two parties as mutual and conditional, upon the other party assuming the same obligations.

Spirituality in business is to have and to *share* values, but also to have values which are true to oneself.

BECKY H: "It's good to have an internal compass and to know what to do. But I didn't all of a sudden just develop my values, I developed them over some years."

GEMMA H: "The difference being, from my spiritual approach and *my* organisation's approach, is both *I* and they will review my/its values every year, to make sure that they are still valid and fresh—good and worthwhile. All of these values are then lived out every day, through the work which we do and as long as everyone sticks within those perimeter[3] values, they will always come across in everything that we all do. For instance, we have a few key phrases such as, where most call it customer service we call it compassionate service, because you are not only being understanding and displaying empathy to the customer, but *you* are also compassionate to all of your different stakeholders."

Spirituality cannot just be paid lip service to—otherwise it just becomes farcical:Pharisaical.[4] *It* has to 'spread like an antibiotic'—a kind of spiritual antimicrobial—and have a multiplier/ricochet effect which is influenced and encouraged by identity, empathy and relational factors within all functions of the organisation for it to work both effectively and affectively (see Chapter 4, Section 4.1 Culture including Figure 4.1 Petri Dish of 'culture' cells). This is the start and the beginning of the *it* . . .

HEATHER P: "Others saw what I got out of *it* [spirituality] and liked it. So, the change in me must have been huge."

Spirituality spans anything from functional issues such as: "How do I deal with this sort of customer?" "How do I lead people? "How do I lead different people from a different culture?" "How do I get the best out of people?" "How do I manage?" Spirituality can assist with professional issues regarding relationships between employees, between managers and leaders; supporting the employee's ability to grow in both their psychological and their functional competences; individuals overcoming their limiting beliefs and/or blockers, which are stopping them from maximising their business career and promotional opportunities. This relationship between spirituality and leadership provides a springboard for developing a leadership and management style, which integrates character and behaviour, motivation and performance on a global cross-cultural model.

These individuals—these leaders—are regarded as being positive and truthful people, who promote openness and honesty. *They* lead by example through their behaviour. They display consistency, stoicism and remain steadfast without being stubborn. This is all underpinned with *self-discipline*, self-awareness, empathy and integrity. It is also important, for every individual, to distinguish between what real choices there are (however difficult) and are to be made around which are true dilemmas.

For organisations to compete within interconnected markets and to achieve their desired results within them, this requires leading with vision and making assertive, justifiable decisions. Couple this with catering for and encompassing interconnected and connected relationships (and in an effort to keeping it simple), all of this can be described as, 'simply', leaders (as do ourselves within our daily lives), having a binary choice between the bad and the good and the right and the wrong. However, these choices, in themselves and however strange this may seem, requires a certain discipline.

Within this discipline it is also important to realise even very prideful or very angry individuals can sometimes be right and tell the truth while the calm and humble can often be mistaken, even lie. On all occasions we ought to listen, whilst asking ourselves, "Do they mean it, or do they think they are fooling *me*?" Distortion, dissimulation and deception cannot be allowed and all cards must be put on the table.

Spirituality isn't all or nothing. It is a workable emotional balance and perspective, where it is accepted that mistakes are naturally going to be made, by both ourselves and others, whilst freely admitting those mistakes and more importantly learning from them, before moving on without any fear, grudges and/or negative judgement. To develop genuine patience with other people is a large order and sometimes we will fail to make good on it, but nevertheless we must try. Now is the time to invent the wheel.

5.11 Inventing the Wheel

Max Weber (1958) predicted bureaucratic features would create an organisational 'iron cage', which would sap the flexibility and responsiveness of the individuals who work within it (Weber, 1958). Michels's (1962, 1915) 'iron law of oligarchy' stated that a circle of leaders *will* obtain control of all decision-making and ultimately eliminate any internal democratic control (Michels, 1962, 1915). Such actions crush individuality, together with self-esteem, aspirations and dignity, individual power and prestige; when combined this can result in shackles, consisting of fear and restrained talent. This, together with coercion and over-control, stunts (overall) growth and contributes to organisational (cultural) ineffectiveness and failure. *Modernising* a global business with local integrity and ability emerges through having a values framework, which provides some mutually shareable and understandable points of reference, which are designed and intended for identifying and evaluating challenges, judgements and appropriate behaviour.

Matching a global organisation with local integrity and ability where such values, attitudes and conduct towards each other are not just a fancy idea, this has been in existence for over 90 years and yet this particular 'wheel' still needs to be recognised, even invented within today's business world.

Max Weber's 'iron cage of bureaucracy' and Michels's 'iron law of oligarchy' have failed to materialise within AA, or in any other spiritual 12-Step Fellowships (Borkman, 2006). Crucially, the temptations of leadership and management power have also been truly avoided and even 'professional*ism*' (another ism in itself) has been significantly removed and positively discouraged.

"Does this mean these Fellowships are not generally business-like?" Yes—it does—well sort of!

"Does this mean, then, they are unprofessional, below or contrary to the standards expected in a particular professional?" Yes—it does—but no . . . sort of.

By default, then, "Does this mean these Fellowship organisations consist of an unruly rabble, with a mob-like mentality?" No—it doesn't. But these individuals are in a state of chaos.

"They must, to this, then, all have a manner which is not pertaining to, or characteristic of, a profession? *What on earth does that mean?*"

"Does this mean they are all non-professional?" Yes—it does! Strictly non-professional. This is a golden rule within these organisations.

With that, non-professional*ism*, clarified, "Does this mean, then, they are not exhibiting a courteous, conscientious standard or ethic, with language, behaviour, or conduct not befitting of a professional?" No! It certainly doesn't.

"So they are, in effect, all amateurs?" Yes! They certainly are.

By rejecting the notion that leaders and managers of these Fellowships are inherently more superior and understanding that any learning and influences are multi-directional, these organisations have a distinctive co-op leadership style. This approach, uniquely, accommodates for dispersed groups of people via a decentralised power-based cell standardised structure, which provides the organisation with the ability to operate not just at a local base group level, but also function on a global scale as well. This (tried and tested) formula allows individuals to attend and fit into any 'local' group, whilst also being welcomed and being able to fit into *any* other, relevant, group (appertaining to the same problem/common cause requirement) around the world.

Having a values-based authority, these Fellowship organisations display and follow significant beliefs, where all of its members have and share a common cause, intention and aim.

The individual, as part of the group, has an interest in learning not just from others, but also invites (and listens to) input from all levels (in or outside of their Fellowship) and importantly, as an individual, they then apply all of this learning (taking what they like and leaving the rest out, at that particular point in time) into a self-development process for themselves. Through their own development processes, they utilise and realise (as outputs) the uniqueness of their own individual talents and abilities for their own greater good, whilst also delivering the overall aim of the organisation. To have well-being they also, through leading through attraction, inspire other people as well, not only outside of their Fellowship, but they also give something back into their group/s by sharing their experience, strength and hope with others. Even, maybe, becoming a sponsor within it. So, *it* all comes back full circle.

People such as psychologists, doctors, dentists, lawyers, judges, police, politicians, 'famous' people in music, sport, stage and screen, etc. also attend Fellowships. These are all professionals within their own chosen fields. But, regardless of any profession, nobody can be or is a professional within the field of spirituality. Even if it were remotely possible, this would lead to this person's being revered and others looking towards them to be *told what to do* by them, rather than *figuring out their own life choices*. However, although some individuals have been around spirituality and spiritual groups longer than some others and as such, they know some ropes (whilst remaining truly humble in their knowledge and experience), nobody in the subject of spirituality is an expert, everyone, to a degree, is an amateur or amateurish, to reflect where they are on their pathway. As a side note to all of this, all of these individuals come together as complete strangers and unless they become friends outside of their Fellowships they don't, in the main, even know each other's surnames. They are truly all true and separate individuals fitting into and acting as one group. "What is wrong with and how relevant is that within a place of work?" But this side note, in turn, can then trigger off thoughts of them being all non-professional i.e. amateurish and so "How does this part of the (spiritual) offering fit into the scheme of things?"

Going back to "Does this mean these Fellowships are not generally business-like?" Yes—it does—sort of. Although the individuals themselves are in a state of chaos and suffering, the Fellowships themselves are not in a state of chaos. The Fellowships have a long history and pedigree of structure and discipline via the 12-Steps, Concepts, Traditions and Principles and all of their meetings are business-like, formally opened and closed with a, albeit loose, agenda (as everybody is free to share what they like, as long as it is relevant to the goal) and although autonomous they have to follow some rules in order to keep a certain and common standard, approach and understanding, again, not just on a local level but also on a worldwide one.

Although each of these groups are fully self-supporting (i.e. they pay their own rent and buy their own literature, tea and coffee, etc.), they invite individuals to make a monetary contribution (there is no pressure to do so) to the main hub of the organisation. The main hub employs a core team of specialists for support purposes and any donated money is used to further the aims of the appertaining Fellowship, rather than used as profit for shareholders, etc. In this context, the main Fellowships generate a respectful (not-for-profit) annual turnover, within their own rights. See Tables 5.1a and 5.1b, for example.

Table 5.1a Financial (UK) snapshot of Organisation A: Alcoholics Anonymous (AA)

Alcoholics Anonymous*	Company no: 00587316	Turnover: 1.4M GPB	Net Assets 2.4 M	Debt to Capital (%) 6.55%	Liquidity Ratio: 6.32

* Figures correct at the time of writing.

Table 5.1b Closely related (UK) financial snapshot of Organisation B: Al-Anon

Al-Anon (UK) GBP*	Company no: 00984912	Turnover: 326.6K	Net Assets 375.3K	Debt to Capital (%) **34.51%**	Liquidity Ratio: 4.61
Al-Anon Inc. (USA) USD*	Income tax exempt	Revenue 5,550,952	Net Assets 9,529,001		

* Figures correct at the time of writing.

Changing tack slightly, but still relevant, the founding father to all of these (12-Step) Fellowship organisations, Bill W., turned down the opportunity to appear in *Time* magazine. He also declined at least seven honorary degrees from prestigious (from the likes of Yale) Ivy League universities, who wanted to award him *directly* for the recognition of his endeavours and achievements. He also turned down a number of overtures from the Nobel Prize Committee, who were 'sounding him out' for 'the prize' itself. "The reason?" He refused them all on the basis that it wasn't just *directly* him, but the organisation as a whole and all those within it that should be recognised. In keeping with this, his gravestone does not link him to either AA or any of his life achievements and successes. A true and humble, but zealous pioneer.

Alcoholics Anonymous (AA) has and is, described as being 'one of the great success stories of our century' (Mäkelä et al., 1996, p. 3).

These Fellowships balance being human with having leadership traits.

Leadership is an interpersonal relation in which others comply because they want to, not because they have to. Leaders are individuals who refuse to use manipulation or deceit; achieve personal and professional goals; freely admit mistakes; value integrity over profit and material growth—all without having a requirement to obey them. All this requires this individual to have moral integrity which inspires trust and promotes transparency and honesty throughout organisation life and life itself.

"What is it, then, about the 'S' word, which throws 'dust' into people's eyes?" "Where somehow it doesn't cut through their thinking; creates considerable resistance and prevents serious consideration towards its relevance and applicability, in both life and mainstream business?" These problems are abundantly recognised, as, after all, plenty of people have tried to overcome this by simply rehashing, repackaging and relabelling spirituality, but to no real avail.

It is, perhaps, understandable then, that most people, especially executives, proceed with a degree of caution where any new ideas and business/conceptual models are met with (the art of) scepti*cism* and resistance. It is only after consistent and persistent efforts to inform and educate, that some of these ideas and paradigms, finally, receive and gain some attention to where they then eventually, may, become accepted and implemented in some way, shape or form. "So why should this book and the subject of spirituality be any different this time?" "How can it state the benefits of spirituality without over-selling it, commoditising it, rebranding it, or watering it down but still remain valid enough to bring into the business world?" Here lies the dilemma.

SANDRA C: "It is about sharing and informing people—but of course, only if they are interested. I'm not going to force it on people and say, 'You sit there and listen to me'."

5.12 Attraction Rather Than Promotion

Spiritual support Fellowship groups are regarded and renowned for their organisational structure. Their 'local' groups not only span the world but are also autonomous and self-managed, whilst also being in sync with and complementary to the main organisation (hub) itself. In effect these local groups are all Micro-Groups, operating (and dynamically complementing) inside a Macro-Group, which/who all share the same culture—values and behaviours, goals and aims—whilst also containing a multitude of inter-connected individuals and (when they are sponsoring each other, or if they become friends outside of the meetings) connected individuals.

By default, we are back to "Does this mean these organisations consist of an unruly rabble, with a mob-like mentality?" No—it doesn't. Although the individuals are themselves, in a state of chaos, it can be safely said there are absolutely no sub-cultures which exist within 12-Step Fellowships. The, overall main, culture is recognised and respected by all and where the Steps, Concepts, Traditions and Principles are also and equally adhered to. Behaviour throughout is kept to a required and decent standard and the overall intentions, goals and aims are notably progressed towards. If someone is being unruly and/or are flagrantly and frequently breaking the rules, without any hesitation, they are simply asked, immediately, to leave the group.

A non-hierarchy, where everybody is equal and nobody is in charge, is an essential method where peers convey hope and strength to one another on the same terms and under the same (natural) conditions as each other. This creates the right conditions and environment for each individual to be a creation of the culture and for the culture to be the creation of each

individual. In turn, these right conditions and environment create a result-
ant 'pull' (attraction), not a forced 'push' (promotion), an energy which
drives individuals in a positive direction in their lives. (All of . . .) this
is what motivates an individual to leave their home in the snow and ice,
lightening, hail, wind and rain, in order to attend a meeting with the aim
to be better versions than themselves and to help others to do the same for
themselves. Imagine a business being able to capture this highly motive,
steely determination and ambition in the pursuit of their goals!? The good
news . . . it doesn't have to be imagined! This is a setting where real leadership emerges, but not in a hierarchal sense, but by learned example.

Spirituality is considered within servant leadership to be selflessly serving
others. Frequently confused with servant leadership, spiritual support groups
encourage individuals to give service, to give something back into their group,
but not only in monetary terms (they can contribute towards rent, tea and
coffee, but only if they can). This encouragement is designed to repair broken people, broken characters, broken relationships and broken systems
and so bring social unity. Many individuals when asked "How are *you*?"
tend to automatically and politely reply that they are "Fine" (even though
they are clearly not), where, in this instance—especially within Fellowship
Groups, 'fine' stands for Fucked Individual, No Emotions! From organising
the meeting room, making the tea/coffee, ordering literature and tidying up
afterwards, no gift of service is better or less than others, they are all equally
valuable. Through this aspect of service work the esteem of every person is
acknowledged, together with their individual talents and abilities. It also starts
to build confidence and involvement. Participation in this particular work is
an individual decision, with some people so broken (sick and suffering) in
their thoughts, emotions and physical feelings; through being constantly on
the receiving end of negative actions, caused by living in a dysfunctional environment and/or relationship, they feel that they have absolutely nothing to
offer, to either themselves or to others. This is also relevant and applicable to
business organisations trying to function with broken processes, systems and
dysfunctional people, together with the increasing exponential levels of sickness absence and lost productivity, the similarities are there to be regarded.

Spiritual support Fellowship groups are there for anybody, whether
they are religious or not religious. They do not read from the Bible or
sing hymns; they are purely neutral. Nor are they a cult,[5] individuals are
free to come and go as they please. Described as either a 'Group' and/or
'Fellowship',[6] there is a sense of belonging within these spiritual support
systems, which are also termed as programmes.

SANDRA C: "Every week I was going to some sort of spiritual gathering,
with people who I wanted to connect with."

SHELLY M: "One of the things regarding spirituality is coming together,
with similar hearted and minded people, because there is strength in
numbers."

Although there are some guidelines contained within the Fellowship Principles, Concepts and Traditions, their format and content consists of people sharing their varied experiences, good and bad, around different things, for others to reflect upon. Golden rules include no lecturing or intention to moralise or condemn. There is no cross sharing, which means there is never any advice given, or comments directly aimed at any individual. As testified by . . .

JAMES P: "There is no advice given, so it's basically a self-help group."
Hence, these meetings are designed and intended to be honest; individuals are free to say what is in their hearts and minds, whilst stimulating (self-)reflection within others. "Do I agree with that, or don't I agree with that?" "Can I accept that, or not accept that?" "Why is that being said and does it contradict with my views and if it does, will it help to develop my own views?"

These group sessions provide a clearer understanding of what's important to the individual and what's not important to them—stressing the point—that moment in time. Thus, those who attend any Fellowship meetings are involved, through being attentive, engaged and keeping an open mind to what is being said. They share and they listen; they then listen and then share.

Through all of this interactive, (collective wisdom), participation, as individuals we (in some cases even just *start* to, as we may have never done it before) share, listen and learn from each other and from this we gain our own perspective and balance for our own action. As such, this sharing and listening is considered to be a crucial blueprint for progress for the individual—the 'I' in finding your *authentic self*—the real you—the I—*your self* (see Chapter 2, Section 2.17). This individual can then lead by example in all areas of their/your life and to provide hope and encouragement to another individual—the (connected) 'we'—when asked to do so and/or as part of the collective group 'strength—the 'us'—before coming back to the 'I' again, the 'I' being the newcomer and/or the lost and disillusioned individual. To begin and start the continuous loop again.

As a whole, this is due to timing. Just as everybody progresses, some people are further along their pathway than others are, (hence what distinguishes between the amateur and the amateurish), so they can metaphorically say, "Hey listen, mind that 'hole' there, I just fell down that!" Or, this is how I approached things (note *not how I would, but how I did*) and this is what happened to me. These individuals are helping to set a direction by helping others to see what (possibly) lies ahead . . . (possibly as, for example, you can read, look at pictures and listen to someone else about how to climb a mountain, but you cannot experience and appreciate it without actually doing it and even then you will have to take your own route/pathway up it, together with your own, specific, equipment, and the weather may be different, the season/time may be different, etc.) . . . all by sharing with well meaning reason and intent. Where the main intention is to lead by example; leading with actions, as well as words. This stimulates everyone's potential, and encourages and inspires those around them. These are the traits of a true leader and, more importantly, to which *anybody* can aspire.

By conveying practical experience, together with hope and faith in this way, carries/sends a message (see Chapter 3, Section 3.6.3 The 12-Steps: The Message to Be Carried) that things will be alright—situations and circumstances can be gotten through, regardless of where you have come from and what you will go through.

It makes sense, therefore, this has to be a frequent, recurring cycle of inputs and outputs; as our attitudes, behaviours and situations are changing all of the time—so we may not be ready to hear 'the message' which is being carried/given at the moment, but we may be ready to 'hear it' when we are further along our pathway. Take what you like and leave the rest, until you are ready to like it, that is! For example, through continuous self-reflection and improvement, we can then start to join the dots up within ourselves; this is what makes me do what I do. "Why do I do this?" "Why do I continue to do it/things this way—which seems to never work, or does work until it no longer does so, then I will change it!?" "How can I do something different—maybe take some (further exciting) risks?" Then by also listening to other people's experiences or their ways of dealing with things, then you make your own activity, or action, which makes you the unique and authentic you—the self!

Through interacting in this way with others, all individuals can bring some positivity into both somebody else's life and their own life. Articulated by:

CLAIRE S: "I think of others and I particularly think of newcomers and hopefully I can be of some help to them. I can always remember when I first walked into a meeting and thinking, 'I've got to have some of what they've got!' It was so calm—so serene—and everyone believed me when I was telling them *my* story. Everyone was going 'Yep, yep' and you think 'They are actually listening . . . they actually believe me!' For me, this was a big thing and now if a newcomer is up on the ceiling . . . in the corner, then hopefully, I can help to bring them down a little bit. That's why I'm with Al-Anon today. I also sponsor three people separately [separately—to maintain their connection with them as an individual, on a one-to-one basis] and while I'm sponsoring those people and attending meetings . . . I am still very active in the/my meetings . . . and also very active in putting my programme to use for everyday life—cos it's not just about other people, it's all about me! So yeah it's huge—it's [spirituality is] massive in my life! I'll never not have it in my life, ever!"

THERESA F: "It's a way of helping myself and incidentally it also helps other people, at least I hope it does occasionally."

MAGGIE C: "By sharing the three nouns of experience, strength and hope, I help other people. But whether I do or not, I don't know, that is debatable, but at least I am doing it."

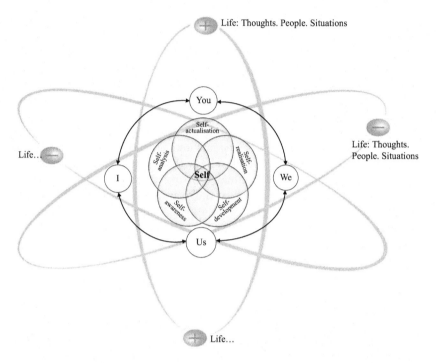

Figure 5.4 Atomic life of the *Self*.

RACHEL M: "I remember coming away from my first meeting and kind of collapsing on the floor and just feeling a glimmer of hope! That there was *something* out there, that might be a way forward."

To give, to carry a message . . . to help other people who are looking for some answers, looking for a change in their life. To move to being well, realising that life doesn't have to be the way it is for them, that there is a way out.

IAN P: "To give whatever I need to give, to help those people to have some hope."

This is the point where *we*—the individual comes together in ourselves to build and form the important *Self*. By placing our self at the centre of our 'nuclear' lives we can—will respond, not to volatilely react, to life and its, trying/testing, influences. This is where our new found selfishness ensures first and foremost not only our own wellbeing but, paradoxically, that of others as well (Figure 5.4).

HEATHER P: "I was so happy . . . and I was in this bubble and I couldn't believe my luck . . . how lucky I was to have found this group . . . and to be changing and . . . it was just the room itself . . . it even just . . . this room became just a safe haven for me . . . a place where not everything was doom and gloom . . . a safe and confidential place . . . being amongst people who I could trust."

Overall, this collective wisdom and support involves two or more people being co-operative, collaborative and creative, in many different ways, for the sole purpose of accomplishing any given objective.

VICTORIA W: "Do I believe in something? Yes! It's about how you relate to your higher power and the higher power, for me, is the wisdom I get from the people in my group."

PAUL J: "To be fair, with what is going on in my life, the people who are helping me are all from Al-Anon and that says something in its own right. That's power in its own right, of a higher power, of whatever that is."

Just 90 minutes once a week (the time and duration of a Fellowship meeting) supports and assists the individuals' capability to deal with *any* issues in both their home and work lives. As stated by . . .

YVETTE T: "It [spirituality] helps me to function in all areas of my life, by giving me the tools and techniques for coping."

These types of spiritual support programmes, and together with leadership by example, create a vision and value congruence across both the strategic (autonomous) macro-group and the (self-autonomous and empowered) local micro-group functions; right down to self-empowerment and autonomy on an individual level. It is all of these areas which provide a mixture of opportunities for establishing a common ground as humans where, as individuals, we are capable of developing and applying forms of intelligence and logic to manage and overcome any problems, risks and challenges.

Simon P. and Shelton D., both suggested starting a Fellowship meeting at their places of work.

SHELTON D: "I asked my manager if we could have a *Group* session once a week, where we could just offload?" Immediately he said, 'No!— People would just be moaning and groaning all the way through it'. I think that's a very old-fashioned way of looking at it and I don't think that would actually happen."

Simon P., was also met with, virtually, the same response but as he expressed. "It's better to have a go, [at anything], than not bother at all." 'To start a Fellowship meeting all you need is a resentment and a coffee pot' (Bob, 1980).

Spirituality cannot be considered as an all or nothing. Going through the motions of everyday life, living in our heads (and where the head is either quite a boring and/or destructive place to live in), a lot of people just become robotic. It's people's fears which run with them and once you are aware and in control of these/your fears, and volatile emotions, nothing can phase you—too much. Therefore, we all have a choice of which frequency we want to live on, where no matter what life throws at or deals us, we always come back to a healthy—positive default setting, pretty quickly. However, there is help and support out there when needed; if you care and want to find it and/or if you want to give *it* in order to help others who are trying to find *it*. The quality of our human character is dependent upon the many traits which contribute to both the way in which we think and our overall behaviour which results from our thinking. Therefore, it all starts and ends with you—the *self*.

A new generation of leadership needs to be sought, those who will both relate and respond to the global economic environment, interconnected markets and increasing competition; who will encourage both individual and group capability and ability together with both interconnected and connected relationships; who will be willing to contribute to the success of the organisation; who will intellectually improve and empower individuals; who will equip and enable them with strength, risk and value-based approaches to survive in the struggle of life. For the benefit of one. For the benefit of all. For the benefit of all. For the benefit of one.

After going through and experiencing (horrendous) suffering and misery, the qualities of spirituality and surviva*lism* both, together, provide a means in which an individual can continue to live **and** (please note this is worded 'and' not 'or') exist with well-being. This can occur in spite of any hardships which have been previously endured, where any future trials and tribulations will be suitably lessened through the individual having a different way of thinking and acting upon (where and when appropriate action is required) their circumstances.

Spirituality bridges the gap between serenity and having emotional, social, ethical and moral elements and combines them with knowledge from sociology, psychology and philosophy to create a new leadership. A new leadership—from a new individual who leads with courage and through example and so attraction—who uses three main aspects: 1) Personal and professional development, 2) a (new) different way of thinking and living and 3) relationship (personal and professional) leadership. This person also has the ability to create a positive vision for both the self and for others to follow—with hope and faith that everything will turn out to be alright. Spirituality has the ability to initiate and drive affective change, together with development and growth and the desire for continuous improvement of both the self and others; through attraction and the multiplier/ricochet effect, so enhancing (a loop of) mutuality and reciprocity across all levels. This . . . spirituality is progressive and ongoing and as such, there is no conclusion to where this can and will all end. But when it actually starts and actually begins is, however, up to *you*!

Notes

1 In the USA 'giving somebody the sack' (sack meaning bed) means having sex with another person. Thanks for pointing that one out Penny B., four days after *I* had said it to everybody!

2 a. Relativistic: philosophy—any theory holding the belief that different things are true and right for different people, at different times.

   b. A theory that knowledge is relative to the limited nature of the mind and the conditions of knowing.

3 The word 'perimeter' has been derived from the Greek word 'peri' meaning around.

4 Pharisaical: It is what the Pharisees did. They were very good at just standing there with saying their prayers outwardly, but they did not bother with decent actions if they were not going to be noticed.

5 A relatively small group of people having religious beliefs or practices regarded by others as strange, or as imposing excessive control over members.

6 A Fellowship is defined as: 'A Friendly association and community, especially with people who share one's interests, feelings and/or experience; the quality or state of being comradely; with meaningful communication and mutual support for building trust—a community bound together in fellowship' (Stevenson & Waite, 2011).

6 An Ending Without a Conclusion

It may seem pedantic, but by the very nature of spirituality there cannot be a hardwired conclusion[1] to this script. The reason is because this conforms (and confirms) with the subject matter i.e. spirituality provides a pathway that facilitates a steady and continuous line of progress, not perfection, of which there is no end point.[2] We could also (for those people, and there are some, who also skip straight to the end of a book—naughty!) just read the next couple of pages and so miss out on the all-important, actual 'devil' in the details[3] and *voila*! We would think we are all spiritualled up and ready to go. *It* certainly and really doesn't work like that![4]

Everyone has different lives and so, it makes sense, even if we make the same (confident) decisions and take the same (well intentioned) actions (by the Law of Variation[5]) these situations and events, where conclusions to such—will turn out somewhat different and varied, good or bad, for all of us, even when we apply a spiritual approach and application. So, to be able to write a conclusion on what a spiritual outcome on these variation's might be, to cover for each and every one of us, is nigh on impossible. However, a sure-fire ending that can safely be offered is, spirituality provides a quality of thinking and attitude to life that consists of serenity throughout all the situations that we find ourselves in. This serenity—this quality of emotion and well-being, is based upon need not want and doing the best we can with what we are given. This is all whilst accepting any negative, (however disappointing some may be), outcome by regarding it as a, sometimes hard, lesson—as temporary defeat to reflect and to improve upon where we can, whilst also accepting any positive outcome with gratitude, to be appreciated and enjoyed for what it – this good time is.

From seemingly hopeless cases the *message to this* is one of hope, courage and confidence and that there are answers to those who are seeking them. Spirituality alleviates suffering and brings people together on a global scale, to all act as one, local, group for the progress of all and the benefit of each individual; to share a common aim and purpose, to discover and have the 'priceless gift of serenity' (Al-Anon, 2006, p. 35) and to achieve well-being. This has been successful the world over through interconnected and connected active support, communication, co-operation and collaboration, where nobody is in charge and everybody is equal. Spirituality has helped a multitude of individuals to overcome their suffering by addressing *their* isms, issues and problems. Spirituality isn't religious and so is literally *free* to anyone who cares to *find it* and *wants* to *do it* 24 hours/7 days a week/365 days a year. Spiritual support/ Fellowship groups are always open (including Christmas Day and New Year's Day) and are welcoming; full of empathy, knowledge, experience, wisdom and hope, whenever both *it* and they are needed. Although spirituality is free it isn't possible to 'give' people spirituality, but it is true that what the mind can conceive it can and will achieve, always providing that you have the tools and techniques for the job (Hill, 2011). Spirituality doesn't tell you what you should, shouldn't, or must do and yet it is progressive and realistic—and importantly, it works!

Despite the commercial and academic discourse on spirituality being awash with all sorts of (outdated) promises, misdirection and misunderstandings, there *still* hasn't been an agreed dominant paradigm or prevailing framework within which the discussion on spirituality, in the workplace, can be duly (seriously) considered and (practically) carried out. Managing the moral complexity of globalisation requires the construction of a flexible, breathing and adaptive framework which links diverse values, *everyone's* requirements, wisdom and well-being. This, will, is based upon both the rational and reasonable, as well as provides viable access to the various tools and techniques which spirituality offers to individuals, groups and organisations alike. Spirituality says "Keep it simple," as this allows for creativity and interpretation, thus allowing everybody to understand what *it's* all about. Keeping it simple, the challenge, therefore, is/was to strip away the misconceived and irrelevant associations with the subject of spirituality and identify the strengths and truth in the actual theory and practice of it. Through integrating all of these into a practical paradigm which offers a fresh and new (business) perspective and a clear vocabulary, this can be applied to and prepare the individual, the employee, business leadership and management for both the *now* and the *future now*.

This, however, leads to a viable consideration of influencing spiritual behaviours and values towards achieving a corporate advantage: "Surely the very idea of adopting spirituality in this way could be considered a cynical attempt by the organisation to manipulate its employees, through (false) pretences, purely for its intention to achieve shareholder and stakeholder gains?" The single-minded pursuit of materialistic success has produced a number of corporate scandals and a widespread feeling of anger and mistrust, so from this perspective, perhaps there is a reason to be sceptical of what appears to be an emerging all-inclusive, all-encompassing view of spirituality, which is being offered as a 'cure' to the plethora of business issues. The question therefore needs to be asked,

"Is it appropriate to focus on the many gains which will be reaped from integrating spirituality into organisation life, through using it as either a means to attain organisation profit, or for professional gain?" If so, "Is not the real connotation of spirituality lost?"

Within Chapter 5 we spoke of 'creating a win/win situation' . . . and if we consider this in line with Figure 5.1, The meaning and purpose of work (see Chapter 5, Section 5.3 Work: Spiritual Drivers and Motivators), where it was suitably determined that there is no one discernible section, or inter-section which spiritual individuals could (mainly) be identified as 'occupy-ing' and so could be pigeon holed into . . . this makes considerable sense, as most people acquire most of their material possessions through working. Although spirituality emphasises that there is more to success than materi-alistic values and attainment and where practices such as mindfulness[6] (it is also worth noting, the selling of mindfulness has become a business in its own right[7]) have failed, now is the time to balance and accept both materi-alistic and spiritual aspirations and integrate them, both, into the *business world*. Spirituality can so comprise within it a set of *interpretive* moral and material practices, which makes this world visible and realistic for all. This 'what's in it for me and what's in it for you' has to start somewhere and it really has to begin now.

6.1 A Breathing Paradigm

Social exchange theory describes relationships as a series of exchanges aimed at balancing rewards—benefits against costs. These relationships are created through repeated exchanges, which both constrain and enable individuals to both influence and exercise power within social structures (Cook & Whitmeyer, 1992). Social structures are viewed as networks of connected social relations between individuals and/or groups (Cook & Whitmeyer, 1992). The fundamental concept of social exchange theory is cost and benefit where, through making comparisons, this drives human behaviour and decision-making. Costs are the negative consequences of a decision such as the amount of time, money and energy required and/or spent, versus the level of/return on investment of achieving a positive out-come. Subsequently, rewards are the positive results of social exchanges. The overall purpose, therefore, is to maximise benefits and minimise costs. Cost benefit also plays a major part in the social exchange process, in determining any associated risks and benefits within economic rela-tionships, where each party has goods or skills which other parties either value or don't. If the costs of the relationship are higher than the rewards, such as when a lot of effort, time or money is put into a relationship and is not reciprocated, this can lead to problems in terms of a return on investment or desired expectation from the transaction. Spirituality within the workplace is often associated with social exchange theory, as it endeavours to provide an explanation of the relationship between job satisfaction and deviant workplace behaviour amongst employees. Minor deviant behaviours include deliberately working slowly, arriving late/leaving early and showing favouritism to others. Serious deviant behaviours include stealing from the organisation, abusing privileges and taking fake sick days to gain some, unauthorised, time off. Servant leadership has long been 'tied' to social exchange theory (Liden, Wayne, Zhao, & Henderson, 2008) but, frankly, it has been largely voided[8] i.e. there is nothing interesting or worthwhile to say about how the servant leaders' behaviour actually influences their followers' well-being or any associated organisational outcomes.

6.1.1 Leadership Theories

According to Clark's (1997) theory of leadership, many leadership theories fall under the domain of philosophy, as they deal with knowledge, beliefs, concepts, attitudes and values mostly in the ways that leaders should treat others (Clark, 1997). Spirituality is also described as a philosophy . . . as it deals with knowledge, beliefs, concepts, attitudes and values, although mostly in the ways that individuals should treat, firstly, themselves and then others.

Leadership styles describe the manner and approach of providing direction, through implementing plans and motivating people (Clark, 2010). Leadership traits describe a person of honourable character. Ethos and leadership designate moving beyond the talk of ethics, by actually displaying core beliefs (Clark, 2010). Motivational leadership allows the needs of *your* team to synchronise with the needs of *your* organisation (Clark, 2004). Leadership through diversity and inclusion creates an atmosphere in which all people feel valued, respected and have the same opportunities as others (Clark, 2004). Change and leadership reshape the organisation in order to meet a rapidly changing world (Clark, 2004). A learning organisation describes the level of performance and improvement which is needed in today's ever-changing environment and is one that requires both full-time and continuous learning (Clark, 2004). Leadership through mentoring involves identifying the different types of mentoring, finding the appropriate mentor and creating a mentorship programme, which suits both the individual and the situation (Clark, 2004).

Through exploring the role of spirituality and the self, Maslow (1964) realised that theories of leadership and motivation weren't adequate for the tasks of today's organisations. There are five categories appertaining to Maslow's Hierarchy of Needs Theory (Maslow & Lewis, 1987). The first level consists of physiological needs; the second level safety needs, especially with regards to failure. The third level is belonging. The fourth level is self-esteem and the fifth level is self-actualisation, which also leads onto and includes self-realisation. These levels describe the pattern through which human motivators generally move and as previously determined, will be successfully influenced by spirituality.

Transformational leadership is a theory of leadership where a leader works with teams to identify needed change, whilst creating a vision to guide the change through inspiration and relevant action, in tandem with committed members of a group. McGregor Burns (1978) defined transformational leadership as 'a process where leaders and their followers continuously raise one another to ever higher levels of morality and motivation'. Transformational leaders are ones that lead by example. This type of transformational leadership is not just expected to be found in leaders and managers, but at all levels of the organisation. Transformational leaders are visionary, inspiring, daring, risk-takers and thoughtful . . . creating a style that encourages, inspires and motivates others to be innovative and create change, which will help to grow and shape future success. Not unlike a sponsor within a Fellowship programme (see Chapter 1, Section 1.8 Introducing: *Paracoaching*). House's (1971) path-goal theory is based upon the employee's effort and performance within the workplace being greatly affected by the leader's behaviour. Here the goal is to increase employees' motivation, empowerment and satisfaction so they become productive members of the organisation. These leaders help group members by clarifying and clearing the paths to the organisational goals, by removing any obstacles which affect their performance. The Path-Goal theory advocates that leadership is not viewed as a position of power, but rather these leaders act as coaches and facilitators to their team members. Not unlike a paracoach (see Chapter 1, Section 1.8 Introducing: *Paracoaching*).

Similar to an Ishikawa diagram, considering all of the previous theories and styles, the construct in Figure 6.1 has been developed and determined for ease of reference, to outline the different areas/steps that will formulate a 21st-century leadership conceptual framework, which may also help to determine which resources are required at specific times to enable this, new found, initiative.

Over time, through adopting spirituality, the individual begins to develop all of the traits contained within Figure 6.1. They may not, initially, know that they are starting to do so and they may not set out with the intention to do so, but they will start to develop them. They may also not be able to (immediately) recognise or academically label them as such, but they will *all* start to manifest themselves, nonetheless, subtly and progressively. Then comes the day when everything starts to come together and becomes readily apparent not only with the individual realising the change and difference within themselves, but also *others* seeing the *it* in terms of improvements in their character, confidence and self-esteem as well! This is attraction rather than promotion—living every day and leading by example. From then onwards, these skills can be even

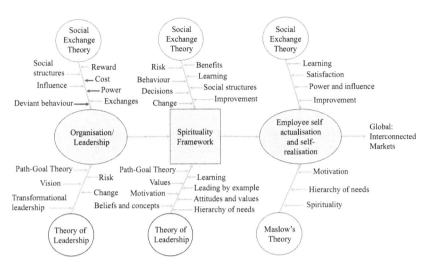

Figure 6.1 21st-century leadership framework.

further developed, strengthened and progressed into whole realms of possibilities and opportunities.

6.2 Bringing *It* All Together

As a reminder, the primary purpose of a business is to fund the costs of operating the business as well as maximising profits; therefore, the employee's role and requirement within that organisation is to complete their work to a fit-for-purpose standard which, in turn, contributes towards the overall business aim. In return for this transaction, the employee receives a wage or salary for undertaking this/their function. This, could be argued, is where the contractual arrangement between the two parties suitably ends! However, every employee is capable of adding more value to the organisation—iron cages and iron laws, or lack of leadership ability and poor management skills must no longer stand in the way of an employee's ability and willingness to contribute, further, to the purpose and intention of the business aim.

To be able to confront any external competitive challenge, inevitably, contemporary organisations must create a work culture—an environment which provides a sense of challenge, purpose and meaningfulness for all. This and in turn will help them, the organisation, to attract, keep and motivate a team of high-performing employees to not only survive amongst the cut and thrust of interconnected markets, but to thrive within them as well.

Going forward, therefore, the questions "How do you involve people?", "How do you convey through others how to build a shared vision?", "How do we reconcile how we work, lead and manage, with an equally powerful desire to grow?" all need to be considered and asked.

EDWARD P.H: "It was just a gradual intervention. After years of doing it the same old way, I adopted a different style where both myself and the group started to gain more and more confidence."

SIMON P: "Setting the standard and being that standard for other people to refer to and work by, ultimately means the work environment can be less stressful and employees go home a lot happier. It also means that everybody will be more productive, because this approach provides the motivation, where everybody's contribution is equally valid."

Levels of motivation respond in conjunction to the organisation's environment, but such motivation may also adapt to it, such as when desire reaches satiation,[9] or diminishes when satisfaction is chronically unavailable (Baumeister, 2016).

Motivation within the workplace is one of the most important topics for both future economic business goals and general well-being. Defining motivation is difficult. Kleinginna and Kleinginna (1981) alone reported and categorised 140 different definitions, including humans being simply motivated to increase pleasure and avoid any pain. For the purpose of workplace motivation, having such strong desires for the material things money can buy the individual is prepared to work long and unsociable hours, which ultimately means having less leisure time and quality in terms of a real meaningful life. Intrinsic motivation takes the form of personal satisfaction, in other words living to work, where work itself is the reward. Separating work from extrinsic reward, in this way, eliminates the motivation for labour and as such, motivation is replaced with compulsion, which equates to business slavery.

Extrinsic motivation removes intrinsic motivation, by rewarding for any work done through working to live via a combination of (and increases of) pay, promotions, bonuses, (better) company cars, insurance benefits and holidays when either meeting or exceeding the expectations *of others*. In relation to incorporating wants and needs, now is the time to balance organisational profit against material and spiritual/individual aspirations and integrate them all into the business world. Experiencing real purpose and meaning, at work, also goes hand-in-hand with pay (monies) and performance reviews to form an equilibrium between all of these sought-after factors. Therefore, any motivational theory framework for future leadership must consist of the components and processes which support and develop both intrinsic and extrinsic motivations.

Through exploring the role of spirituality and the self, Maslow (1964) realised that current leadership and motivation theories weren't adequate for today's organisations' tasks and requirements. Although attempts to link and integrate spirituality into leadership theories have been made much of, both spiritual and management literature suggests—says—what leaders should do and should be, together with must do and must be, which can be highly misleading and off-putting. Therefore, as spirituality is being offered as central to a new organisational framework (see Chapter 6, Section 6.1.1 Leadership theories, Figure 6.1 21st-century leadership framework), then what is required is a totally authentic and unique approach to leadership.

6.3 Transforming Leadership

Leadership and leadership development have been around all through-out the written history of humankind. Some leaders and managers 'rise up' in times of crises and challenges, others in the form of charisma, while others in the form of skills which have been acquired through training, knowledge and experience. Another (and add to, expand upon and amplify these others), leadership type is a process of spiritual forma-tion, through philosophical tenants like 'knowing one-self'. Such leaders become aware of their environment and their limitations and seek to change their behaviour and establish a work-in-progress attitude towards intellectual growth and maturity, for both themselves and others.

No business can function without capable leadership and now, more than ever, a new generation of leadership needs to be encouraged and sought out. These individuals are trusted to manage in a way which relates to the general economic conditions and increasing competition, by encouraging both individual and group capability, whilst also seeking and capturing their willingness to contribute to the required changes and (needed) success of the organisations. As the individual and group are expected to work hard and produce quality products and services, then leading by example is the way forward.

HANNAH H. (MANAGING DIRECTOR): 'It's about the way you treat people, the way you look at the bigger picture . . . I am the bigger picture! When I say 'I am the bigger picture', I mean, specifically, what I do and how it affects everybody else around me. So, it isn't just thinking about what I'm responsible for and how it's going to affect me inter-nally, I also always think about what I'm responsible for and how it's going to effect everyone around me externally and how everything, what I do, ricochets out there."

Good leadership can flow from having a focus on the strategic require-ments of the organisation's aims, ambitions and its customers to hav-ing a pragmatic hands-on delivery. This leadership can bring experience and expertise through group meetings, lead and manage with empathy and warmth, whilst also maintaining a healthy and respectful distance through established boundaries. These leaders can be/are approachable by employees and seek others' valued input and perspective by allowing employees—individuals—to have a voice that matters and is both listened to and is heard. But also to be nobody's fool. There is certainly no room for co-dependency in spirituality, or in business. This means having the courage to set aside emotions whilst making hard decisions and having no desire to have the 'love', approval or validation of others. On that, there is also no room for altruism in spirituality, or in business. Spirituality means having courage, believing in something strongly enough where you will not turn back, regardless of circumstances. There is no room for servant leadership in spirituality, or in business. Spirituality stresses the importance of being human and leading through example; having morals and integrity and good values like empathy, understanding, compassion and knowing good from bad behaviour and right from wrong actions. There is no room for ego in spirituality; keeping it real helps your staff know that you're a human too. Spiritual leadership requires admitting to your mistakes and taking responsibility for things that *you* do wrong whilst also appreciating that other people have bad days and also make mistakes as well. When this authenticity flows throughout leadership, a real transformation of others (also) begins. This is a win which will ultimately facilitate higher levels of organisational commitment and productivity. This is a win which provides not only a salary, but also real meaning and purpose and well-being for the employee—the individual.

RUSSELL W: "You gradually become more morally grounded and more and more authentic."

Being authentic is also to be authoritative.

NICK G: "In the end, I let the local groups lead all the initiatives. As long as it is all going in the right direction, in line with the strategies that the organisation wants to go in and if that's the way they [the group] wants to do it in order to achieve it then fine! That's okay! I would be leading and [*para*]coaching from around the outside and if there was something which wasn't happening, or needed to be done, then I would step in and directly deal with it, in order to get them all back on the right track. Together with gaining more confidence, I also started to be become quite authoritative and learned to start saying 'No!—this is non-negotiable' (see Chapter 2, Section 2.26 Yes vs No!), especially when things had to be done, or go a certain way in line with say governance, or due diligence requirements, or when an unexpected event arises."

Empowering groups through delegation of authority and control and allowing team member participation in the decision-making process of course should be complemented with proper accountability and performance metrics, which have to be, and are, put in place to ensure fairness, whilst also supporting the efficiency and effectiveness of the group.

MICK P.: "Even though I am ultimately accountable by giving them [the operators] the responsibility, authority and control of what they need to do, it is completely theirs—it's not mine; but in my being there, all I do is lead, facilitate and [*para*]coach the process, to guide them, to get them where they need to go to."

MANDY H.: "People get to a point where they know that they can trust me, they know that whatever they say to me is going to be confidential."

PAUL J.: "You have got to trust yourself and then others will start to trust you and then you can start to trust other people. The feedback I get from people says, 'He is easier to do business with now'. That has to be credibility in its own right."

RUSSELL W.: "By giving people the trust, the responsibility, the authority and control of what they need to do and where the quality of listening is there for when they want it, for them to become all what they are capable of becoming."

CLAIRE S.—MANAGER: "I now do 10% of the work and they [the group] do 90% of the work, but actually what we all end up doing is something which is extremely functional, affective and satisfying."

A community without hierarchy is a catalyst for powerful change. Bringing individuals/people/employees together in a judgement-free peer group to discuss change initiatives creates accountability, positive attitudes, responsibility and security. In turn, these individuals and subsequential groups become nimble and creative, with the power to help organisations and each other to progress.

A degree of autonomy is work in which *all* are charged with accomplishing; this creates equality between all employees and links their values and those of the organisation together. This then creates an overall natural and vibrant culture as opposed to an artificial, stifled and imposed one, as Hannah H. expressed.

HANNAH H.: "If you give them the power to do so people will manage themselves, this also makes them feel that they are worthy in any organisation." Additionally . . .

RUSSELL W.: "It gives *me* a huge amount of motivation and great pleasure when I see people make a fundamental change in themselves."

NICK G.: "We are there to do a job, we all know that's what work is—but if you treat everybody equally you gain respect and so more work out of them, which leads to better productivity and so everybody goes home happy!"

Through acquiring this interdisciplinary, spiritual outlook and application which (as previously discussed, debated and determined throughout the previous chapters) not only bridges and encompasses (what is conceded to be needed) the different and isolated streams of thinking and research (Karakas & Sarigollu, 2013), but also (goes right back to [one of], the aims contained within Chapter 1) brings everything together to form the important and relevant, interconnected and connected links; ones that truly form and link relational behaviours, through having a more centred and balanced (sharing of) values. This so achieves a healthy (business) *pathway* between and beginning with and from the 'I' (the individual), to the you (who you actually are—the real *you*), to the we (the connected, but not co-dependent), to the us (the recognised interconnected individual*ism*), to the group (but not emmeshed) collectiv*ism*, to all come back to the *I*, the free-willed, authentic, *Self* . . . to then start over again with the *Self and by the knowing of one's self* to being able to lead by example and so to 'carry the(ir) message' to the 'I', another individual (who may be suffering, lost and/or disillusioned), to then go on to follow the process and progress their lives, who will then, eventually, go onto help another 'I', all in a continuous improvement loop/cycle. Therefore, to further enable this, Figure 6.2 has been constructed to bring the required elements (albeit at a high level, as the devil is, afterall, in the detail) together into one pictorial representation.

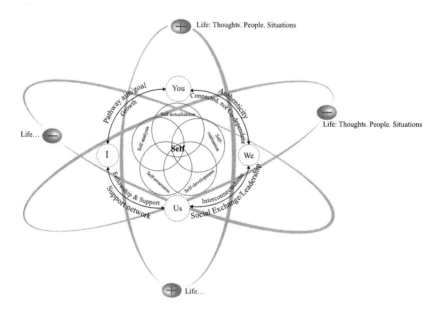

Figure 6.2 Spiritual and leadership conceptual framework.

Additionally . . .

PAULINE H: "Especially when work is stressful, I now make sure that at lunchtime I just go for a walk, just listening and looking at the world around me, just to give my brain a bit of a rest between places."

EDWARD P. H: "When I am feeling a tad stressed, or I'm not focusing properly, just for a few minutes, I simply sit, look out the window . . . look at the sky and breathe in . . ."

JO C: "I will never not be without my spirituality, it's fantastic! I'll come to these companies who have got stressed workers and they'll never have a day off sick again, there's no need to! There's no need to take days off sick—don't be sick—trust me—there are better, brighter and other ways."

STEVEN I: "Stay calm and just look after yourself."

KATHRYN W: "I wish everybody had *it* to conduct their life by."

6.4 Culmination, Prior to Suggestion

Before *we* even start to contemplate spirituality there are the obstacles of denial and excuses, issues and challenges to be overcome, not just for ourselves as individuals, but also within both the academic and corporate/organisational worlds alike, before they can/will even begin to entertain the subject and take the idea of spirituality and its benefits seriously.

This, together with the pre-existing stagnated views of spirituality, has meant that the whole subject area (desperately) wanted and needed a reboot—fresh and creative thinking, together with a new integrative construct . . .

. . . which catered for the individual ("What's in it for me?") as well as for connected and interconnected relationships ("What's in it for them?") as well as recognising and reflecting within it this global trading world and its interconnected markets ("What's in it for us?") and the need for organisations to, both, effectively and affectively operate and survive within them . . .

. . . to this purpose and end, the various elements of Figure 6.2 Transformational Leadership (illustrated above) have been previously and duly debated, then constructed and delivered.

Amongst the various issues and challenges of spirituality in the workplace is the description of its being of a selfish nature. All spiritual support Fellowship members are *specifically* taught to be selfish through their spiritual support programmes. This is significant—in that it is not only a new contribution, but is also directly contradictory to what is primarily the domain of servant leadership and its, steadfast, relation to spirituality. Going further, it was also determined, as spirituality advocates progress rather than perfection, that servant leadership and altruism are not only tantamount to self-abuse, but both are akin to the destructive illness co-dependency. Perfection, servant leadership and altruism are all spiritual super struggles for deluded idealists and have absolutely no place in spirituality.

Another issue which was identified is the experience of great suffering and trauma as being the *starting* point of an individual's spirituality. In relation to leaders and managers, a recurring issue is the growing numbers of dissatisfied workers who are increasingly complaining of bullying, harassment and poor relations which, in turn, are leading to sickness and unplanned absenteeism through workplace suffering and trauma. Complaints of this nature, together with this category of unplanned sickness absence, are both exponentially rising across corporate businesses the world over. All spiritual support participants aspire to function healthily, remove stress and have overall well-being. To enable this, they have learned the importance of 'putting their own oxygen mask on first', before they are able to help others. Spirituality, as is business, is fundamentally all about looking after the *self*. If an organisation doesn't look after itself it ceases to exist. If an individual doesn't look after themselves, they cease to exist. Spirituality is both holistic and integrative and has different gears to suit each individual and organisation alike, so finding the appropriate support vehicle/group/individual is an important beginning (i.e. an important precursor) to the start of the beginning.

Two primary challenges were difficulty in the different ways of defining spirituality, together with the various ways of measuring it. Therefore, together with a real and relevant measure being given as *serenity*, the following new definition was discussed, built and determined: 'Spirituality is an awareness that you are on a pathway that it is expanding and that you are moving into different areas of yourself, so it is really becoming aware of who you are and all of what your potential is' (Broadhurst, 2019, p. 86).

From the very beginning of our, new, way of thinking to the start of our, new, way of doing and through continuing along our, (new), spiritual pathway culminates in a series of events, where both individuals and groups can and will continually stretch themselves, challenge and grow in their capabilities and abilities. As is in life, these situations and events will consist of both good and bad experiences, but both these ups and downs equally contribute to who we are and what we are capable of becoming. It is how we view these different experiences, by accepting the good times with gratitude and enjoyment and the bad times with both courage and (where, if you are going through absolute hell, *for fuck's sake*,[10] don't stop! Keep going through it, or you will just stay there) as only temporary defeat at that particular moment in space and time. For it—spirituality—is, indeed, a steady but progressive pathway which we tread. With serenity, rest assured we do, eventually, come out of defeat and everything else on the other side to be a better, all round, individual—*I*—for it.

A prime benefit of applying spirituality for any individual and within any organisation, is its contribution in the development of both the self and others. An interesting point is Abstraction A, in what seems to be an individual phenomenon, spirituality is, in reality, a holistic phenomenon (Davis, 1971). This is in relationship to individuals who attended spiritual support Fellowships by *speaking directly*—both subjectively and objectively affecting those people around them. Through attending Fellowship support groups and by having and keeping an open mind, sharing, listening and learning (wisdom) from others, of both their pitfalls and successes, theses participants changed their *own* lives through self-help, whilst knowing that they had readily accessible and appropriate support when they required it. Spiritual support participants stress the importance of learning not only that they were human, but accepting that other people were human as well.

This is also interesting, consistent with Abstraction B, that what seems to be a spiritual holistic phenomenon is, in reality, an individual spiritual phenomenon (Davis, 1971). Courage is required as part of the individual's self-help programme/transfiguration, as it is at this stage of their framework and pathway which entails a fundamental reconstruction and (re)testing of the individual's own (sometimes new) core beliefs and values but, as a consequence, this leads to the individual's own brand of authenticity. Authenticity: being human—a view of who *you* really are, built on genuine statements and authentic actions (i.e. the real person and not an artificial construct) which, in turn, inspire trust and confidence in both the *self* and in and from others. In addition, these spiritual support participants didn't speak directly about their spirituality within the public domain, but through displaying their spiritual values and behaviours—subjectively and so *unintentionally*—positively affecting those people around them, through leading by example.

6.5 Virtues

Any economic organisation and social system is only as good as the people within it. Virtues are universal and recognised by all cultures as being the basic qualities of well-being. Virtues support and actively encourage the development of our character, by enabling us to direct our behaviour towards an aim.

Personality is the combination of qualities which form an individual's distinctive character, the individual differences in characteristics and our patterns of thinking, feeling and behaving. A person can have either dominantly good or dominantly bad character traits; however possessing a virtue is a matter of degree (see Chapter 2, Section 2.25 Boundaries). It also makes sense that there is a little bit of bad in good people and a little bit of good in bad people. The opposite of virtue is vice (a behaviour generally considered immoral, sinful, criminal, rude, taboo, depraved and/or degrading), and virtue, as a disposition—moods and attitudes toward the life around us—means having a choice between virtue and vice. This is free will.

The concept of a virtue is of the individual possessing something internally, which makes them feel good. A virtuous person is considered to be morally good, by doing what is right and avoiding what is morally wrong. However, we may also say of this someone that they are generous or honest 'to a fault', so others can and will take advantage of them. Equally, "Would it be right to tell somebody a lie as telling them the truth would significantly 'hurt' them?" "Do we avoid telling another individual the truth as we are aware that they might go into a defensive mode and/or trigger a flying rage (possibly caused by denial on their part, or even ours for that matter) and then they, potentially, seek revenge and/or sulk for a period of time afterwards?" Then we would feel bad about it all (as what we have, after all and in effect, caused this discomfort within them) and then we backtrack on, or apologise for what we have said and/or cave in due to their sulks or threats, in order to 'keep the peace'. "So, is it really worth (the distinct possibility of) falling out over it/something as being the truth and the 'damage' that this may/will cause to our relationship?" We, therefore, have to consider "Does this honest dishonesty—in which we are protecting ourselves and so preventing others from being hurt, whilst we experience uncomfortable protracted silences or any consequential retribution— mean we are being morally good by avoiding what is wrong, or is it *us* being morally wrong by avoiding the truth by not telling them what could, ultimately, be for their own good, regardless of the fallout this may cause?" Consequently, does this avoidance then make us morally bad!? Other individuals can be described as dishonest, self-centred, cheating, lying, greedy, and if these characteristics make these individuals feel good, "Does this make them a virtuous person?" These bad or good traits/virtues (depending upon how *you* view them) are (also) commonly bounded about in regard to describing individuals in business and often go hand-in-hand with the pursuit of bottom-line goals and 'success' (of both the individual in terms career and via the organisation's reportable accounts and/or annual reports), related to profit. The answer to these examples, therefore, appears to lie in a ready acceptance to the ordinary usage of the word 'virtue' and its measure and what it can and actually means.

All organisations can make room for virtues. Virtues incorporate both value and profit creation, which also align and bring together operational integrity and human virtues.

Multi-national corporations are able to frame and link opportunity to a strategy of social virtue and growth through social investment.[11] An interconnected market environment calls for flexibility, responsiveness and adaptability to (connected and interconnected) human needs where, in this context, strategic investment is regarded as a social transaction, that is, a joint venture where the organisation supports, for example, spirituality, with a view to gaining an (honest) financial return and employee effectiveness. Through having a valid input, it is the employees' effectiveness, capability and ability which leads this strategy of value creation and through significantly reduced suffering through stress, the individual's well-being will improve as well. To fully ensure this, it goes without saying, this will also include good governance around the appropriate involvement of decision-making and the (timely) process by which these decisions are implemented. From this, it is envisaged, the role of the (business) leader is to orientate them, the operators/group, towards making, by virtue, profitable business decisions, whilst incorporating and aligning their human values and virtues to achieve them.

It isn't easy to get our out-of-control emotions in harmony with rational thinking, let alone have the recognition for the need for certain, spiritual, action to overcome them. Few people enjoy suffering and trials and tribulations of any sort or kind and we certainly should not and are not expected to within spirituality to 'joyously' *experience* any difficulties and happily 'skip' down the road whilst we are going through them. However, it has to be said that there is something particularly admirable about people who manage to act well when it is especially hard for them to do so. Great big horrible situations require great big necessities which call out for even greater and bigger virtues as well as tru*isms* such as courage, faith, hope, strength of will, perseverance, endurance and maturity as it is from all of these that our true great and big characteristics are formed.

6.6 Nitty Gritty Tru*isms*

Previously stating and describing our negative isms (see Chapter 2, Section 2.18 Nitty Gritty *Isms*) and herby forming our, opposingly termed, nitty gritty tru*isms*, the following traits are an extension to and form part of our Figure 6.1 21st-century leadership framework (see Chapter 6, Section 6.3 Transforming Leadership). Loyalty—a sense of obligation. Sincerity—self-respect and genuineness. Always responding, never reacting to people and situations. Kindness—especially to and including oneself, then to others. Having patience and tolerance—living and letting live. Displaying common courtesy. Having balance and gratitude—laughing and appreciating life. Having and showing integrity and the ultimate tru*ism*—to be true to oneself! To be an authentic and well-being individual, to be ones *Self*. This is the heart of—the building blocks of a, both yours and mine, spiritual framework (see Figure 6.3).

It has been determined spirituality isn't religious, it's a (multi-cultural) philosophy. A vast majority of spiritual people, even atheists and agnostics, replace a belief in a metaphysical God and instead have *their higher power*. For the majority of spiritual Fellowship individuals, their *higher power* is the people who make up *their* spiritual support group . . . the collective wisdom, strength and support which they get from those who have the experience and so have an empathy with them and as such who understand what the individual has truly gone through or is going through. Having awareness

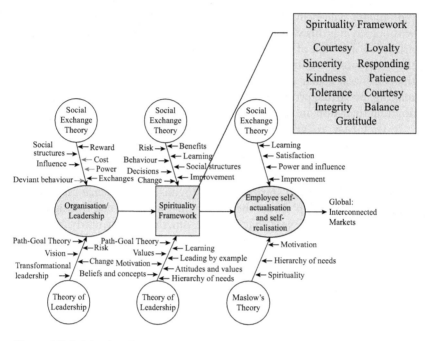

Figure 6.3 Spiritual truisms.

and access to Fellowships and/or dedicated groups are positive additions to the individuals' own spiritual support system (to include a true and good friend and/or sponsor). Many people are not aware of this, or have misconceptions of what these groups, these Fellowships are, what they consist of and who (as in the types/kinds of people) frequents them, even where, in the world or just around the corner, they are located and what they *actually* do within them. These group participants also stress the importance of learning through reading and sharing, so creating overall awareness through the distribution of (organisationally) approved books and (usually) free flyers and pamphlets on the subject of the various Fellowships might, specifically and initially, help in good favour with issues 'closer to home', as when home life suffers work suffers as well. Whilst the distributing of literature is a way of exposing and educating others about what these various groups are and do, as in Step-12 ('tried to carry this message to others and to practice these principles in all our affairs'), they may also serve as a precursor to spreading the benefits of the application of spirituality in the workplace as when work life suffers, home life suffers as well.

This leads into another benefit. As a result of their spiritual values, beliefs and actions, spiritual individuals express that they acquired greater psychological benefits, greater job satisfaction, enhanced empowerment abilities, a better work/home life balance, had less stress and anxiety, which resulted in less (unplanned) time off work from being sick. This is consistent with physical, psychological, personal (selfish-based) well-being being an all-important attribute of this contemporary spirituality. This is evidenced as a positive contribution to all of an individual's issues, supplemented by the establishment of healthy boundaries and having no fear, stress or desire of engaging in conflict with others. However, although the participants brought as much compassion into their work as possible, none 'would (any longer) tolerate being treated like a doormat', or leave their 'vulnerable chin' exposed for others to freely aim at.

By influencing free-thinking and speaking and together with proven and progressive spiritual practices, one recommendation is for the organisation to provide, as stipulated by Heather P., "A place where not everything is doom and gloom . . . a safe and confidential place, to which anybody can go to—to just let off some steam." Further to this, this room can also be utilised to hold types of formatted meetings in accordance with a formal spiritual support system (i.e. utilising a non-hierarchical support system structure) and by adapting their (Fellowship) readily available guidelines around conducting local meetings—within which individuals/groups are considered equals and so they can share freely, listen and learn, regardless of who is attending, on any chosen, consensual topic, or just simply to offload!

In turn, for business purposes, these types of meetings could be extended to work related themes and initiatives, to being facilitated by an appropriate and experienced *paracoach* leader who, in addition, also has the appropriate authority to remove any blockers and to make things happen at work in a timely manner and to a fit-for-purpose quality standard.

Leading from and building upon this, a suggestion would be to empower teams through delegation of authority and control and also allow team member participation in the business/objective decision-making process. This, of course, is complemented with proper and relevant accountability and performance metrics which will ensure fairness, whilst also supporting the, timely, efficiency and effectiveness of the group and to make sure that they were going in the right direction.

In the face of (any) economic downturn and (increased) global competition for companies to survive in this century, this is the time where organisations can no longer afford to ignore, or compromise on human values and their—the individuals'—ability to add value through an innovative approach, such as what spirituality offers. Such personal and professional growth doesn't require a radical personality makeover, just incremental changes in the way we carry ourselves, the way we communicate and the way we interact—this can make a world of difference in how affectively we lead. Following a 'spiritual model', like spiritual support programme Fellowships, will enhance the levels of leading (by example), development and motivational factors, thereby enhancing both known and unknown capabilities—the untapped potential of the individual/others/the workforce.

Further, taking this Fellowship/spiritual support structured approach would also be affective and so benefit the overall level of productivity and

Table 6.1 Suggestions of how to integrate spirituality into an organisation

Suggestion 1	Suggestion 2	Suggestion 3	Suggestion 4	Suggestion 5	Suggestion 6	Suggestion 7
Keep it simple. Keep an open mind. Show positive action, not just empty words.	Create awareness: Obtain and distribute Fellowship—spiritual support programme—literature and contact details.	Be human. Ask self-effacing questions. Be authentic. Display consistent values and virtues and admit when you are wrong.	Lead by example. Develop the human capital through multiplier/ ricochet effect.	Provide a safe and confidential space. You share, you listen! Learn and apply without fear of failure. Measure serenity.	Have and conduct non-hierarchical meetings, where every input is valid. Higher power = wisdom of the group.	Everybody is equal. Remove managers and empower/ trust the team with business initiatives. Employ a paracoach. Have a reciprocal agreement.

improve the overall quality in the organisation's products and services, together with its positioning within interconnected markets and economies alike. This would be accomplished by levering off and utilising interconnected relationships, where the connected employee/individuals positively contribute to their working life and the customer subsequently gains ever more value, leading to both repeats of orders and new business opportunities. In other words, the more the individual and they—everybody—puts in, the more they—everybody—and the individual—will get out.

To enable these benefits, through overcoming denial and finally surpassing any hurdles, a (in the spirit of keeping things simple) summary of the recommendations of how to integrate spirituality within any organisation is provided within Table 6.1.

As with any addiction and/or unhealthy behaviour, spirituality facilitates healthy well-being and good behaviour; but *not* the pursuit of happiness, just the 'priceless gift of serenity' (Al-Anon, 2006, p. 35). Spirituality and serenity not only provides a means upon which an individual can live *their* own daily lives by, but also enables them to be part of their community and their place of work and their home life. It is through the correcting of one's own shortcomings that they will not only improve themselves, but also establish healthy, connected and interconnected, relationships and improve matters when dealing with others. The future of anything, never mind spirituality, cannot be accurately predicted or determined, but we are capable of foresight and we should use it.

Notes

1 Conclusion: the finish, close or last part of something.
2 The terminal point of something in space or time.
3 Chapter 3, Section 3.5, Figure 3.3 The Devil is in the detail, of happiness.
4 If it did, this would be a very short book!
5 The Law of Variation is defined as the difference between an ideal and an actual situation.
6 Mindfulness is a skill: It doesn't come naturally—it requires instruction and practice.
7 Mindfulness-based stress reduction is an eight-week evidence-based programme which offers secular, intensive mindfulness training to assist people with stress, anxiety, depression and pain.
8 Voided: having a section, or area, that has been cut out or omitted.
9 Satiation: To completely satisfy a need, so that you could not have any more and where further increasing the amount of a good thing reduces the worth of each individual unit of it and so it temporarily loses its meaning.
10 Yep! Spiritual people are allowed to swear. Within this context, this word is well associated the world over with emphasising the seriousness of the occasion.
11 Social investment is the use of repayable finance, to help an organisation achieve a social purpose. Social enterprise can use repayable finance to help them increase their impact on society, by growing their business, providing working capital for contract delivery and/or buying assets.

7 Leviticus
Now vs the Best Guesstimate

Predicting the future of spirituality (within the workplace, or otherwise) could be interesting (to say the least) as trying to predict it is considered to be a mortal sin (see Chapter 1 Setting the Scene). The past has gone and predicting the future is in the realms of spiritualism together with its 'spiritualists' (so you can see where the confusion with 'spirituality' comes in?), mediums and mesmerists together with the use of tarot cards, horoscopes and crystal balls, etc. are all definite no-nos! Leviticus 19:31 NIV: 'Do not turn to mediums or seek out spiritists for you will be defiled by them' (The Holy Bible. New International Version, 1988, p. 122). Leviticus 20:27, NIV: 'A man or woman who is a medium, or a spiritist among you, must be put to death' (The Holy Bible. New International Version, 1988, p. 124).

Many people are fascinated by all of this spiritualism and death and thereafter 'stuff', mainly to seek reassurance that there is life after death and/or to 'see' if they have either a bright or foreboding future ahead of them—because they simply 'cannot wait' to know the unknown, of which can never actually be known. Ironically, these individuals are more interested in and fascinated with what *could* happen to them and with death and the *possibility* of a thereafter and *all of these unknowns*, rather than living *this life* and its *possibilities in the now*; as we only have the now to live in—*the known*! Yesterday is history and tomorrow is, certainly, a mystery! Either way and according to Leviticus we would be in danger of committing a mortal sin—treading upon hallowed ground in even trying to predict the future of spirituality (or anything else for that matter), so we need to be very careful within this particular chapter but, then again, spirituality does encourage us to take exciting risks, whilst skilfully avoiding hell . . . !

Sir Isaac Newton is regarded as creating the scientific revolution. Before, Sir Isaac, life was explained through mystics, healers, spiritual teachers, theologians, priests, magicians and storytellers. Short of anything else, these were our guides where we relied upon folklore, wisdom and myths to explain the mysteries of our lives and to provide us with 'data/information' upon which to make *our* informed decisions. Even royalty, in the day, sought the use of these 'mystical' people and their methods. Sometimes, even today, with all what goes on in the world, rather than so-called scientific methodologies, it feels like we are still consulting the rune stones and using haruspicy[1] to predict the future, but that would be ridiculous. . . .

A majority of political parties base their political actions and programmes on ideology. Political ideology comprises of ideals, principles, doctrines and myths appertaining to a social movement, institution, class or a large group of people. Ethics, or moral philosophy, involves concepts of right and wrong behaviour and matters of value. Ideals are a principle or value, propositions which guide behaviour. Doctrines are taught principles, beliefs, teachings or instructions. A myth is folklore consisting of narratives and/or stories which are considered to play a fundamental role in society, the main characters of which are gods, demigods or supernatural humans. Political ideology explains how a society *should* work, whilst also offering a political and cultural blueprint which subscribes to a certain social order. Social order is a fundamental concept which refers to the way the various components of society work together. As a result of say . . . self-isolation and social distancing and . . . common occurrences of job losses, depression amongst the populace, divorces as well as domestic violence, drinking alcohol and drug taking all of which are all significantly increasing. It is safe to say we are not exactly heading to the land of social order Oz anytime soon!

Spirituality advocates that we learn from the past—not stare at and obsess over it—but look at it in the 'rear-view mirror' (see Chapter 2, Section 2.18 Nitty Gritty *Isms*) and that there is only the *now* to be had and so to be considered and lived in. So by basing predictions on both the past and what is happening in the now, perhaps, we can 'get around' the sin proclaimed by Leviticus through thoughtful guesstimate (after all, isn't this what science really does—guess!?), regarding what the future for spirituality could consist of. On that loophole, it's *now* time to sacrifice the chicken and study its entrails!

Death and taxes are the only sure thing in life. They also say that when we die our lives flash before our eyes—"What will yours rerun?" As in co-dependency/servant leadership, will it be *others'* lives and/or your regrets that flash before your eyes!?

The top five regrets of the dying?

- I wish I hadn't worked so hard
- I wish that I had let myself be happier
- I wish I'd had the courage to live a life true to myself, not the life *others* expected of me
- I wish I'd had the courage to express my feelings
- I wish I had stayed in touch with my friends

Any ring a bell?

Tenuously, but unashamedly linking this, the ringing of a bell is also an old Victorian séance way of communicating with the dead. . . .

. . . Against a backdrop of the inside of an old historic house, in the dim parlour we sit around a large round table . . . as Madame Maggie Greening-Smith calls for spirits to appear. Soon, a bell rings! Then someone—or something—knocks, then raps under the wooden table and it slowly starts to tremble and begins to tilt—backwards then forwards . . . and a cold chill of air is felt across the room and everybody shivers. . . . Madame Maggie goes into a trance. . . . "Is there anybody there?" . . . *"Is there anybody there!?"* and surely there is . . . it's . . . *you!* "What will *you* say to the assembled—what would be *your* regrets? What would you tell yourself to stop, or start doing? Do less or more of?" The good news is—it isn't too late to change your answer(s).

By taking this different, off vision, perspective the intention is to (apart from show the difference between spirituality and spiritualism) spark a thought—a thought which can be developed into a different future for yourself. Suffice to say, building upon your past and based upon your choices in the now, the rest of your life should be the best of your life.

By experiencing and going through suffering, through spirituality we learn to not only persevere, but also to significantly increase our resilience. Nobody, spiritual or otherwise, happily 'skips' through any trauma but such is the human spirit, even when going through sheer hell . . . through truly horrendous and tragic situations we also, amazingly, learn and make room to truly change . . . where any adversity breeds innovation!

7.1 Neo-Evolution*ism*

The Black Death (1347–1351) caused the demise of 70–200 million people, but it also led to a change in the ways humans fundamentally think and act. Although catastrophic, the Black Death pandemic marked the end of the late Middle Ages and the beginning of the Renaissance and by that, the start of the modern era. The scale of death and the subsequential economic depression from the Black Death caused a transference from obsession with the afterlife to the realities of existence here on planet Earth. In essence, the Black Death pandemic changed the entire course of European history, for the better. Smallpox is responsible for over a half billion deaths (and it is still a threat to today's civilisation), but it also paved the way for technical instruments such as the microscope, the hypodermic syringe and vaccine initiatives. Spanish flu (1918–1920) infected 500 million people worldwide, but changed attitudes to pave the way for women to enter into medicine and formed what became hygiene-based nursing and medical care. Incidentally, the Romans were obsessed with handwashing and after their departure from Britain the use of soap significantly declined, possibly removing one defence against the Black Death. Sound familiar?

History tells us, after the pandemics of the past, economies rebounded fairly quickly and robustly and as such, over time, employment rose again. Everything and anything, is just temporary defeat.

7.2 The Industrial Revolutions: Surely, the End Game?

The First Industrial Revolution (1760 to 1830) instigated the growth of coal, iron, railroads and the textile industries. The Second Industrial Revolution (1870–1914) oversaw the expansion of electricity, petrol and steel. The Third Industrial Revolution built upon the widespread availability of digital technologies and the rise of electronics, telecommunications and computers. It also opened the doors to space expeditions, research and biotechnology. The Fourth Industrial Revolution was/is driven largely by the convergence of digital biological and physical innovations (i.e. Internet of Things, robotics, virtual reality [VR], 3D printing, genetic engineering and quantum computing and *some* artificial intelligence [AI]).

Believe it or not, The Fifth Industrial Revolution is now upon us! Industrial Revolution 5.0 focuses upon co-operation between employee and machine, where human intelligence works in conjunction with cognitive computing and nanotechnology, to find the optimal balance of efficiency and productivity.

But wait, the excitement doesn't end there! The Industrial Revolution 6.0 consists of more 'good, the bad and the ugly' claptrap but this time *full* AI, along with 5G robots and food replicators. All nicked off Star Trek basically. The 7th Industrial Revolution—molecular engineering and fabrication and . . . on it goes. . . . Incidentally, at which point did you blink and miss Industrial Revolutions 4 and 5 and even know about the 6th and 7th ones!?

This is all well and good but *all* of these *Industrial Revolutions* still (suitably) avoid confronting and solving the real and (still) existing (connected and interconnected) people issues which are inherent amongst all organisations, and regardless of technological promises, organisations still need people—individuals to enable them to function, perhaps now more than ever, if they are even going to survive never mind thrive these, *in the now*, turbulent times and competitive interconnected markets.

At the beginning of the Industrial Revolution (1750) there were 1 billion people living on the planet. Now there are 7.8 billion people. It is not another Industrial Revolution which is needed but an *Industrial Evolution*, an evolution which necessitates for the changing of human nature and the meaning of (inter)connection and (relational) interaction itself. This, self-styled, Industrial Evolution proposes and points to the need for both new ways of thinking and new ways of doing.

Thousands upon thousands of individuals all come together, as employees, to work in organisations in which the employer can know little or nothing about them. Meaningful and constructive communications break down and sub-cultures and cliques are born and formed—this, in turn, breeds mutual ignorance and mutual distrust of one another. These 'us's and them's' have little or no sympathy and want no truck—no dealings with the other—ready to discredit others, (the 'them's'), and be awkward at any given opportunity; thus friction, tension, torsion and stress is created and ever present. This is neither healthy or productive for anyone to even try and operate (or live at home) affectively within.

Considered as never paid enough for what they do these 'us's'—individuals/employees within these companies are desperately unhappy, to not only the point of themselves being sick, stressed and suffering, but also to the point of committing sabotage. Yet they are reluctant—even defiant—to find, apply and so move into other employment elsewhere. This, in any respect, beggars belief. This, together with disjointed and no longer fit-for-purpose leadership and management, with one and all appearing to point the finger of responsibility of the/their problems at the 'others', and rather than sharing the blame and sorting things out together, leads to the question "Is it the very fabric of the organisation, the sweat, the sanity, or the very identity of the self—even all four—that are truly at stake here?"

As spirituality alleviates suffering within the individual's personal life and leaders and mangers are cited as being responsible for suffering at work i.e. within their professional life, doesn't the answer/s to both of these problems seem obvious!? "Why don't we be proactive in significantly reducing, (note, it would be nice to think we could remove suffering but it is an inevitable part of life—part of the being human experience), the prospects of suffering, in our personal lives, from an early age and/or educate future leaders and management (as organisations, even going forward, do and will still need able leadership and management) in spiritual tools and techniques, before we start our intended careers—our professional lives, before the seemingly inevitable happens?" Shamelessly speaking, do we just need to go back for the future?

7.3 The Industrial Evolution = Back for the Future

THERESA F: "The primary school children who I work with can be aged anywhere between the ages of 3 to 11, and especially the younger children have a real sense of right and wrong. If somebody is doing the wrong thing, they will report that person to you very quickly— 'She's not doing that . . . there is something going on over there and you're in charge and you need to be putting it right'."

Additionally *and initially* supported by Rachael D.-S.:

RACHAEL D.-S: "I came into the Fellowship programme when I was 27 and I wish I'd had it from birth type of thing . . . however . . . I wasn't mature enough for it. I wouldn't have accepted it! I wouldn't have understood it!"

From birth to 5 years old—it is readily apparent those first five years of life provide the greatest capacity for learning, together with the sense of reasoning between right and wrong behaviour and conduct; therefore it would make considerable sense to introduce the concept of spirituality to children—*these individuals*—within this age range, as they have the potential to be encouraged and developed into having a better understanding of what *it* is all about and so significantly alleviate their chances of suffering in their future. Many of these children will also have the potential and will subsequently become future leaders and so all of this feels, on the face of it, like a win/win situation for the teaching of the subject of spirituality at an early age!

However, the 'mature enough' together with the 'acceptance and understanding' comments, previously made by Rachael D.-S., have been duly noted and are not lost amidst the following further thoughts for discussion. . . .

Although there does seem to be merit in introducing and teaching spirituality within the *compulsory* educational curriculum, teaching youngsters a way of dealing with (life) issues and situations will, perhaps at best, allow them to avoid the prospects of horrendous suffering whilst, at least, providing them with a means to recognise and mitigate any future unpleasant situations and events. At first glance there appears to be nothing wrong with this; however this intention, although laudable the aim might be, would be open to widespread criticism from all sides of the discussions.

Within any school age and environment, pupils are, in effect, *being made* to sit and listen to lessons, and nobody within a spiritual group is made to either listen and/or learn. They are there because they want to be and importantly, spiritual practices have to be undertaken under the individuals' own free will to do so.

These 'spiritual parameters' or 'Standard Spiritual Operating Procedures', however, are not applicable to Alateen members. For 12- to 17-year-olds, Alateen is a spiritual support programme Fellowship but for children of relatives and friends of alcoholics (so not unlike like Al-Anon—but Al-Anon is for adults) and as such, these attendees are (also) suffering as a result of other people's behaviour and the environment which these people are causing them to live in. However, particularly from the ages of 11 to 16, these individuals are somewhat restricted in their choices, as they cannot just leave where they are (or they can to become, in effect, homeless) due to their age, and they cannot ask the adult alcoholic to leave, because they haven't got the authority to do so—this boils down to either the alcoholic has to die, get sober or the Alateen individual has to learn to cope with this horrific situation, at least until they are old enough to be able to execute a full range of available, their choices. Alateen also follows exactly the same format as all of the other 12-Step Fellowships and as such, these individuals are also free to come and go (from their meeting) as they please, whilst also taking what they like and leaving the rest from what they have heard from the, various, individuals shares, in terms of 'food for thought' and appropriate action for *me*, rather than be given advice as to what *we* should and must do. Also, by default, although they will lead by example in their lives, some of these (young) individuals will also go into leading within an organisation. However, as justified this may seem, this doesn't in anyway encourage a corporate stampede to recruit these truly remarkable individuals who are having to cope with truly horrific situations. Even if it was encouraged to do so, these individuals would be hard to find due to the surrounding anonymity of this (as in all of these) Fellowship.

A compromise, maybe, to not directly being able to recruit Alateen individuals, might be to recruit from universities and business schools, where individuals are older and who might also, possibly, be receptive to the teachings and application of spirituality in both a theoretical and practical sense. These institutions are the principal suppliers of leaders and managers into corporate organisations. Therefore, "Couldn't these establishments be considered as being a suitably 'more mature' place to benchmark and teach spiritual practices as part of a core module?" Afterall, these student participants are not being forced to listen, as their attendance is (also) voluntary and as such they are free to come and go as they choose. The tools and techniques of spirituality would just become part of their career-management toolbox!

However highly educated, individuals can still have a negative mindset and be narrow-minded in the crucial area of thought and application, just as many less-educated individuals can have a positive outlook and a broad-minded approach in the crucial area of thought and application. Additionally, there would still remain the tremendous task of convincing highly influential academics as well as corporate leaders that a different kind of organisational chemistry is needed to progress the spiritual initiative.

RACHEL M: 'It's almost like relearning a language and I do sometimes feel like I've stepped out of one world and into another and my family, friends and colleagues are still in that old world and it's difficult to watch this sometimes, because you want people to have the peace—the serenity—that you get from the programme; but you can't force people. No, they've gotta want to come for themselves."

Rachel M.'s testimonial highlights the difference between (the previously virtually 'underlined') 'compulsory' and 'made to' comments and spirituality—where individuals are free to come and go, through their own free will, to and from their respective spiritual support groups, but, aside from that, although it—spirituality—is free, you cannot give spirituality to somebody, they have got to both want and even need it (funnily enough) for themselves. Neither can you, your self, go backwards in order to help them or, equally, force spirituality onto others.

CHARLOTTE D: "It's like walking across a bridge from a dark place to a light place and you can stand in the light place and encourage them [others] over, but you don't go back to the dark place to fetch them, because you'll just end up staying there."

This all (and no 'perhaps' about it) comes down to a brutal reality of life, that as part of our lives we *simply* have to experience suffering where, paradoxically, this suffering provides us, in many cases, not only with (at least) a grain of learning from these tremendous lessons to be had from these really unpleasant experiences—these horrendous situations—but it is also through the consequential suffering from such that leads us onto seeking spirituality and so our own further learning and (continuous) improvement. Both the bad and good news: the bad news is it is well known that individuals learn more from failure rather than success and as long as they do not give up, we have to go through failure to ensure success. The good news, ironically, is these failures can teach us how to overcome any adversity, which then leads us to moving onto even more future success.

7.4 Moving On

With the arrival of globalisation and (its associated) technology around, almost, every aspect of human life, modern societies and organisations have to extend, grow and function away from being *isolated—cocooned* in their own corporate world and way of doing things, into broadening their horizons—extending their vision into distinct areas of learning how to function, operate, interact and have (healthy) relationships with, not only, other organisations, but also culturally diverse groups, entities and customers, from not just all over the world but also closer to home. This requires learning how to have healthy relationships within their very own internal environments—with their own employees. This breaking through of internal and external boundaries, seeking the required connected and interconnectedness, will affect the role of not just leadership and management as a phenomenon, requirement and a practice, but also the employee themselves, as a phenomenon, requirement and a practice to them as an individual.

With the drive from all sides supporting employees working from home, this is almost like going back to the pre-Industrial Revolution times where a business, service or otherwise is conducted within people's homes. It certainly does appear that what goes around comes around! With many individuals wanting a better work-life balance and blaming leaders and managers for their workplace suffering, "Is the prospect of working from home a viable solution which will solve all of these, previously cited, problem areas once and for all—whilst also overcoming the non-acceptance/acceptance of spirituality?"

7.5 (Work-Life Balance vs Home-Life Balance) vs Spirituality

Reminding ourselves of work absenteeism reason number two, the suffering of stress, depression and anxiety (see Chapter 3, Section 3.7 A Fully Considered Spiritual Measure . . .), the pressures and demands of today's work expectations and 'hardnosed' business environment are a pressing challenge to the lifestyle of a huge number of people. Individuals, *at least*, want to have a *sense* of control over their own lives, to do what they want to do when they want to do it and as such, the answer seems to 'scream' out—either win the lottery, or work from home, which *they think* could be as equally freeing. Although both winning the lottery and working from home could be (initially) considered to be highly worthwhile, both can bring both benefits and challenges. Lottery aside, working from home does, at least, seem to address the main issues which have been highlighted throughout the previous chapters, but does it really?

7.5.1 Pros of Homeworking

When sitting at home in your jammies or onesie all day you are free from the office politics and have minimal interaction with leaders and managers, organisation culture or sub cultures. So far so good. Add in 'specialist workers' who are employed to support the main business hub, together with regular face-to-face get-togethers (higher power) meetings for group strength and support, on the face of it, this *appears* to be *close* to a Fellowship organisational model. But, hastening to add, this organisational model is not a spiritual model. However, the pros of working from home could be considered to be:

- Working from home is *close* (with suitable and realistic add-ons) to a support Fellowship organisational model
- There is little to no management interaction/interference with the employee
- There is a removal of and/or less emphasis on organisational culture
- No destructive sub-cultures exist
- Better/increased Wi-Fi and technology accommodations for working from home
- Fewer costs incurred by both the employee (travelling) and employer (utilities)
- The employer has access to a wider pool of job applicants
- The employee has access to a wider pool of job roles

- Motivation can also be increased, due to the cut in commuting and travelling time, time which can be invested into more 'quality' personal activities
- It is environmentally friendly, due to the reduction in travelling and commuting

7.5.2 Cons of Homeworking

Whilst at least (initially) considering that working from home could be freeing for people who become too stressed at work and/or for those who are also seeking a work-life balance, home working can also significantly increase anxiety and also may not, in the main, be all that it is cracked up to be. Humans are, generally, social beings and are designed to function within groups. Social and professional (and increasing over time) isolation and even solitude—with no workplace camaraderie, no exposure (or involvement in) to interpersonal dramas and the illicit organisational romances—is a stable mate of (remember 'HALT' [see Chapter 5, Section 5.9.2 First Act: Neutral Darkness—Some New Awareness]) and as such, doesn't bode well with individuals *living in their head*. Working from home does not solve the deep-rooted and denied traits—our isms which need to be rooted out of us at an individual level. Working from home is merely a distraction—a sticking plaster (which quickly falls off)—an excuse to the real issues that the individual has. These individuals, as employees, also need to be able to self-motivate and manage themselves every day, as well as ensure proper monitoring of and control over their own work performance and yet they cannot, they fail to self-motivate and address their *own* issues and personal performance, every day.

Many individuals find this self-motivation and performance monitoring difficult, in even setting their own parameters, of knowing what even constitutes good work well done. Yet they do not, at any level, start to consider "Well if it is hard for me to do this for myself, it must be even harder and more difficult for leaders and managers, who also have to motivate and monitor the performance of a multitude and diverse set/team of individuals!?"

Being remote from the workplace, individuals usually feel a sense of guilt with being at home, because they feel a constant need to at least appear to be busy, to justify that they are being productive and so worthy of being at home and employed and being paid to be and do so. However, appearing busy is not the same as actually being busy.[2] We could also be busy fools, not distinguishing and confronting our true dilemmas (See Chapter 5, Section 5.10.2 Part 2: The Truth, Is It so Far Removed?, p. 149). Couple this 'self-induced pressure' with advances in technology, this pressure can be significantly magnified, as employees are all too readily accessible, as they can now be remotely 'seen' and so monitored by their employer. Demand for surveillance software—used to track employees' working hours, (even) keystrokes, mouse movements and websites visited, whether they are logged on or not, 24 hours 7 days a week—is currently 'going through the roof'. Sneakily, this technology can also offer photos of workers taken remotely through their laptop and uploaded for their colleagues to see if they are at their 'desk' and just what they are 'up to'. "So just what could they be up to?"

Popular and well-known online sales auctions' profits are exponentially increasing. Some people are even citing *addiction* to online shopping as a potential cause of this increase—but, either way, addiction or not, the lure is extremely tempting just to have a 'quick' dabble when you are at home all day—with nobody, seemingly, watching! If we avoid this rather cynical 'fact' and surrounding 'big brother' paranoia, employees can, to a certain extent, create their own working schedule. Therefore, if they want to take a three-hour 'break' and (potentially) make up for this time late into the evening/night, or during weekend, they can do so. This is where the lines between a work-life and home-life balance start to become somewhat blurry. Being at home means never being able to leave, physically and mentally, the 'office', as the laptop and mobile/cell phone are always 'calling'; how many times have we said to ourselves and to others (partners at home) "I am just going to have a quick look at my emails"? Then two plus hours later . . . but we can, physically and mentally, leave the office and go home and at least try and switch off from it all—the madness—and at least try and talk to/interact with our cohabitees!

Of course, all of this, from a working-from-home perspective, now becomes highly dependent upon technology, where some parts of the world cannot support the internet speeds, required for this type of 'enriched' communication. We also need to consider not everyone is comfortable with collaborating online, and conflict amongst individuals can become readily apparent. Task conflict is less personal and although not easy, it is easier to deal with than if the problem/issue is an interpersonal one. Interpersonal issues are difficult to resolve, as they can lead to avoidance tactics like logging off, simply ignoring one another, or being deliberately vague in content on, for example, an email. Task-related conflict can often quickly become relationship conflict where, caught in the moment, unedited and brutally honest email exchanges can occur—once written . . . there is no deleting. This can leave the perpetrator with a large portion of regret from acting in haste and they may repent with leisure, which can also often result in disciplinary procedures.

For any worthwhile *employee* this combination of constant watching, justification and their organisation—their employers—their managers requirement to keep tabs on them, can make for a toxic work environment and by extension, for any worthwhile *individual* this combination of constant watching, justification and requirement by the manager, can make for a toxic home environment. Either way, this isn't healthy in any shape or form.

An individual player in a group game, being isolated from others is far from realistic and as previously stated, everything has a cause and effect and everything has a cause and affect!

Separation is a major challenge for living in our heads as well as for building trust, forming positive (connected and interconnected) relationships, maintaining group strength and cohesiveness and positive communication and interaction with others, which also includes the giving and sharing of *needed* hope to each other. Separation also prevents the build-up of empathy—empathy relieves tension and working through a machine does not build real understanding of either ourselves or of others.

All of these factors and together with our tru*isms* (see Chapter 6, Section 6.6 Nitty Gritty Tru*isms*) being components of spirituality, then all act as ingredients to our own brand of authenticity . . . our uniqueness, our ability to communicate face to face coherently and affectively, rather than using 'lols', 'amazeballs', 'awks', 'l8ters' and/or conveying our desires with images of 'peaches' and 'aubergines'—apparently— whatever they mean! All curses on the language which we speak,[3] but if this is the reality of the now (and in the spirit of keeping an open mind), is there going to be an app, or a demand for one in the future, for all of the required *it* in spiri*t*uality?

7.6 Is There An App for *It*?

Technology has brought us closer to each other in terms of geographics and by blurring/stripping all the time zones away, so making it easier (or harder in some cases—remember Paul J. who previously stated: "My boss, at that point in time, was in the USA and he was always calling net meetings at 8 o'clock at night, because this was 2 o'clock in the afternoon to him") to communicate with one another. It can also drive us further apart in terms of human/emotional relational contact (i.e. concerning the way in which two or more people, or things are connected). As humans we value our individuality and how we relate to others, but being connected to someone through a machine is not the same as being connected and interactive in someone's actual physical presence. Namely . . .

- When technology breaks down, it cuts off all interface with the outside (business) world
- It is difficult to monitor both our own and others' performance
- *We* cn be spied upon 24/7
- It causes a significant decrease in staff integration
- It becomes difficult to self motivate and to consistently perform
- It is more difficult to solve problems, especially interpersonal ones— being online may even exaggerate them

- There are more distractions at home than, previously, thought of—so productivity and concentration levels may drop.
- You never leave work; staying at home will mean that you will never leave the 'office', making it (even) more difficult for *you* to 'switch-off' from work as it is always present and around you via the laptop and/or mobile/cell phone. This may increase your overall worry and stress levels
- Those working from home are not likely to be promoted as much as their office-based colleagues are
- Not every job can allow for working from home, for example, nurses, teachers, production and manufacturing personnel, etc.
- Individuals are also more likely to feel isolated and lonely
- Working from home does not produce a work-life balance
- Working from home does not solve the root-cause issues of individual suffering and misery—it may even exacerbate them
- Working from home does not help group empathy and cohesiveness, or spiritual tru*isms*

The Mental Health Foundation is concerned that a significant and sizeable group of people are neglecting the factors in their lives which make them resilient or resistant to mental health problems. Suffice to say, working from home and mental health (and spirituality aside for the moment) do not look like (and balancing the pros with the cons) too good a combination. In this instance, organisations who are striving towards achieving a successful, global-level, interconnected market also have to examine this, working from home, requirement at a more granular—local—level and of course, vice versa. In other words, achieving an interconnected market becomes a struggle for achieving not just *interconnected employees* on a *global* scale—but also *interconnected individuals* at a *local* level, who can and will connect to not just each other, through shared values and aims, but also to their own organisation, together with its values, as well as its intentions and purpose for being (i.e. to cover its costs and to make a profit) and an individual working from home does not support this. Although, from an organisation perspective, the requirement and quest for profit through interconnectedness and connectedness is completely understandable and reasonable and spirituality certainly supports this; this is assuming and depending upon the whole being greater than the sum of its parts, where on one hand it is and the other—it isn't!

GENERALISATION B: What seems to be a general global phenomenon is in reality a local phenomenon (Davis, 1971).

'Weak' individuals are weak individuals as they—we, as in all individuals—are flawed on any one given level (see Chapter 4, Section 4.2 Organisational Culture) and as an organisation is only as strong as its weakest link, it therefore makes sense that the organisation is—it must be—

considerably weak at a multiple, individual, level. In turn, these flawed weaknesses are also magnified with regard to all of these, multitudinous, individuals working from home as, by default, they are isolated and so are not and never will be part of any overall group strength so, again spirituality aside, this alone doesn't positively support the lone individual working from home debate.

Considering that these existing (natural) flaws are inherent weakness which are in the *me*, then these weaknesses have to be and are the root cause of the problem(s) which have to be recognised and addressed in order to trigger off the beginning of the change of the 'I' at the individual level, before any successful solution, whether it be personal or professional, can be reached in any given objective, aim and/or goal undertaken by the 'us' (i.e. the organisation). However, by *beginning* with the 'I' means overcoming denial, and having and keeping an open mind (and this is where spirituality comes in) means being able to recognise these change requirements, both on a personal and a professional level, as being the necessary precursors to the *start* of the solution (i.e. to themselves—ourselves becoming the *authentic Individual*—the *Self*). This denial and lack of an open mind makes, regardless whether the employee works from home or not, achieving organisation connectedness and interconnectedness even more difficult in achieving the '*us*'—*the all in it together* mantra, if we cannot get the *pathway* from the 'I' to the 'you' and to the 'we' right in the first instance. To this, this further confirms and makes the case for spirituality being ultimately all about the *selfish me* (in order to achieve—the *I*—the authentic *Self*) even more significant and relevant if we are to achieve stability within any turbulent environment and/or suffering relationship. This is where the spiritual framework comes in (see Chapter 6 Section 6.3, Figure 6.2: Spiritual and leadership conceptual framework), which has been designed with the intention to be able to identify both weakness and strengths and so bridge the gap/s—through targeted and supported action—to form the effective, healthy, relational links between the 'I' to the you—to the we—to the us—to then come back to the *I*, before starting again with the 'I', both at a local and on a global level.

GENERALISATION A: What seems to be a local phenomenon is in reality a general global phenomenon (Davis, 1971).

The whole is greater than the sum of its parts; this means that a group of people is considered to be better together, because the way they come together adds a different quality and strength to the overall offering and requirement of an initiative. This is the essence of teamwork.

Further to this, when *you* are truly suffering, when *we* are truly at our wits' end, *you* are prepared to literally do *anything* that is required (see Chapter 2, Section 2.14 Why Find the Spiritual '*It*' . . .) to set yourself free from it. Sharing a common aim, spiritual support groups can be found at a local level, close to home when the individuals want it, but also these individual 'local groups' are a successful, global phenomenon spread all across the world, so anybody anywhere can physically (and mentally) be within reach of one 24 hours a day/365 days a year. These groups provide empathy, understanding and camaraderie, where the individual is not alone in what they are going through and experiencing. As humans we want this central message, a message that also calls for a need in social cohesion and unity i.e. we are all in it together.

There are over 50 *existing* 12-Step Fellowship groups and in the very near future, with the appropriate awareness, these will become frequented with many, many more people—individuals seeking help to alleviate their suffering. This suffering will, in turn and with no doubt, negatively affect both the individuals' home and work lives in equal measures. Also, for many of these individuals, even though spirituality is a 'local' self-help initiative, their higher power (see Chapter 1, Section 1.7 Higher Power) is the support and strength which they receive from their 'local/global' Fellowship/group. Subsequently, organisations need to recognise this local and global balancing act and encourage and facilitate, as previously discussed (see Chapter 6, particularly Section 6.6 Nitty Gritty Tru*isms*), a similar, bespoke, internal model, together with a supported external awareness and/or attendance within a Fellowship support group, in an effort to get the spiritual ball rolling.

Predicted *future* Fellowship support groups are envisaged and will exist for (and is now very much teetering on the edge of) is addiction to technology, including mobile/cell phone addiction, which is ideally reflected in the use of them still being used whilst driving—still a frightening trend, despite the increasing consequences associated to this illegality—and walking, seemingly forever hunched over their phones all of the time regardless of where or when. This, together with social media addiction (in some part driven by the desire for 'likes'), including online dating, gaming, auctions and shopping addictions are all potentially, readily primed, problem areas to our psyches. Perhaps, (persuaded and driven by accumulating and so gaining validation from 'likes'), social media has so much influence on us, (it even makes us panic-buy alcohol and stockpile toilet roll and instant, pot/cup, noodles in case of an impending, virus related, Armageddon), which is sheer madness when you think about it!? This, and together with being significantly (mentally) disturbed by other people 'unfriending', trolling[4] and on-line bullying us, and rather than 'just' quit social media, are ideal examples of the power of addiction . . . to negative communication and unhealthy disruption . . . to both our rationale thinking and actual constructive doing. Suffice to say, in the main, technology, our laptops and our phones, now rules our irrational thinking—our negative *ism* emotions and dictates our everyday 'abnormal' practices – with an increasing, and accepted as being completely normal, frightening effect and affect on us as individuals'. <u>This is addiction in its purest form!</u>

As with any and all addictions, addiction to technology begins with and satisfies a want—a 'tool' of convenience to obtain necessities, but ends in vanity and the need for validation, which altogether soon becomes a slippery slope of indulgence, which only provides a quick and temporary fix of feeling good, but a longer-term affect of negativity but, as with any addiction, enough is never enough!

People do bond on weakness (see Chapter 4, Section 4.1.2 'Us and Them' Now Becomes 'Us' vs 'Them') and spiritual support groups recognise this. In spiritual terms, these groups are deemed to be a higher power—a, physical, gathering of people consisting of empathy, strength, support and hope to enable individuals to become stronger, within their own right and time.

With the preference being to physically attend these Fellowships groups, so the benefits of warmth and nuances are experienced—appreciated and gained directly by the attendee. As remote technology, together with its associated content and apps, is determined to be the next great addiction, then technology and spirituality and support groups as a combination, therefore, do not fit the spiritual remit. This is because, although technology addiction will be an issue for some individuals, just as somebody who is suffering from an addiction to sex (Sexaholics Anonymous) wouldn't attend, for example, a spiritual support group meeting specifically for a gambling addiction (Gamblers Anonymous), these tech addicts wouldn't (and couldn't) attend an online meeting. If they did it would be rather ironic and counterproductive to their recovery, if attending an online support meeting is a solution to their online/tech addiction! It would be like Alcoholics Anonymous holding a meeting in a pub/bar, it just wouldn't happen, as, the metaphor goes, if you sit in a barber's/hairdresser's chair long enough at some point in time you're going to 'want a haircut!'

For others, as opposed to online meetings of any kind (as you cannot beat, as previously discussed, direct physical and mental group interaction), perhaps the advent of VR (i.e. a computer-generated simulation of an environment like a virtual 'room' which can be interacted within, in a seemingly real or physical way) would, partly, fit the bill. There is also a lot to be said for attending a meeting/s outside of your own 'home group' (a home group is termed as the one which you frequent the most); say, for example, if you live in Macclesfield England and this is your *physically attended* home group, there would be nothing to stop you from also *virtually attending* a meeting in Macclesfield North Carolina in the United States of America ("How cool would that be!?"). This/any Fellowship virtual experience would still consist of the same warm welcome, (but without the coffee/tea or nuances), common ground and format of your 'home' group Fellowship meeting, but also has the advantage of increasing both diversity, together with a more enhanced experience and understanding for the participant/s, as a result of new blood amongst them as, understandably, different individuals and groups will share different experiences and fresh perspectives on the subject matter, which provides even more richness and depth for the individual/s to (further) consider. This all helps in furthering *your* understanding of spirituality, whilst also stretching the elasticity of taking what you like and leaving the rest. Although, rest assured, as both time and progress are forthcoming and by keeping an open mind we do, eventually, start to examine why we 'don't like the rest' and whether we are being too judgemental—even considering if we are *denying* what we don't like and its actual applicability to us. Thus, we can then start to develop these thoughts into potential areas to further explore and progress into. Brilliant! Regardless, there is really no substitute for direct effectiveness with regards to attending the real thing (i.e. actually walking into a group meeting and appreciating all of the nuances which are contained within them).

Without exception, spirituality is applicable and affective the world over and across all of the social classes; however, within any gathering of humans, there must be a certain amount of (atomic level) chemistry and behavioural traits that brings individuals together to form a group (see Chapter 3, Section 3.4 All Sorts Attract All Sorts). Amongst this 'soup' of required spiritual group/individual ingredients is the development of trust and acceptance of others. This means constructive interaction with those that you both like and dislike, accepting that we are all different and displaying tolerance and understanding towards them. This doesn't mean that we actually have to like, or love, everybody and anybody, but we have to deal with both the like and dislike through creating boundaries and not simply logging off, sending (regrettable) emails, ignoring others and falling out and arguing with them—this behaviour, particularly, does not bode well in the workplace . . .

. . . if we want to achieve healthy connectedness and interconnectedness between us.

Spiritual traits can only be forged through interaction, awareness, realisation and action, which are further honed through our own experience and application. Through technology, this interaction, awareness and realisation is certainly being lost, and particularly, through text messaging, we are also losing the art of conversation and articulation. "How many people do you see walking—looking down at their phones not watching where they are going, or simply not looking/showing an interest at the world around them?" "How many friends and families, 'loved ones' all together, do you see either on 'holiday', or in a pub/bar, or in a restaurant not talking to each other but just on their mobile/cell phones (and probably just complaining, amongst themselves and to the establishment, about signal strength—vowing to never go back to that place ever again)? This, it seems, is all somewhat shockingly common and somewhat disturbing in occurrence!" With this steadily increasing fixation to technology, rich, interesting verbal communication and both subtle and not-so-subtle nuances that go with good conversation are all being lost in translation, dispersed across the airwaves. Actually meeting people face to face and talking to them cannot be beaten in any shape or form. "How good it is to actually meet people and see the whites of their eyes?" This way you can learn about their habits and (sometimes annoying) quirks and read their non-verbal cues, ticks and body language; after all "Isn't 55/65% of affective communication considered to be non-verbal?" This is the very stuff—the very fabric—the very subtleties and abilities which drive the very function of spiritual support groups. Technology, therefore, will either kill all of the Fellowships stone dead, or cause a resurgence in them, where all of the safe money is on the latter!

Technology has its place in the world order and is great for what it does and can do, but lousy at what it can't do, which is replace human interaction and connectedness. Without this human element, the/any strategic initiative will fail. Technology will, no doubt, play an important part in the organisational strategy of formulating *part of* today's interconnected markets, but it will not solve the undercurrent and (generally strategically ignored) *part of the problem* of connected and interconnected relationship alliances. Rather than grasp and address the real people issues, organisations are groping around for 'easier' off-the-shelf technical solutions to try and bypass the root causes around the distinct lack of skills and abilities of their leadership and management and around the lacking engagement, well-being and motivation of their employees taboot.[5] A strategic sticking plaster isn't the answer, as plasters tend to come off very quickly, once again, allowing picking as if at a scab and so exposing the raw wounds of suffering in the future.

7.7 The Future of Spirituality—Is in the *Now*

It would be very easy to fall into the (various) Industrial Revolutions' '(clap-)trap', in predicting all sorts of weird and wonderful directions which spirituality could go in—in the future, however, spirituality advocates both keeping it simple and living in the now. The now is particularly apt, with the need to sort out what is wrong in the now due to the complexity of our nitty gritty isms (see Chapter 2, Section 2.18 Nitty Gritty *Isms*), which are stubbornly central and entrenched within our complex minds. As even spiritual support Fellowships consist of a very simple programme—after all, there are only 12 Steps—spirituality has to be simple for us complex individuals to easily understand and follow. This enables us to both recover effectively and move forward, into the future, with confidence, one step at a time.

The effort to which *you* both want and need to apply to spirituality is an active choice, as the amount of effort that is invested into spirituality has a direct impact upon the return on investment—the results which you will achieve from it. In effect, this is cause and affect! Alongside playing to (and building upon) our strengths, we also have to actively work on our weakness—our negative behaviour and attitudes which we find hard to acknowledge and accept; not acknowledging them is denial, whilst accepting them is change readiness. Learning to adjust and overcome our various isms requires positive action, in other words change for and within *our-selves*—not change for and within others. This is cause and effect. Para-doxically, positive change doesn't guarantee the avoidance of failure, or even the guarantee of success, but within spirituality, we do acquire a dif-ferent way of thinking and gratitude from all events and situations, which we may/will find our future selves in. This change of attitude requires courage, in accepting success with a "Yippee!" but without any associ-ated arrogance and ego, and any failure as *just* temporary defeat. Courage, because our admission of vulnerability helps us to recognise and address our failings and failures, and we are grateful to do this, by recognising that we are being given the opportunity to address them—so becoming a better, more authentic individual. This courage and mindset, together with the substance of what *you* do in relation to the results which *you* deliver, is fundamental to the growth within your self and today's economy and society in which we all live and work. Working your spiritual programme by stretching yourself and taking exciting risks will no doubt set you on a—*your*—pathway to a different realm of *unknown*, not *expected*, success. Any success is proportionate, to not only the effort that is put in but also to the results which you get out of it, so you are not just *appearing* to be successful but you *are actually being* successful.

Spirituality is about stepping into the unknown and creating condi-tions which don't yet exist. Leaders envision a better future for their peo-ple which doesn't yet exist; where these people—these individuals—in turn either do not or can choose to not (i.e. ignore) recognise and under-stand this vision of the future. As a consequence, a leader within the workplace faces considerable resistance along the way to achieving their vison—their intention of success for all.

To treat individuals' motivations, requirements and outcomes in their entirety means understanding and responding to both their material and immaterial needs. It is, therefore, proposed that the 'best' vision for success is a balance between outward-facing materialism and inward serenity—knowing that all is well. This balance between material and non-mate-rialistic values and virtues must be real enough to provide a basis upon which individuals can and will be able to construct a coherent identity for themselves and furnish some solid motivation for action; only then will a satisfactory outcome occur. Of course, distinguishing between actual moti-vations, actual reasons and actual outcomes is even more difficult.

Some businesses, employees and individuals, in the main, dwell in and maybe even (secretly) 'enjoy' working and living—thrashing—around in chaos, but have, so far, 'skilfully', avoided enjoying and thriving in personal and professional challenge and change. Now the time has come to distinguish between the status quo, wishful fantasy, unforeseen woe and future progress.

We find ourselves in a new—economic, interconnected and connected—age, where employees tend to keep quiet through fear of losing their wage packet, and (turbulent) economics is used by employers to keep people in this fear and as such in 'their place', where this 'place' causes individuals to be unhappy, both at home and at their place of work. This is no longer fit for today's lifestyle and purpose. Whilst yielding tangible benefits and (perceived) success to at least some individuals and employers, organisations are facing tremendous challenges consisting of pandemics, political changes, volatile global markets, privatisation, vulnerability of their supply chains, cold wars and political tensions, reduced investment levels, shrunken markets, stalled emerging markets, advancing technologies (cyber-attacks, mass redundancies), whilst also trying to achieve social growth. Individuals, employees, leadership and management alike must awaken to and learn to take responsibility for required change, flexibility and adaptability to these, whether unexpected or expected, events, situations and circumstances in not just work, but in all areas of their—*our*—lives!

It is now important, more than ever, to distinguish between challenges that are true dilemmas of competing within the corporate world and those choices, behaviours and attitudes which are understood to be right and those which are equally understood to be wrong. Then we must refrain from anything or anybody avoiding or contradicting a positive choice of action in achieving a vision of success for ourselves. These negative, *individual*, blockers, after all attempts have been made and have failed, must be removed from the process. This is part of spirituality, keeping what is needed and removing what is no longer fit for purpose.

The failure of business leaders to navigate this moral territory may exacerbate the ever-deepening dangers of widespread workplace suffering; however leaders who allow you to learn from failure are those who are keen for you to grow. These *true* leaders are sponsors—ones who guide and encourage you through the worst experiences of failure—in your career—without holding one mistake, or major error as a negative judgement or grudge against you for the rest of your career.

Rethinking business correlates to rethinking leadership and no business can function without capable and able leadership. The future undoubtably belongs to a different kind of person, to not only lead and manage, but also to join all of the dots up. This person balances the need for a business to function in order to make a healthy profit, with that of the health and the function of the employees. This requirement is enabled by delivering balanced immaterial and material—intrinsic and extrinsic reward—which is applicable and relevant to the individual/employee. To enable this innovativeness to thrive in their organisations, leaders will have to develop a *fearless* culture, which will support adaptation and allow for both creativity and the individual/employee to grow. Meeting such a challenge requires a change in attitude and approach towards lifelong learning, alertness and good conduct, not just by the few but by the many, 'Many' as the all wouldn't be possible, as there is always one! This can be achieved through *paracoaching*, where an individual, who has a well-built subconscious, knows how to lead within the organisation and manage both the strength of a group and its contained 'weaker' individuals within it, by responding and certainly not reacting to both the inside and outside environments and their associated benefits and challenges, all within a well-maintained natural culture. Employee empowerment, within this natural culture, will allow those members to take ownership of their part of the organisation's initiative and through their participation within a focused and strong group, (start to) feel, form and build confidence and trust and so be motivated and be committed to the goals and objectives which they have both set themselves, as well as that of the group's requirements and by extension, that of the strategic aims and so success of the organisation. This empowerment will only require the leader's attention for guidance and direction in critical situations. The leader will have also gained the appropriate authority and respect to remove (as, again, there is always one!) any individuals and/or blockers to make sure things happen in a timely manner and to ensure a fit-for-purpose quality standard is continuously strived for and maintained by all of the remaining employees.

Spirituality is about attraction rather than promotion and as such, this book is not, crudely or otherwise, attempting some sort of evangelism as, in all instances, anything that an individual either chooses to do or doesn't do, all boils down to their free will.

Free will and progress is fast and loose when applied to the material world, but is painfully slow when applied to the business world and even slower, even non-existant, to our own behaviours, habits, attitudes and desires. 'Self-education is a life-long affair. There cannot be mental atrophy in any person who continues to observe, to remember what he observes and to seek answers for his unceasing how's and why's about things' (Dr Alexander Graham Bell [1847–1922]).

Being quick to sign up for professional education (especially if the organisation is paying for it) as, after all, it looks good—great—on the CV or resume and keeps us ever ready for our next career move or job change. But our own personal development, where there is no certificate or graduation ceremony to be had, is very little thought of; however, the overall value (and investment in) of our personal development is invaluable!

Leaving the individual/employee to be free to undertake their own self-discovery and determine their own boundaries and development is, indeed, a lifelong affair. Self-discovery and development are a way for individuals to assess their own skills and qualities and so to consider their, own, aims in life. This, in turn, allows them to set themselves goals in order to realise and maximise their potential and this should—must—be encouraged, for the benefit of all, by leading through example and via the multiplier/ricochet affect. Within this positive environment they—no *you*—can plan to make relevant, positive and effective life choices and decisions for *your* future aims as, never forget, you are empowered to do whatever you want to do. The choices are all yours: Stay in the situation you are in. Remove yourself from the situation, or remove the situation from you, or have courage to change your own situation. *Personal development* covers activities which improve awareness, as well as identifies and *develops* your talent and potential. Professional development builds human capital, together with both your own and others' talent and potential, which, in turn, facilitates employability; where both combined leads to meaningful and purposeful work; which also satisfies the very existence of the organisation and its intention to make a profit; which will, all in all, deliver an enhanced quality of overall life; which all contributes to the realisation of, *nearly everybody's* dreams and aspirations. This is making sense so far, so "What is stopping all of this from happening?"

'*Nearly everybody's*'—as (and despite having dreams and aspirations) when approaching any change, people will only measure what they will lose, even the bad stuff and not what they will gain by letting things go. This is particularly prevalent when it comes to money. Money can only, at best, buy temporary happiness and yet most people continuously try to plug the empty gaps appertaining to 'fixing' their emotional state by accumulating more and more money and spending it accordingly. This is what they think achieving actual happiness means within their lives, by them having and 'throwing' money at material aims and gains and most individuals, sadly, die without ever achieving any happiness, or even contentment. We cannot 'buy' a life and death offers no refunds on our purchases; we also cannot take money with us when we die as there are no pockets in shrouds and there aren't many tombstones with the word 'success' and £, $ or ¥ written on them.

Within this life, a shift in our mindset will change all that . . . spirituality encourages you to throw all of your sceptical (stinking-thinking) thoughts into a metaphorical box and either throw the box away completely or, if that is a step too far, put the 'box' into your 'loft or garage', but either way the intention is to free yourself from *dis-ease*. *Now* is the time to take stock of ourselves and prepare whole-heartedly, without despair or undue worry, for an exciting and positive future, where instead of "It's all or nothing," try "I will make a balance in my life." The 'priceless gift of serenity' (Al-Anon, 2006, p. 35) is free and permanent to all who care to want and *find it*, together with the appropriate support, on their/your doorstep, for those who *need it*. This is the required action!

Aside from this book's objective to shine a fresher, better and more practical perspective on what spirituality both is and isn't—and in doing so bringing everything together to build a new . . . spiritual framework, a conceptual model which truly links the 'I' right through to the *I* (see Chapter 6, Section 6.2 Bringing *It* All Together), together with a realistic definition (see Chapter 3, Section 3.2 A Fully Considered Spiritual Definition . . .) and an apt spiritual measure (see Chapter 3, Section 3.7 A Fully Considered Spiritual Measure . . .)—from the very beginning the intention and aim of this endeavoured script was—is—to, at the very least, create a spark of interest in this fascinating subject. If it has achieved any of this, even for just *you* dear reader, then this is the beginning of the start to the future. At best it has, significantly and realistically, moved the whole subject of spirituality forward, by converting *it* into a manual for further thought against a progressive framework which, together with the appropriate and practical action, can be used as a tool for surviva*lism*, well-being, sustainability and growth, in all areas, of not just an organisation and their associated interconnected markets, but also in overall life, a life which can be developed into a different, connected and successful future for *your self*.

Life isn't about how we can 'take all of the punches', (on our vulnerable chin), which everyday living throws at us, it's about learning to 'duck' from them when we can and where we can't fall over, get back up (before we are 'counted as out'), wonder "what the hell just happened!", dust ourselves off and keep moving forward—learning and progressing one step at a time. This is the action for the now, to ensure the future. Suffice to say, the past is history and from this moment on, the rest of your life is endeavouring to be the best (but not perfect) version of yourself and so to be considered as going to be the most successful and serene that it has ever been before. This is spirituality!

Finally, with nothing to lose and everything to gain, always remember life and any associated thinking, action and the success and serenity that go with it, are all about how you handle *your* Plan B!

Sincere and best wishes to you and thank you for both contemplating and reading my efforts. Steve.

Notes

1 The study and divination of (sacrificed) animal entrails for the purpose of seeking/attempting to foretell events and/or obtain (hidden) knowledge of the future or the unknown, by supernatural means.
2 Busy fool: Avoiding difficult things by occupying oneself with trivial things. To deal with urgent trivia instead of what's really important i.e. True dilemmas. Keeping busy in this way allows us to avoid having to make important decisions.
3 Although, to be fair, language has been generally diluted and has suitably evolved to include all types of speech over history and influences through social settings.
4 Trolling: Creating discord by starting quarrels or upsetting people by posting inflammatory or off-topic messages on an online community. A social media troll is someone who purposely says something controversial in order to get a rise out of other users.
5 Taboot: meaning as well as; the presence of something.

Appendix

Appendix A
Participant demographics

Interviewee/ Identifier	Age	Gender	Highest Academic Qualification	Organisation/ Department	Direct/ In-directs	Spiritual	Religious	12-Step
Simon P.	41–50	Male	PhD in Organic Chemistry	Senior Scientist Researcher: Global Pharmaceutical Company, Analytical Department	3	No	No	Yes
Paul J.	51–60	Male	Advanced Diploma	Director: Major Global Oil and Gas organisation	None	Yes	Yes*	Yes
Edward P.H.	51–60	Male	Diploma	Director/ Contractor: Business Coach and Mentor	None	Yes	Yes	No
Heather P.	31–40	Female	GCSE's	Managing Director/ Owner: Drainage Company	22	Yes	No****	Yes
Judith K.	31–40	Female	A level's	Project Manager: Global Engineering Consultants	12	Yes	No	No
Steven I.	51–60	Male	Post Graduate, DMS	Independent Consultant: Prestige Motor Co., B*** M******	None	Yes	No	Yes
Gemma H.	41–50	Female	Masters in Leisure Management	2 Directorships: Sports and Neuro rehab	9+	Yes	Yes***	Yes

Name	Age	Gender	Qualification	Job				
Josephine B.	41–50	Female	Degree: BA Hons in Youth studies	Higher level Teaching Assistant: Secondary School	1+	Yes	No	Yes
Charlotte D.	31–40	Female	Degree in Health and Social Care	Managing Director: Sub Post Office	4	Yes	No	No
Rachel M.	31–40	Female	Degree in Business Management	Care Assistant: UK National Care Home Organisation	None	Yes	No****	Yes
Robert A. G.	51–60	Male	HNC Mechanical Engineering	Director: LOT Aero Services Ltd.	2	Yes	No	No
Laurence W.	31–40	Male	CEng	Account Manager: Engineering recruitment consultancy	1+	Yes	No	No
Sarah H.	41–50	Female	Post Graduate Diploma in Law	Solicitor and Legal Counsel	3+	Yes	No	No
Joanna B	41–50	Female	Associate degree in nursing	Director/ Owner: Private Medical Clinic	6	Yes	No	No
Hannah H.	41–50	Female	BA Honours in Communication Media	Managing Director/ Owner: Digital Marketing Company	4+	Yes	No	Ex
Jannine B.	31–40	Female	Degree in fine art	Independent Artist	None	Yes	No****	Ex
Shelton D.	41–50	Male	Degree in Psychology	Sales Assistant: Major UK Supermarket	None	Yes	No	Yes

(Continued)

Interviewee' Identifier	Age	Gender	Highest Academic Qualification	Organisation/ Department	Direct/ In-directs	Spiritual	Religious	12-Step
Lauren C.	41–50	Female	Bachelor of Science (B.Sc.). Mathematics grade 1.1.	Finance Manager: Engineering dept., 'Prestige' motor producer	4	Yes	Yes	Yes
Rachael D.-S.	41–50	Female	Fellow in Mathematics at Royal Institution of Great Britain	Cloth and clothes worker	None	Yes	Yes	Yes
Nick G.	41–50	Male	Site Manager Training	Contracts Manager: Construction and Utilities	30+	Yes	Yes	No
Sandra C.	41–50	Female	Certified in Art Intelligence Coaching	Director: Spiritual Change Agent/ Catalyst for Change	1+	Yes	No	No
Katie D.	41–50	Female	Bachelor of Arts (BA) History	Countywide Pathways and Engagement Lead	3	Yes	No	Ex
James P.	41–50	Male	Degree in Psychology	Sales Assistant: Major UK Supermarket	None	Yes	No	Yes
Theresa F.	51–60	Female	Degree	School Teacher: Primary School	None	Yes	Yes	Yes
Russell W.	51–60	Male	Business HNC in financial planning	Life Coach: Director	4	Yes	No	No
Ffrancon W.	50–60	Male	Graduate in Electrical and Electronic Engineering	Group Chief Executive: Quality Homes and services provider	8+	Yes	No	No

Name	Age	Gender	Qualification	Occupation				
Sue P.	41–50	Female	Diploma in occupational safety	Health and Safety professional	None	Yes	No	Ex
Michelle O.	51–60	Female	Doctor of Philosophy (Ph.D.)	Director/Owner: ***** Consulting Ltd	6	Yes	No*****	Yes
Yvonne T.	51–60	Female	Level 5 Management	Director: Childcare	17	Yes	No	Yes
Alison R.	41–50	Female	GCSE's	Clinical Manager: C*** in M***	None	Yes	Yes	Ex
Jayne B.	41–50	Female	Book keeping	Director/Owner: Dog Groomer and Walker	2	Yes	No	Yes
Jo C.	51–60	Female	Care Management	Care Manager: Care Home Owner	10	Yes	Yes**	Yes
Jim N.	51–60	Male	'O' Level	Director of Sales EMEA: Global aviation distributors	5	Yes	No	No
Yvette T.	51–60	Female	'O' Levels	Freelance IQA, Consultant: Assessor and EPA	None	Yes	No	Yes
Rozalin F.	61–70	Female	CSE's	Owner: Market retailer	None	Yes	No	Yes

(Continued)

Interviewee' Identifier	Age	Gender	Highest Academic Qualification	Organisation/ Department	Direct/ In-directs	Spiritual	Religious	12-Step
Rowena N.	61–70	Female	Bachelor of Arts (BA) History (Hons)	Customer Advisor: Sub-Post Office	None	Yes	Yes	No
Victoria W.	41–50	Female		Singer Songwriter, Producer. Actress and Entrepreneur	None	Yes	No	Yes
Janice D.	51–60	Female		Senior Support Manager: ICT strategy. C******* E*** Council	3	Yes	No****	No
Karen A.	41–50	Female	CSE's	Retail and Warehouse operative: International industrial distributer and supplier	None	Yes	Yes	No
Stephanie W.	31–40	Female	Bachelor of Arts (BA): French studies with international relations	Secondary School Teacher: Languages	1	Yes	No	Yes
Chris H.	51–60	Male	'A' Level	Managing Director/ Owner: Haulage and Distribution	45	Yes	No	Yes
Syd B.	61–70	Male		Insurance Advisor	1	Yes	No	Yes
John W.	61–70	Male	'O' Level	Managing Director/ Owner: Precision Engineering	25	Yes	No	No

Julia T.	51–60	Female	Pharmacy Degree and a Post Graduate Diploma	Clinical Pharmacist in NHS. Locum in Retail Pharmacy	1+	Yes		No
Christine S.	41–50	Female	A Levels	Events Co-ordinator: D**** Club	None	Yes	Yes***	No
Linda R.	61–70	Female	MSc Risk Management	Safety Systems and Business Continuity Manager: National television production Co.	2+	Yes	No****	Yes
Maggie C.	51–60	Female	Diploma in Relationship Counselling	Relationship Counsellor	None	Yes	Yes	No
Claire S.	51–60	Female	CIMA: Advanced Diploma	Senior Accountant Manager: S*** Accountants	6	Yes	No	Yes
Kirsty R.	31–40	Female	Bachelor of Science (BSc)	Global Programme Manager: Health and insurance	2+	Yes	Yes	Ex
Ian P.	51–60	Male	M.B.A (Honours) Business Admin.	Financial Director: K****** Housing Trust	4	Yes	No	No
Alan T.	51–60	Male	Masters in Engineering and Computer Science from Cambridge	Business Angel. Entrepreneur and Technology Investor	1+	Yes	No	Ex

(Continued)

Interviewee' Identifier	Age	Gender	Highest Academic Qualification	Organisation/ Department	Direct/ In-directs	Spiritual	Religious	12-Step
Raymond H.	41–50	Male	City & Guilds in Aero Engineering	Head of Customer Services/ Engineering Queries: A****** Operations Ltd	7	Yes	No	No
Shirley Anne P.	61–70	Female	NVQ in Childcare and Education— level 3	Private Nanny	3 Children	Yes	Yes	Ex
Linda O.	61–70	Female	Certificate III in health support services	Orderly: The NHS	None	Yes	No	Yes
John S.	61–70	Male	BA (Honours) Engineering	Interim Director: St****y Press Equipment	30	Yes	No	Yes
Lee K.	41–50	Female	Bachelor of Science (BSc) 1st Class Hons	Lean Six Sigma Training and Consulting	None	Yes	No	No
Kathryn W.	51–60	Female	M.B.A.	Solicitor	2	Yes	Yes	No
Paula B.	41–50	Female	'A' Levels	Dept. Manager: International Pharmaceutical Company	4	Yes	No****	No
Peter J.	51–60	Male	Degree: English language and Literature	Teaching Assistant: Private Grammar School	None	Yes	Yes	Yes

Mick P.	51–60	Male	City & Guilds in electrical installation	Maintenance Manager: A****Z*****	18	Yes	No	No
Becky H.	41–50	Female	BA Hons. Multi-Media Journalism	Lead Business Improvement Manager: The B**, Broadcasting Company	2	Yes	No	Yes
Shelly M.	51–60	Female	MSc in Finance	Commercial Banking Advisor: H**C	None	Yes	No	Yes
Ian P.	51–60	Male	M.B.A. Operations Management and International Business	European Operations Director: I******** Brands PLC	9	Yes	No	Yes
Mandy H.	41–50	Female	M.B.A. Banking and Finance	Banking Executive: H**C	4+	Yes	No	Yes
Pauline H.	51–60	Female	'A' Level	Senior Banking Advisor: H**C	None	Yes	No	No

Key:

Ex: Used to attend a spiritual support Group.

* After his Christian upbringing, Paul J. became an Atheist and then an Agnostic and whilst still not believing in God, 10 years ago become a practicing Buddhist, of which he describes Buddhism as "A religion".

** Capturing this as a 'yes', as although Jo C. made a comment about spirituality being 'her religion', this was regarded as a 'tongue in cheek response' and as such, the researcher has determined her response as not to be taken literally.

*** Gemma H. and Julia T. are only 'a little bit religious.' "I wouldn't say I agree with everything they [Clergy and Church] do, but it's a way to introduce my children to other worldly thoughts and morals." Julia T. "Some of their [Clergy] values do hold with me."

**** Lapsed

References

Adams, D. W., & Csiernik, R. (2002). Seeking the lost spirit: Understanding spirituality and restoring it to the workplace. *Employee Assistance Quarterly, 17*(4), 31–44.

Al-Anon Family Group UK & Eire. (1992). *UK & Eire service manual*. London: Al-Anon Family Group Headquarters Inc.

Al-Anon Family Group UK & Eire. (2006). *UK & Eire service manual*. London: Al-Anon Family Group Headquarters Inc.

Al-Anon Family Group UK & Eire. (1997). *Paths to recovery: Al-Anon's steps, traditions and concepts*. London: Al-Anon Family Group Headquarters Inc.

Anonymous, A. (1952). *Twelve steps and twelve traditions*. New York: Alcoholic Anonymous World Services Inc.

Anonymous. (1978). *Guide to 4th step inventory*. Minnesota: Hazelden Publishing.

Bachelard, G. (1927). Essai sur la connaissance approchée. *Continental Philosophy of Science, 176*.

Baumeister, R. F. (2016). Toward a general theory of motivation: Problems, challenges, opportunities, and the big picture. *Motivation and Emotion, 40*(1), 1–10.

Bob, D. (1980). *The good old-timers: A biography, with recollections of early AA in the Midwest*. New York: Alcoholics Anonymous World Services.

Broadhurst, S. (2019). *Application and benefits of spirituality, within the British workplace* (EDBA dissertation). Ecole des Ponts, Champs-sur-Marne.

Borkman, T. (2006). Sharing experience, conveying hope: Egalitarian relations as the essential method of Alcoholics Anonymous. *Nonprofit Management and Leadership, 17*(2), 145–161.

Buchman, F. N. D. (1961). *Remaking the world: The speeches of Frank ND Buchman*. London: Blandford Press.

Burns, J. M. (1978). *Leadership*. New York, NY: Perennial; London: HarperCollins.

Chesnut, G. F. (2011). *The first Roman Catholics in alcoholics anonymous* (G. F. Chesnut, Ed.). Minnesota, US: Hazelden Publishing.

Clark, D. R. (1997). Concepts of leadership. In *Big dog & little dog's performance juxtaposition*. Retrieved April 3, 2006, from http://files.eric.ed.gov/fulltext/ED384695.pdf

Clark, D. R. (2004). The art and science of leadership. In *Big dog & little dog's performance juxtaposition*.

Clark, D. R. (2010). Big dog & little dog's performance juxtaposition. In *Big dog & little dog's performance juxtaposition: Case study*. Retrieved from http://www.nwlink.com/~donclark/hrd/bloom.html

Cook, K. S., & Whitmeyer, J. M. (1992). Two approaches to social structure: Exchange theory and network analysis. *Annual Review of Sociology, 18*(1), 109–127.

Davis, M. S. (1971). That's interesting! Towards a phenomenology of sociology and a sociology of phenomenology. *Philosophy of the Social Sciences, 1*(2), 309–344.

Ebenstein, L. (2014). The increasingly libertarian Milton Friedman: An ideological profile. *Econ Journal Watch, 11*(1), 81–96.

Foucault, M. (2005). *The hermeneutics of the subject: Lectures at the Collège de France, 1981–1982*. New York: Springer Publishing.

Friedman, M. (2007). The social responsibility of business is to increase its profits. In *Corporate ethics and corporate governance* (pp. 173–178). Berlin and Heidelberg: Springer.

Fry, L. W. (2003). Toward a theory of spiritual leadership. *The Leadership Quarterly, 14*(6), 693–727.

Fry, L. W., Matherly, L. L., Whittington, J. L., & Winston, B. E. (2007). Spiritual leadership as an integrating paradigm for servant leadership. *Integrating Spirituality and Organizational Leadership*, 70–82.

Fry, L. W., & Smith, D. A. (1987). Congruence, contingency, and theory building. *Academy of Management Review, 12*(1), 117–132.

Gotsis, G., & Kortezi, Z. (2008). Philosophical foundations of workplace spirituality: A critical approach. *Journal of Business Ethics, 78*(4), 575–600.

Greenleaf, R. K. (1998). *The power of servant-leadership: Essays*. San Francisco, CA: Berrett Koehler Publishers.

Greenleaf, R. K. (1978). Servant leader and follower. New York: Paulist Press

Greenleaf, R. K. (1977). Servant leadership: A journey into the nature of legitimate power and greatness. New York: Paulist Press.

Hanegraaff, W. J. (1999). New age spiritualities as secular religion: A historian's perspective. *Social Compass, 46*(2), 145–160.

Heindel, M. (1920). *The Rosicrucian cosmo-conception: Or, mystic Christianity; an elementary treatise upon man's past evolution, present constitution and future development*. Oceanside, CA: The Rosicrucian Fellowship.

Hill, N. (2011). *Think and grow rich: The original classic*. Hoboken, NJ: John Wiley & Sons.

The Holy Bible. New International Version. (1988). *International Bible Society*. Great Britain: Hodder and Stoughton Ltd.

House, R. J. (1971). A path goal theory of leader effectiveness. *Administrative Science Quarterly*, 321–339.

Karakas, F., & Sarigollu, E. (2013). The role of leadership in creating virtuous and compassionate organizations: Narratives of benevolent leadership in an Anatolian tiger. *Journal of Business Ethics, 113*(4), 663–678.

Kleinginna, P. R., & Kleinginna, A. M. (1981). A categorized list of emotion definitions, with suggestions for a consensual definition. *Motivation and Emotion, 5*(3&4), 263–291, 345–379.

Koenig, H. G. (2008). Concerns about measuring "spirituality" in research. *The Journal of Nervous and Mental Disease, 196*(5), 349–355.

Koenig, H., Koenig, H. G., King, D., & Carson, V. B. (2012). *Handbook of religion and health*. Oxford: Oxford University Press.

Liden, R. C., Wayne, S. J., Zhao, H., & Henderson, D. (2008). Servant leadership: Development of a multidimensional measure and multi-level assessment. *The Leadership Quarterly, 19*(2), 161–177.

Mäkelä, K., Kurube, N., Arminen, I., Bloomfield, K., Eisenbach-Stangl, I., Bergmark, K. H., . . . Rehm, J. (1996). *Alcoholics Anonymous as a mutual-help movement: A study in eight societies*. Madison, WI: University of Wisconsin Press.

Maslow, A. H. (1962). Some basic propositions of a growth and self-actualization psychology. *Perceiving, Behaving, Becoming: A New Focus for Education*, 34–49.

Maslow, A. H. (1964). *Religions, values, and peak-experiences*. Columbus: The Ohio State University Press.

Maslow, A. H., & Lewis, K. J. (1987). Maslow's hierarchy of needs. *Salenger Incorporated, 14*, 987. *Originally Published in Psychological Review, 50*, 370–396.

Michels, R. (1915). *Political parties: A sociological study of the oligarchical tendencies of modern democracy*. New York: Hearst's International Library Company.

Michels, R. (1962). *Political Parties: A Sociological Study of the Oligarchical Tendencies of Modern Democracy/4ctranslated by Eden and Cedar Paul; Introduction by Seymour Martin Lipset*. Free Press.

Moberg, D. O. (2002). Assessing and measuring spirituality: Confronting dilemmas of universal and particular evaluative criteria. *Journal of Adult Development, 9*(1), 47–60.

Neal, J., & Biberman, J. (2003). Introduction: The leading edge in research on spirituality and organizations. *Journal of Organizational Change Management, 16*(4), 363–366.

Paloutzian, R. F., & Ellison, C. (1982). Spiritual well-being scale. *Measures of Religiosity*, 382, 385.

Parkinson, C. N., & Lancaster, O. (1958). *Parkinson's law or the pursuit of progress* (p. 48). London: Murray.

Ratnakar, R., & Nair, S. (2012). A review of scientific research on spirituality. *Business Perspectives and Research, 1*(1), 1–12.

Ruse, M. (2010). *Science and spirituality*. Cambridge: Cambridge University Press.

Schutte, P. J. (2016). Workplace spirituality: A tool or a trend? *HTS Theological Studies, 72*(4), 1–5.

Sheldrake, P. (2013). *Spirituality: A brief history*. Hoboken, NJ: John Wiley & Sons.

Shenhav, Y. A. (1995). From chaos to systems: The engineering foundations of organization theory, 1879–1932. *Administrative Science Quarterly*, 557–585.

Sills, D. L. (1968). International encyclopedia of social sciences. *International Encyclopedia of Social Sciences, 17*, 495–495.

Smith, L. (2014). *Can we be obliged to be selfless? Philosophical foundations of fiduciary law*. Oxford: Oxford University Press.

Stevenson, A., & Waite, M. (Eds.). (2011). *Concise Oxford English dictionary: Book & CD ROM Set*. Oxford: Oxford University Press.

Waaijman, K. (2007). What is spirituality? *Acta Theologica*, 27(2), 1–18.

Weber, M. (1958). *The protestant ethic and the spirit of capitalism* (T. Parsons, Trans.). New York: Charles Scribner's Sons.

Wilson, B. (1988). *Language of the heart: Bill W.'s grapevine writings*. New York: Alcoholics Anonymous World Services.

Index

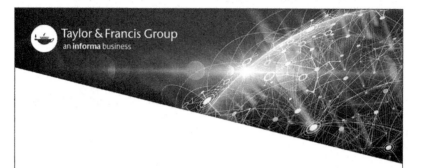

–

Printed in the United States
by Baker & Taylor Publisher Services